HOW TO BE AN EVEN BETTER MANAGER

HOW TO BE AN EVEN BETTER MANAGER

FOURTH EDITION

A complete A-Z of proven techniques and
essential skills... reveals the secrets of
successful managers

MICHAEL ARMSTRONG

KOGAN
PAGE

Note: Masculine pronouns have been used in this book. This stems from a desire to avoid ugly and cumbersome language, and no discrimination, prejudice or bias is intended.

First published in Great Britain in 1983, entitled *How To Be a Better Manager*
Second edition, 1988, *How To Be an Even Better Manager*
Third edition 1990
Fourth edition 1994
Reprinted 1994, 1995

Kogan Page Limited
120 Pentonville Road
London N1 9JN

© Michael Armstrong 1983, 1988, 1990, 1994

British Library Cataloguing in Publication Data
A CIP record for this book is available from the British Library.

ISBN 0–7494–1383–2

Typeset by DP Photosetting, Aylesbury, Bucks
Printed and bound in Great Britain by Clays Ltd, St Ives plc.

Contents

Foreword to the Fourth Edition

This edition takes account of the approaches to management that have been developed in recent years and were not covered in previous editions. They include new thinking on such aspects of management as:

- Benchmarking
- Business process re-engineering
- Change management
- Coaching
- Conflict management
- Continuous improvement and the learning organization
- Counselling
- Empowerment
- Improving organizational effectiveness
- Leadership
- Objective setting
- Organizing
- Performance management
- Strategic management
- Team management
- Total quality management.

Introduction:
On being a better manager

However good you are – or think you are – you can always improve. That's the theme of this book. It is about self-development and as Peter Drucker wrote in *The Effective Executive* (15).*

> Self-development of the effective executive is central to the development of the organization.

You may already be a good manager, but to be an even better one it is worth spending some time increasing your understanding of:

- What management is about
- The aims of management
- The processes of management
- Managerial roles
- Managerial qualities
- The role of experience
- The role of personality
- The phenomenon of change
- What you can do.

This introductory chapter reviews each of these overall requirements as a lead to the 50 specific areas of management covered by this book.

What is management?

Essentially, management is about deciding what to do and then getting it done through people. This definition emphasizes that people are the most important resource available to managers. It is through this resource that

---

* The numbers in parenthesis after authors' names refer to the General bibliography, see page 320.

all the other resources – knowledge, finance, materials, plant, equipment, etc – will be managed.

However, managers are there to achieve results. To do this they have to deal with events and eventualities. They may do this primarily through people, but an over-emphasis on the people content of management diverts attention from the fact that in managing events managers have to be personally involved. They manage themselves as well as other people. They cannot delegate everything. They frequently have to rely on their own resources to get things done. These resources consist of experience, know-how, skill and, most important, time – all of which have to be deployed not only in directing and motivating people but also in understanding situations and issues, problem analysis and definition, decision-making and taking direct action themselves as well as through other people. They will get support, advice and assistance from their staff, but in the last analysis they are on their own. They have to make the decisions and they have to initiate and sometimes take the action. A chairman fighting a takeover bid will be given lots of advice but will personally manage the crisis, talking directly to the financial institutions, merchant banks, financial analysts, City editors and the mass of shareholders.

The basic definition of management should therefore be extended to read 'deciding what to do and then getting it done through the effective use of resources'. The most important part of management will indeed be getting things done through people, but managers will be concerned directly or indirectly with all other resources, including their own.

The aims of management

Management is a process which exists to get results by making the best use of the human, financial and material resources available to the organization and to individual managers. It is very much concerned with adding value to these resources, and this added value depends on the expertise and commitment of the people who are responsible for managing the business.

The processes of management

The overall process of management is subdivided into a number of individual processes which are methods of operation specially designed to assist in the achievement of objectives. Their purpose is to bring as much system, order, predictability, logic and consistency to the task of management as possible in the ever-changing, varied and turbulent environment in which managers work. The main processes of management were defined by the classical theorists of management as:

1. *Planning* – deciding on a course of action to achieve a desired result and focusing attention on objectives and standards and the programmes required to achieve the objectives.
2. *Organizing* – setting up and staffing the most appropriate organization to achieve the aim.
3. *Motivating* – exercising leadership to motivate people to work together smoothly and to the best of their ability as part of a team.
4. *Controlling* – measuring and monitoring the progress of work in relation to the plan and taking corrective action when required.

But this classical view has been challenged by the empiricists, such as Rosemary Stewart (54) and Henry Mintzberg (39), who studied how managers actually spend their time. They observed that the work of managers is fragmented, varied, subjected to continual adjustment and governed to a large degree by events over which the manager has little control and by a dynamic network of interrelationships with other people. Managers exist to control their environment but sometimes it controls them. They may consciously or unconsciously seek to plan, organize, direct and control but their days almost inevitably become a jumbled sequence of events.

To the empiricists, management is a process involving a mix of rational, logical, problem-solving, decision-making activities and intuitive, judgemental activities. It is therefore both science and art.

Managers carry out their work on a day-to-day basis in conditions of endless variety, turbulence and unpredictability. A single word to describe all these features would be chaos. Tom Peters (46), however, in *Thriving on Chaos* has suggested that it is possible for managers to thrive on this.

Managers also have to be specialists in ambiguity, with the ability to cope with conflicting and unclear requirements, as Rosabeth Moss Kanter (30) has demonstrated.

Managerial roles

During the course of a typical day a chief executive may well meet the marketing director to discuss the programme for launching a new product, the personnel director to decide how best to reorganize the distribution department, the production director to ask why costs per unit of output are going up and what is going to be done about it, and the finance director to review the latest set of management accounts before the next board meeting. These activities could be categorized under the headings of planning, organizing, directing and controlling, but the chief executive would not have attached these labels when deciding how to spend his or her time (in so far as there was any choice). The fact that these processes took place was imposed by the situation and the need to exercise one or more of the roles inherent in the manager's job. These roles are fundamentally concerned with:

- Getting things done – maintaining momentum and making things happen
- Finding out what is going on
- Reacting to new situations and problems
- Responding to demands and requests.

They involve a great deal of interpersonal relations, data processing and decision-making.

Henry Mintzberg (37) in *The Nature of Managerial Work* has suggested that managerial activities can be divided into ten roles within the three groups of interpersonal roles, informational roles and decisional roles.

Managerial qualities

Pedler, Burgoyne and Boydell (43) in *A Manager's Guide to Self-Development* suggest, on the basis of their extensive research, that there are 11 qualities or attributes which are possessed by successful managers:

1. Command of basic facts
2. Relevant professional knowledge
3. Continuing sensitivity to events
4. Analytical, problem-solving and decision/judgement-making skills
5. Social skills and abilities
6. Emotional resilience
7. Proactivity
8. Creativity
9. Mental agility
10. Balanced learning habits and skills
11. Self-knowledge.

The role of experience

'How can I develop these qualities?' A familiar answer to this question is to say that 'managers learn to manage by managing under the guidance of a good manager'. But can experience alone be the best teacher? Several writers have expressed their doubts on this score. Tennyson called it 'a dirty nurse'. Oscar Wilde noted that 'experience is the name everyone gives to their mistakes'. And the historian Froude wrote that 'experience teaches slowly and at the cost of mistakes'.

Experience is an essential way of learning to improve but it is an imperfect instrument. We also need guidance – from a good manager *and* from other sources such as this book – which will help us to interpret experience, learn from our mistakes and make better use of our experience in the future.

The role of personality

'Managers are born not made.' This is the discouraging answer which has been given to managers who seek ways to improve themselves. The implication that neither experience nor study can be beneficial is of course unacceptable, but the statement does contain some truth in that our personality strongly influences the way in which we manage and our effectiveness as a manager.

Studies carried out on the qualities displayed by successful top managers as quoted by Rosemary Stewart (54) in *Managers and Their Jobs* show a number of common characteristics, such as:

- A willingness to work hard
- Perseverance and determination
- A willingness to take risks
- An ability to inspire enthusiasm
- Toughness.

Psychologists claim that personality is formed in the early years of life. Apparently it is in the cradle, or at least in the nursery, that we learn to be ruthless. *If* this is the case, maybe there is not much we can do about it when we grow up and become managers. Spending ten minutes every morning before a mirror practising being ruthless may not get us very far. Neither will much good come from our boss's exhortations to display different personality characteristics, or from attending lectures, or reading management textbooks. We can, however, modify the way in which we behave – the way in which we use our personalities. And guidance – not exhortations – from outside sources as well as from within should help. If we know what we are looking for we are more likely to find it.

The phenomenon of change

The economics and business environment has become much more turbulent, uncertain and demanding. Tom Peters (46) in *Thriving on Chaos* has referred to 'an era of unprecedented change' and suggested that 'predictability is a thing of the past'.

Environmental change has taken place in a number of ways as described below:

- Economic and political change has seen the rise in recent years of the enterprise culture and its associated phenomenon, the market economy. However, in the late 1980s in the light of Wall Street and City scandals people were beginning to question whether an approach to management based purely on greed was appropriate. Hence the increasing importance attached to mission and value statements, which are dealt with in this book.
- In the 1980s social change produced a trend towards individualism and away from collectivism, although it is now realized that the flatter, decentralized and flexible firm of the 1990s will have to rely more on commitment and teamwork.
- Consumer expectations are higher than ever before. Consumers want value for money, as always, but they are now demanding, quite rightly, higher standards of quality and service.
- The business environment is changing significantly with an emphasis on growth, a rash of takeovers and acquisitions and increased competition from Europe, Japan and from multinational firms.
- Product life cycles are shorter and firms must innovate to sustain their competitive advantage and to establish and maintain their position in increasingly segmented markets.
- New technology is playing a much greater part in the management process in so far as process is largely concerned with information flows.

The impact of change on attitudes

A new managerial revolution has taken place over the last decade. Attitudes have changed in the following directions:

- *The market place.* It is at last recognized that organizations are market driven and that management must be market orientated.
- *Customers.* Customer care and service have become major features in marketing strategies.
- *Excellence.* Peters and Waterman (45) in *In Search of Excellence* initiated what has become almost a cult of excellence. ICL, for

example, in a message to all employees has stated that 'ICL's sights are now set on world success. That demands excellence in everything we undertake. And excellence will be achieved only by adopting "can do" attitudes and the highest levels of cooperation and commitment throughout the organization.'

- *Turbulence*. Managements are beginning to accept turbulence as a way of life. Tom Peters (46) has redefined his original definition of excellence to read:

> Excellent firms don't believe in excellence – only in constant improvement and constant change. That is, excellent firms of tomorrow will cherish impermanence and thive on chaos.

The impact of change on the firm

Environmental and technological developments have resulted in fundamental changes to the ways in which firms are structured and managed. We now have:

- *The responsive firm* which has to react quickly to changes in the marketplace and in customer needs and preferences.
- *The proactive firm* which has to make markets as well as adapt itself to them.
- *The flexible firm* which has to adjust its structure, its product range, its marketing strategies and manufacturing facilities quickly to respond to and, more important, anticipate change.
- *The information-based firm* which will be knowledge-orientated and composed largely of specialists who direct and discipline their own performance through organized feedback from colleagues, customers, and the strategic business units into which the organization is divided in accordance with the markets it serves. Peter Drucker (16) in an article in the *Harvard Business Review* has suggested that: 'Information is data endowed with meaning and purpose.' And it is on this basis that many organizations are rethinking the ways in which they are managed.
- *The compact firm* which has a flatter organization structure because superfluous layers of management have been stripped away. Peter Drucker followed up his remarks about new technology quoted above with the comment that many organizations have not rethought their structures in the light of its availability: 'Whole new layers of management neither make decisions nor lead. Instead their main, if not their only function, is to serve as "relays" – human boosters for the faint unfocused signals that pass for communications in the traditional pre-information organization.'

- *The decentralized firm* which consists of strategic business units placed firmly in their market niches and capable of responding quickly to opportunities. These units are tightly managed to achieve well-defined goals with the minimum of interference from above.
- *The global firm* which is operating across many international boundaries.

The impact of managers

Managers have to learn to exist with change, like the organizations in which they work. They have to be more flexible and more responsive to new and challenging demands.

In the decentralized organization of today they must be able to operate independently – the very essence of effective managers is that they achieve the goals they set themselves. But in the flatter organization they also have to be good team workers able to deploy a wider range of skills in working with others across organizational boundaries.

These demands can result in role conflict and role ambiguity, which can produce stress, and stress management is a new topic included in this edition. People generally prefer to work in an orderly structure which provides a framework within which they have a fair degree of autonomy. They prefer to know where they stand and where they are going. They like a certain amount of predictability and, although they welcome variety, it has to be within reasonable bounds. But life in organizations is not like that. Change, uncertainty and ambiguity are ever present. Organizations are supposed to behave rationally, progressing steadily from A to B. But they don't. They consist of webs of power and politics and proceed by fits and starts.

The balancing act practised by all managers is between the need for order and continuity and the demands of the situation, which involve flexibility and discontinuity. Organizations suffer too. As Rosabeth Moss Kanter points out in *When Giants Learn to Dance* (30), businesses and managers are continually being bombarded with conflicting advice on these and many other matters.

What you can do

Perhaps Francis Bacon provided the best answer to this question when he wrote: 'Studies perfect nature and are perfected by experience.'

The art of management – and it is an art – is important enough to be studied. The aim of such studies should be to help us to make better use of our natural attributes – our personality and intelligence – and to ensure that past experience is better interpreted and more fully used, and that future experience is more quickly and purposefully absorbed.

How this book can help you to become an even better manager

This book contains 50 chapters, which are arranged in alphabetical order for ease of reference. No book can contain all the answers, neither can it offer prescriptions to cover every eventuality – ultimately, what you do will be largely determined by the situation in which you find yourself. But this book does provide guidelines which will help you to build your managerial knowledge and skills. These cover the following areas:

● *Personal development*

  - achieving results (Chapter 1)
  - assertiveness (Chapter 2)
  - getting on (Chapter 22)
  - stress management (Chapter 46)

● *Factors contributing to success*

  - benchmarking (Chapter 3)
  - corporate culture and how to manage it (Chapter 14)
  - cost cutting (Chapter 15)
  - empowerment (Chapter 21)
  - how things go wrong and how to put them right (Chapter 23)
  - improving organizational effectiveness (Chapter 24)
  - productivity improvement (Chapter 41)
  - profit improvement (Chapter 42)
  - re-engineering the business (Chapter 43)
  - trouble shooting (Chapter 50)

● *Management processes*

  - budgeting (Chapter 4)
  - organizing (Chapter 33)
  - policies (Chapter 37)
  - power and politics (Chapter 38)
  - strategic management (Chapter 45)
  - total quality management (Chapter 49)

● *Management skills and techniques*

  - case presentation (Chapter 5)
  - change management (Chapter 6)
  - clear thinking (Chapter 7)

- coaching (Chapter 8)
- communicating (Chapter 9)
- conflict management (Chapter 10)
- continuous improvement (Chapter 11)
- controlling (Chapter 12)
- coordinating (Chapter 13)
- counselling (Chapter 16)
- creative thinking (Chapter 17)
- crisis management (Chapter 18)
- delegating (Chapter 19)
- developing people (Chapter 20)
- empowerment (Chapter 21)
- getting on (Chapter 22)
- innovating (Chapter 25)
- interviewing (Chapter 26)
- leadership (Chapter 27)
- managing your boss (Chapter 28)
- meetings (Chapter 29)
- motivating (Chapter 30)
- negotiating (Chapter 31)
- objective setting (Chapter 32)
- performance management (Chapter 34)
- persuading (Chapter 35)
- planning (Chapter 36)
- presentations and effective speaking (Chapter 39)
- problem-solving and decision-making (Chapter 40)
- report writing (Chapter 44)
- team management (Chapter 47)
- time management (Chapter 48).

Note: Masculine pronouns have been used on occasion in this book for convenience and conciseness, although feminine pronouns are, in most cases, equally applicable.

Chapter 1
Achieving results

Achieving results, getting things done, making things happen. That is what management is all about.

It can be said that there are three sorts of managers: those who make things happen, those who watch things happening, and those who don't know what is happening. Before finding out how to get into the first category, there are three questions to answer:

- Is getting things done simply a matter of personality – characteristics like drive, decisiveness, leadership, ambition – which some people have and others haven't?
- And if you haven't got the drive, decisiveness and so forth which it takes, is there anything you can do about it?
- To what extent is an ability to make things happen a matter of using techniques which can be learnt and developed?

Personality is important. Unless you have willpower and drive nothing will get done. But remember that your personality is a function of both nature and nurture. You are born with certain characteristics. Upbringing, education, training and, above all, experience, develop you into the person you are.

We may not be able to change our personality which, according to Freud, is formed in the first few years of life. But we can develop and adapt it by consciously learning from our own experience and by observing and analysing other people's behaviour.

Techniques for achieving results, such as planning, organizing, delegating, communicating, motivating and controlling, can be learnt. These are dealt with later in this book. But these techniques are only as effective as the person who uses them. They must be applied in the right way and in the right circumstances. And you still have to use your experience to select the right technique and your personality to make it work.

To become a person who makes things happen you therefore have to develop skills and capacities by a process of understanding, observation, analysis and learning. The four actions you should take are:

1. Understand what makes achievers tick – the personality characteristics they display in getting things done.
2. Observe what achievers do – how they operate, what techniques they use.
3. Analyse your own behaviour (*behaviour*, not personality), compare it with that of high achievers, and think how to improve your effectiveness.
4. Learn as much as you can about the management techniques available.

What makes achievers tick?

David McClelland (35) of Harvard University carried out extensive research into what motivates managers. He interviewed, observed and analysed numbers of managers at their place of work and recorded findings before producing his theory. And before you dismiss anything which comes under the heading of theory, remember what Douglas McGregor (36) of the Massachusetts Institute of Technology, said: 'There is nothing so practical as a good theory.'

McClelland identified three needs which he believes are key factors in motivating managers. These are:

- The need for achievement
- The need for power (having control and influence over people)
- The need for affiliation (to be accepted by others).

All effective managers have these needs to a certain degree, but by far the most important one is achievement.

Achievement is what counts and achievers, according to McClelland, have these characteristics:

- They set themselves realistic but achievable goals with some 'stretch' built in.
- They prefer situations which they themselves can influence rather than those on which chance has a large influence.
- They are more concerned with knowing they have done well than with the rewards that success brings.
- They get their rewards from their accomplishment rather than from money or praise. This does not mean that high achievers reject money, which does in fact motivate them as long as it is seen as a realistic measure of their performance.

- High achievers are most effective in situations where they are allowed to get ahead by their own efforts.

What do achievers do?

High achievers do some, if not all, of the following:

1. They define to themselves precisely what they want to do.
2. They set demanding but not unattainable time-scales in which to do it.
3. They convey clearly what they want done and by when.
4. They are prepared to discuss how things should be done and will listen to and take advice. But once the course of action has been agreed they stick to it unless events dictate a change of direction.
5. They are single-minded about getting where they want to go, showing perseverance and determination in the face of adversity.
6. They demand high performance from themselves and are somewhat callous in expecting equally high performance from everyone else.
7. They work hard and work well under pressure; in fact, it brings out the best in them.
8. They tend to be dissatisfied with the status quo.
9. They are never completely satisfied with their own performance and continually question themselves.
10. They will take calculated risks.
11. They snap out of setbacks without being personally shattered and quickly regroup their forces and their ideas.
12. They are enthusiastic about the task and convey their enthusiasm to others.
13. They are decisive in the sense that they are able quickly to sum up situations, define alternative courses of action, determine the preferred course, and convey to their subordinates what needs to be done.
14. They continually monitor their own and their subordinates' performance so that any deviation can be corrected in good time.

How to analyse your own behaviour

It is no good trying to analyse your own behaviour unless you have criteria against which you can measure your performance. You have to set standards for yourself, and if you don't meet them, ask yourself why. The answer should tell you what to do next time.

The basic questions you should ask yourself are:

- What did I set out to do?
- Did I get it done?
- If I did, why and how did I succeed?
- If not, why not?

The aim is to make effective use of your experience.

Use the list of what high achievers do to check your own behaviour and actions. If your performance has not been up to scratch under any of these headings, ask yourself specifically what went wrong and decide how you are going to overcome this difficulty next time. This is not always easy. It is hard to admit to yourself, for example, that you have not been sufficiently enthusiastic. It may be even harder to decide what to do about it. You don't want to enthuse all over the place, indiscriminately. But you can consider whether there are better ways of displaying and conveying your enthusiasm to others in order to carry them with you.

Learning

There are a number of management techniques that you need to know about. These techniques are discussed in subsequent chapters in this book. The ones you should be particularly interested in are:

- Planning
- Objective and target setting
- Decision-making
- Delegating
- Communicating
- Motivating
- Leadership
- Coordinating
- Controlling.

Conclusion

This process of observation, analysis and learning will help you to become an achiever. But remember, achieving results is ultimately about making promises – to others and to yourself – and keeping them. Robert Townsend (56), in his book *Up the Organization*, has some excellent advice: 'Promises: keep. If asked when you can deliver something ask for time to think. Build in a margin of safety. Name a date. Then deliver it earlier than you promised.'

Chapter 2
Assertiveness

Assertion and aggression

Assertiveness, as defined by Ken and Kate Back (3) in *Assertiveness at Work*, is:

- Standing up for your own rights in such a way that you do not violate another person's rights
- Expressing your needs, wants, opinions, feelings and beliefs in direct, honest and appropriate ways.

When you are being assertive you are not, therefore, being aggressive, which means violating or ignoring other people's rights in order to get your own way or dominate a situation. Aggressive behaviour causes two counter-productive reactions: fight or flight. In other words, aggression either breeds aggression, which gets you nowhere, or it forces people to retreat in a demoralized or dissatisfied way. Inducing this sort of behaviour will not help to achieve your aim of getting them to go along with you.

Assertive behaviour

Behaving assertively puts you into the position of being able to influence people properly and react to them positively. Assertive statements:

- Are brief and to the point
- Indicate clearly that you are not hiding behind something or someone and are speaking for yourself by using words such as: 'I think that . . .', 'I believe that . . .', 'I feel that . . .', – your beliefs and views are important
- Are not overweighted with advice

- Use questions to find out the views of others and to test their reactions to your behaviour
- Distinguish between fact and opinion
- Are expressed positively but not dogmatically
- Indicate that you are aware that the other people have different points of view
- Express, when necessary, negative feelings about the effects of other people's behaviour on you – pointing out in dispassionate and factual terms the feelings aroused in you by that behaviour, and suggesting the behaviour you would prefer
- Point out to people politely but firmly the consequences of their behaviour.

Handling aggression

If you are faced by aggression, take a breath, count up to ten and then:

- Ask calmly for information about what is bugging the aggressors.
- State clearly, and again calmly, the position as you see it.
- Empathize with the aggressors by making it plain that you can see it from their point of view, but at the same time explaining in a matter-of-fact way how you see the discrepancy between what they believe and what you feel is actually happening.
- Indicate, if the aggressive behaviour persists, your different beliefs or feelings, but do not cut aggressors short – people often talk, or even shout, themselves out of being aggressive when they realize that you are not reacting aggressively and that their behaviour is not getting them anywhere.
- Suggest, if all else fails, that you leave it for the time being and talk about it again after a cooling-off period.

Influencing skills

Assertiveness is about fighting your own corner. You have to believe in yourself and what you are doing and express these beliefs confidently and without hesitation. It is about using influencing skills.

There are four influencing styles you can use:

1. *Asserting* – making your views clear.
2. *Persuading* – using facts, logic and reason to present your own case, emphasizing its strong points (benefits to the organization or the

individual(s) you are dealing with), anticipating objections to any apparent weaknesses and appealing to reason.

3. *Bridging* – drawing out other people's points of view, demonstrating that you understand what they are getting at, giving credit and praise in response to their good ideas and suggestions, joining your views with theirs.

4. *Attracting* – conveying your enthusiasm for your ideas, making people feel that they are all part of an exciting project.

Chapter 3
Benchmarking

To establish how well – or badly – you are doing and to identify areas for improvement, it pays to compare your organization with its best-performing peers. You need to study what the 'best-in-class' companies are doing – how well they perform generally in comparison with your business and how well they carry out specific activities and processes.

Asked what he thought of his wife, James Thurber replied: 'Compared with what?' Whatever we are comparing – products, processes, output levels, performance standards – we all seek yardsticks or measures to enable meaningful comparisons to take place. This is what benchmarking is about.

What is benchmarking?

Xerox, one of the first firms to carry out regular benchmarking surveys, defines benchmarking as:

> A continuous, systematic process of evaluating companies recognized as industry leaders, to determine business and work processes that represent 'best practice' and establish rational performance goals.

A survey, conducted in 1993 by the CBI and Coopers & Lybrand, of a sample of 105 Times Top 1000 companies revealed a number of different definitions of benchmarking, but these could be analysed into four categories:

1. *Competitive analysis* – the systematic analysis of competitor activity so that you can improve your performance.
2. *Best practice* – looking for best practice associated with the way companies operate.

3. *Performance comparison* – a means of assessing company and department performance.
4. *Standard setting* – a means of providing guidance on setting appropriate and stretching performance standards.

The underlying logic of benchmarking is compelling: unless you know what the competition is doing, and how customers rate your efforts on a comparative basis, how can you establish meaningful goals for improvement? Without benchmarks, the impact of improvement programmes can be a lottery; raising standards to an industry average, for example, is not the same as leap-frogging rivals. Benchmarking helps to set targets which enable companies to achieve sustainable competitive advantage.

Why benchmark?

The purpose of benchmarking is to identify areas for improvement and to stimulate change.

What do you benchmark?

Anything which drives or measures performance can be benchmarked. Examples include productivity, product quality, standards of service delivery, cycle times, pay, fund management performance and product characteristics.

Benchmarking sometimes concentrates on overall performance indices and ratios but it often produces the best results when it compares operational or process performance levels so that specific standards and targets for improvement can be set. When valid and reliable comparative data are available on, say, delivery times, managers who will not accept that it is possible to improve their performance can be told: 'If they can do it, then so can you.'

With whom do you benchmark?

Ideally, you benchmark with direct competitors, especially those who are operating in similar circumstances to your own. But direct competitors may not be willing to exchange information. In any case, useful comparisons can be made with out-of-sector companies. Xerox, for example, looked at mail specialists L L Bean when it was evaluating customer service.

In some circumstances, it may be valuable to benchmark within the organization, thus spreading best practice from one internal unit to another.

How do you benchmark?

Some organizations seek outside help but it is possible to run your own benchmarking exercise. This could consist of the following stages:

1. *Planning* – make decisions about what is to be benchmarked. You cannot do everything at once so you must focus on those areas which are likely to deliver the greatest returns – the drivers of performance.
2. *Collect data* – decide on sources of data (other organizations and data bases or publications). Approach the selected organizations, making sure you contact the right people, ask the right questions and evaluate the information you receive. You need to be reasonably certain that it is factual rather than propaganda material.
3. *Analyse results* – compare the figures and solutions provided by different organizations, ensuring that as far as possible you are comparing like with like. Make allowances for any significant operational differences which might affect the performance data. Assess, as dispassionately as possible, what can be learned and applied within your own organization, bearing in mind that other people's solutions will not necessarily transplant successfully into your own organization.
4. *Implement changes* – decide what improvements need to be made and plan and execute the change. The change management process will be helped if the people affected have been involved in the planning, analysis and decision-making stages.
5. *Review progress* – take stock of how the change programme is progressing and take corrective action as required. It may be necessary to obtain new information from different sources or to check on the validity of the data you have received.

What factors should be taken into account?

The following factors should be taken into account in analysing and using benchmark data:

- Benchmarking is likely to be most effective if the company has a clear vision of where it wants to go and well-articulated strategies for realizing that vision. It should know what its critical success factors are – the key drivers of organizational performance. Even if like-for-like comparisons can be made between the results achieved by different companies, the ways in which the leading performers have achieved their results may still be unclear. This is why benchmarking should cover processes as well as outcomes.

- What works well in one place will not necessarily work well elsewhere.
- Even if you obtain good, reliable information from a number of sources, it still requires considerable skill to translate this into meaningful terms in your organization.
- Make sure that organizations provide information on what they are actually achieving, not just their intentions for the future.
- There is often as much to be learned from the failures and bad practices of comparator organizations (if you can find out about them) as there is from their successes.

What has been achieved?

The best example is Xerox, the company largely responsible for defining benchmarking in the 1980s. Benchmarking at Xerox has become a way of life, applied as a discipline with its own well-established rules. The practice was initially introduced as a reaction to the Japanese onslaught on Xerox's markets. Xerox set out to find exactly where it was losing out in the price-performance battle and how it could close the gap. The findings underpin its drive for quality and, more recently, the reorganization and re-engineering of its global business.

Another example is Cigna UK, the British arm of the American insurance giant. Cigna knew that it faced an uphill struggle when it started selling employee insurance schemes in a UK market dominated by large, established players such as BUPA and Private Patients Plan. Its strategy was to carry out a comparative assessment of a variety of key aspects of its operations. Its market survey showed where, and how far, the company needed to improve its performance to achieve superior service. The findings set the framework for Cigna's plans to re-engineer its customer service processes. Fourteen months on, the company saw a 40 per cent rise in its revenue.

Tony Macnulty of Hay Management Consultants quotes in *Croners Employer's Briefing* (1 November 1993) the example of a firm with a history of technical excellence, but a tendency to run out of time and money on its projects. Having put in place a matrix structure with the aim of achieving a better balance between time, cost and quality, they decided to conduct a benchmarking survey as part of a total quality initiative. They wanted information on best practices in project management. Was a matrix the best way of organizing? How many staff were needed in the project department? What were the competences of the best project managers?

Because of a shortage of time and lack of contacts, they commissioned consultants to work with them on the survey. Their own staff were asked which companies they would like to see included and what questions they would like asked. All the target organizations bar one agreed to participate in exchange for a summary copy of the overall findings. As a result of the visits carried out by a joint consultant/client team, eight areas for attention were identified and new operating goals and productivity targets were set based on best industry practices.

Chapter 4
Budgeting

The need for budgets

Budgets don't win friends but they do influence people. They can be painful to create and agonizing to manage. But they do translate policy into financial terms and, whether we like it or not, that is the way in which plans must be expressed and, ultimately, performance controlled.

Budgets are needed for three reasons:

- To show the financial implications of plans
- To define the resources required to achieve the plans
- To provide a means of measuring, monitoring and controlling results against the plans.

Limitations of budgets

The main problems in budgeting are:

- An inadequate basic budgeting procedure: imprecise guidelines, unsatisfactory background data, cumbersome systems, lack of technical advice and assistance to managers, arbitrary cuts by top management
- An unskilled or cynical approach by managers to budgeting, resulting from inadequate basic procedures, lack of guidance, training or encouragement or a feeling that budgets are simply weapons to be deployed against them, rather than tools for them to use
- Lack of accurate forecasts of future activity levels
- Difficulty in amending the budget in response to changing circumstances
- The fundamental weakness of basing budgets on past levels of

expenditure which are simply 'plussed up' rather than subjecting the whole of the budget to a critical examination

- Weaknesses in reporting or controlling procedures which prevent the budget being used to monitor performance.

Preparing budgets

Most of the problems concerning the preparation of budgets mentioned above can be reduced, if not eliminated, if the following steps are taken:

1. Prepare budget guidelines which set out policies on where you want to go and, broadly, how you want to get there. These could be expressed as targets, for sales production or activity levels, and as an outline of the major marketing and production plans. In addition, the assumptions to be used in budgeting should be given. These could include rates of inflation and increases in costs and prices.
2. Ensure that those responsible for preparing budgets are given advice and encouragement by management accountants. These experts should be there to help, not to prod or threaten.
3. Get people to think hard about their budgets. They should not be allowed just to update last year's actuals. Wherever there is any choice on how much is spent, they should be asked to go back to first principles and justify what they are doing (zero-base budgeting).
4. Do not accept any significant increase or even decrease from last year's budget without an explanation.
5. Probe to ensure that budgets submitted to you are realistic and do not include a 'fudge factor'.
6. Do not slash budgets arbitrarily. Give reasons. If you don't, you will get 'fudge factors' or a couldn't-care-less attitude.
7. Update or 'flex' budgets regularly, especially when activity levels and costs are subject to large variations.

Zero-base budgeting

The traditional approach to budgeting tends to perpetuate the commitments of previous years. For instance, past levels of expenditure are used as a base from which to project increases or decreases. Only part of the budget is analysed, and managers concentrate on justifying increases, rather than challenging the need for any function or activity in its present form.

Zero-base or priority-based budgeting requires budget managers systematically to re-evaluate all their activities and programmes in order to establish their relative priority and decide whether they should be eliminated or funded at a reduced, similar or increased level. Appropriate funding levels will be determined by the priorities established by top management and the overall availability of funds.

Each activity is broken down into defined decision units, and each unit is analysed to establish:

- Its objectives
- The activities carried out
- The present costs of these activities
- The benefits resulting from each activity
- The standards and other performance measures that exist
- Alternative ways of achieving objectives
- Priorities among the objectives
- The advantages and disadvantages of incurring different levels of expenditure.

This is a fairly exhaustive list, and the amount of detail you want to pursue will depend on the importance you attach to a rigorous examination of expenditure. Zero-base budgeting is no panacea and it has often failed because companies have introduced over-elaborate procedures which have sunk almost without trace in a sea of paperwork. But the approach is right: cost control is about challenging and justifying proposed expenditures as well as monitoring what has actually been spent. The most elaborate control system in the world is useless if its foundation is unsound. Zero-base budgeting techniques should be used by managers to develop an attitude of mind in which they examine and control all their activities and attach priorities to them. The techniques should not be used in a threatening way. The emphasis should be on their value in getting priorities right and ensuring that costs and benefits are thoroughly reviewed to the advantage of all concerned.

Flexible budgets

If it is possible, with a reasonable degree of accuracy, to relate changes in income and costs to levels of activity, the use of flexible budgets is worth while. Budgets are 'flexed' by recalculating income and costs which vary with activity levels by reference to actual activity levels, thus giving an 'expected' level of income and costs. The difference between the original and expected levels is termed an 'activity variance' and the difference between expected levels and actual levels is termed a 'controllable variance'. It is on the latter figure that you must concentrate if you want a realistic picture of how costs are performing.

If a full system of flexible budgetary control cannot be operated because of the difficulty of relating costs accurately to activity levels, you should consider introducing an updating system. This means that periodically during the year the budget is revised to meet changing conditions. This is sometimes called a rolling budget and, while it is not so effective as the fully flexible system, it is easier to operate.

Budgetary control

A budgetary control procedure is not easy to achieve. You have to work at it. There is no problem in designing a system with elegant forms and lots of information. The difficulty is in maintaining the scheme as a useful instrument once it has been set up. The impetus can only come from the top. Chief Executives must insist on a rigorous approach to building budgets and a reporting procedure which is used to make things happen the way they want them to happen. They must also ensure that everyone concerned knows what is expected of them and are accountable for any failure to perform.

Chapter 5
Case presentation

As a manager, you will frequently have to make out a case for what you think should be done. You have to persuade people to believe in your views and accept your recommendations. To do this, you must have a clear idea of what you want, and you have to show that you believe in it yourself. Above all, the effectiveness of your presentation will depend upon the care with which you have prepared it.

Preparation

Thorough preparation is vital. You must think through not only what should be done and why, but also how people will react. Only then can you decide how to make your case: stressing the benefits without underestimating the costs, and anticipating objections.

You should think of the questions your audience is likely to raise, and answer them in advance, or at least have your answers ready. The most likely questions are:

What – is the proposal?
      – will be the benefit?
      – will it cost?
      – are the facts, figures, forecasts and assumptions upon which the proposal is based?
      – are the alternatives?
Why – should we change what we are doing now?
      – is this proposal or solution better than the alternatives?
How – is the change to be made?
      – are the snags to be overcome?
      – have the alternatives been examined?
      – am I affected by the change?

Who – will be affected by the change and what will be their reaction?
     – is likely to have the strongest views for or against the change, and why?
     – will implement the proposal?
When – should this be done?

To make your case you have to do three things:

1. Show that it is based on a thorough analysis of the facts and that the alternatives were properly evaluated before the conclusion was reached. If you have made assumptions, you must demonstrate that these are reasonable on the basis of relevant experience and justifiable projections, which allow for the unexpected. Bear in mind Robert Heller's words (25) that 'a proposal is only as strong as its weakest assumption'.
2. Spell out the benefits – to the company *and* the individuals to whom the case is being made. Wherever possible, express benefits in financial terms. Abstract benefits, such as customer satisfaction or workers' morale, are difficult to sell. But don't produce 'funny numbers' – financial justifications which will not stand up to examination.
3. Reveal costs. Don't try to disguise them in any way. And be realistic. Your proposition will be destroyed if anyone can show that you have underestimated the costs.

Remember, boards want to know in precise terms what they will get for their money. Most boards are cautious, being unwilling and often unable to take much risk. For this reason, it is difficult to make a case for experiments or pilot schemes unless the board, committee or individual can see what the real benefits and the ultimate bill will be.

Presentation

Your proposal will often be made in two stages: a written report followed by an oral presentation. The quality of the latter will often tip the balance in your favour (or against you). Making presentations and writing reports are dealt with in Chapters 39 and 44 respectively, but it is appropriate to note at this stage some special points you should bear in mind when making a case orally in front of an audience:

1. Your presentation should not just consist of a repetition of the facts in the written report. It should be used to put across the main points of the argument, leaving out the detail.
2. Do not assume that your audience has read the written report or

understood it. While you are talking, try to avoid referring to the report. This may switch people's attention from what you are saying. Use visual aids, preferably a flip chart, to emphasize the main points. But don't overdo them – it is possible to be too slick. The audience will be convinced by you, not by your elegant visual aids.

3. Make sure your opening secures people's attention. They must be immediately interested in your presentation. Begin by outlining your plan, its benefits and costs, and let the audience know how you are going to develop your case.

4. Bring out the disadvantages and the alternative courses of action so that you are not suspected of concealing or missing something.

5. Avoid being drawn into too much detail. Be succinct and to the point.

6. An emphatic summing up is imperative. It should convey with complete clarity what you want the board, committee or individual to do.

The effectiveness of your presentation will be largely dependent on how well you have prepared – not only putting your facts, figures and arguments clearly down on paper but also deciding what you are going to say at the meeting and how you are going to say it. The more important the case, the more carefully you should rehearse the presentation.

Checklist

1. Do you know exactly what you want?
2. Do you really believe in your case?
3. Have you obtained and checked all the facts that support your case?
4. What are the strongest arguments for your case?
5. Why must the present situation be changed?
6. Who else will be affected? Unions, other divisions or departments?
7. What are the arguments against your plan?
8. What alternatives are there to your plan?
9. To whom are you presenting your plan? Have you done any lobbying?
10. Have you discussed the finances with the experts?
11. Do you know who are your probable allies and who are likely to be your opponents?
12. Have you prepared handouts of any complicated figures?
13. Have you discussed the best time to present your case?
14. Your ideas were good when you first thought of them: are they still as good?

Chapter 6
Change management

Change is the only constant process which exists in organizations. An effective organization is one that takes deliberate steps to manage change smoothly. It will not always succeed – change can be a traumatic process – but at least it will try, and attempts to manage change can have the minimum objective of mitigating its effects on the organization and its employees.

The approach to the management of change will recognize that the key to success lies not only in a transformational leader, supported by powerful change mechanisms, but also by understanding that change is implemented by people and that it is their behaviour and support that count. The most important aim of change management is to achieve commitment to change.

Successful change management requires an understanding of:

- The main types of change
- How change affects individuals
- The process of change
- How to build commitment to change.

Types of change

There are two main types of change: strategic and operational.

Strategic change

Strategic change is concerned with broad, long-term and organization-wide issues. It is about moving to a future state which has been defined generally in terms of strategic vision and scope. It will cover the purpose and mission of the organization, its corporate philosophy on such matters as growth, quality, innovation and values concerning people, the customer needs served and the technologies employed. This overall definition leads to specifications of competitive positioning and strategic goals for achieving and maintaining competitive advantage and for product market development. These goals are supported by policies concerning marketing, sales, manufacturing, product and process development, finance and human resource management.

Strategic change takes place within the context of the external competitive, economic and social environment, and the organization's internal resources, capabilities, culture, structure and systems. Its successful implementation requires thorough analysis and understanding of these factors in the formulation and planning stages.

Operational change

Operational change relates to new systems, procedures, structures or technology which will have an immediate effect on working arrangements within a part of the organization. But the impact of such changes on people can be more significant than broader strategic change and they have to be handled just as carefully.

How people change

The ways in which people change are best explained by reference to the following assumptions developed by Bandura (4):

- People make conscious choices about their behaviour.
- The information people use to make their choices comes from their environment.
- Their choices are based upon:
  - The things that are important to them
  - The views they have about their own abilities to behave in certain ways
  - The consequences they think will accrue to whatever behaviour they decide to engage in.

For those concerned in change management, the implications of this theory are that:

- The tighter the link between a particular behaviour and a particular outcome, the more likely it is that we will engage in that behaviour
- The more desirable the outcome, the more likely it is that we will engage in behaviour that we believe will lead to it

- The more confident we are that we can actually assume a new behaviour, the more likely we are to try it.

To change people's behaviour, therefore, we have first to change the environment within which they work; second, convince them that the new behaviour is something they can accomplish (training is important); and third, persuade them that it will lead to an outcome that they will value. None of these steps is easy. To achieve them, it helps to know more about the process of change.

The process of change

Change, as Rosabeth Moss Kanter (29) puts it, is the process of analysing 'the past to elicit the present actions required for the future'. It involves moving from a present state, through a transitional state, to a future desired state.

The process starts with an awareness of the need for change. An analysis of this state and the factors that have created it leads to a diagnosis of the distinctive characteristics of the situation and an indication of the direction in which action needs to be taken. Possible courses of action can then be identified and evaluated and a choice made of the preferred action.

It is then necessary to decide how to get from here to there. Managing the change process in this transitional state is a critical phase in the change process. It is here that the problems of introducing change emerge and have to be managed. These problems can include resistance to change, low stability, high levels of stress, misdirected energy, conflict and losing momentum. Hence the need to do everything possible to anticipate reactions and likely impediments to the introduction of change.

The installation stage can also be painful. When planning change there is a tendency for people to think that it will be an entirely logical and linear process of going from A to B. It is not like that at all. As described by Pettigrew and Whipp (47), the implementation of change is an 'iterative, cumulative and reformulation-in-use process'.

The approach to change management

Michael Beer and his colleagues suggested in a seminal *Harvard Business Review* article, 'Why change programs don't produce change'(7), that most such programmes are guided by a theory of change which is fundamentally flawed. This theory states that changes in attitude lead to changes in behaviour. 'According to this model, change is like a conversion experience. Once people "get religion", changes in their behaviour will surely follow.'

They believe that this theory gets the change process exactly backwards:

> In fact, individual behaviour is powerfully shaped by the organizational roles people play. The most effective way to change behaviour, therefore, is to put people into a new organizational context, which imposes new roles, responsibilities and relationships on them. This creates a situation that in a sense 'forces' new attitudes and behaviour on people.

They prescribe six steps to effective change which concentrate on what they call 'task alignment' – reorganizing employees' roles, responsibilities and relationships to solve specific business problems in small units where goals and tasks can be clearly defined. The aim of following the overlapping steps is to build a self-reinforcing cycle of commitment, coordination and competence. The steps are:

1. Mobilize commitment to change through the joint analysis of problems.
2. Develop a shared vision of how to organize and manage to achieve goals such as competitiveness.
3. Foster consensus for the new vision, competence to enact it, and cohesion to move it along.
4. Spread revitalization to all departments without pushing it from the top – don't force the issue, let each department find its own way to the new organization.
5. Institutionalize revitalization through formal policies, systems and structures.
6. Monitor and adjust strategies in response to problems in the revitalization process.

The approach suggested by Michael Beer and his colleagues is fundamental to the effective management of change. It can, however, be associated with a number of other guidelines as set out below.

Guidelines for change management

- The achievement of sustainable change requires strong commitment and visionary leadership from the top.
- Understanding is necessary of the culture of the organization and the levers for change most likely to be effective therein.
- Those concerned with managing change at all levels should have the temperament and leadership skills appropriate to the circumstances of the organization and its change strategies.

- It is important to build a working environment which is conducive to change. This means developing the firm as a 'learning organization' (see Chapter 11, page 76).
- Although there may be an overall strategy for change, it is best tackled incrementally (except in crisis conditions). The change programme should be broken down into actionable segments for which people can be held accountable.
- The reward system should encourage innovation and recognize success in achieving change.
- Change implies streams of activity across time and 'may require the enduring of abortive efforts or the build up of slow incremental phases of adjustment which then allow short bursts of incremental action to take place' – Pettigrew and Whipp (47).
- Change will always involve failure as well as success. The failures must be expected and learned from.
- Hard evidence and data on the need for change are the most powerful tools for its achievement, but establishing the need for change is easier than deciding how to satisfy it.
- It is easier to change behaviour by changing processes, structures and systems than to change attitudes or the corporate culture.
- There are always people in organizations who welcome the challenges and opportunities that change can provide. They are the ones to be chosen as change agents.
- Resistance to change is inevitable if the individuals concerned feel that they are going to be worse off – implicitly or explicitly. The inept management of change will produce that reaction.
- In an age of global competition, technological innovation, turbulence, discontinuity, even chaos, change is inevitable and necessary. The organization must do all it can to explain why change is essential and how it will affect everyone. Moreover, every effort must be made to protect the interests of those affected by change.

See also Chapter 14 on how to manage culture change in organizations.

Gaining commitment to change

These guidelines point in one direction: having decided why changes are necessary, what the goals are and how they are to be achieved, the most important task is to gain the commitment of all concerned to the proposed change.

A strategy for gaining commitment to change should cover the following phases:

1. *Preparation.* In this phase, the person or persons likely to be affected by the proposed change are contacted in order to be made aware of it.

2. *Acceptance.* In the second phase, information is provided on the purpose of the change, how it is proposed to implement it and what effect it will have on those concerned. The aim is to achieve understanding of what the change means and to obtain a positive reaction. This is more likely if:

   - The change is perceived to be consistent with the mission and values of the organization
   - The change is not thought to be threatening
   - The change seems likely to meet the needs of those concerned
   - There is a compelling and fully understood reason for change
   - Those concerned are involved in planning and implementing the change programme on the principle that people support what they help to create
   - It is understood that steps will be taken to mitigate any detrimental effects of the change.

   It may be difficult, even impossible to meet these requirements. That is why the problems of gaining commitment to change should not be underestimated.

   During this phase, the extent to which reactions are positive or negative can be noted and action taken accordingly.

   It is at this stage that original plans may have to be modified to cater for legitimate reservations or second thoughts.

3. *Commitment.* During the third phase, the change is implemented and becomes operational. The change process and people's reaction to it need to be monitored. There will inevitably be delays, setbacks, unforeseen problems and negative reactions from those faced with the reality of change. A response to these reactions is essential so that valid criticisms can be acted upon or reasons given why the change should proceed as planned.

   Following implementation, the aim is to have the change adopted as, with use, its worth becomes evident. The decision is made at this stage whether to continue with the change or to modify or even abort it. Account should again be taken of the views of those involved.

   Finally, and after further modifications as required, the change is institutionalized and becomes an inherent part of the organization's culture and operations.

Case study

Managing change in the Benefits Agency

Ann Robinson, formerly a director of the Benefits Agency, reported at a conference in 1993 how they managed change in the Benefits Agency.

The Benefits Agency was established in 1991 as a Next Steps Agency. It inherited a very large organization with 60,000 staff, an annual administrative budget of two billion pounds and it paid out £60 billion a year in benefits.

The old organization had seen a lot of change, including major benefits reform and computerization. It did not want to know about becoming a Next Steps Agency and it did not want to know about any further change. There was tremendous resistance to change throughout the organization, and who can blame them? Staff wanted to know what was going to happen to them and were concerned about job losses. It was not a good atmosphere in which to introduce change.

But the government's expectations were clear. The Benefits Agency was the biggest of the Next Steps Agencies and the government's policy depended on it being successful. It was also clear that we were set up as a Next Steps Agency to do two things: first, to provide a better service; and second, to provide better value for money.

The image of the organization was poor, and quite rightly. It was poor because an inferior and inefficient service was being provided in a number of places, particularly in areas like London which arguably were the most vulnerable parts of the community.

So there had to be change and the expectation was that we would achieve a significant shift in the first year. A number of steps had therefore to be taken quickly, as I will now describe.

Organization

The first step we took was to flatten the structure. Many people hold the opinion that nothing should be done about structure until the issues of mission, values and strategy have been sorted out and in most circumstances they are right. But we were in the position of having to create a new organization so we took the opportunity to take out two layers of management. This was essential at that stage because we knew that we had to maximize devolution as the only way in which we could get problem-solving and decision-making to take place effectively at the sharp end. This gives the front-line staff freedom to define their own jobs and provide the service required and helps them to feel that they have a real stake in the organization.

Risk-taking and innovation

One of the important reasons for this approach was that it would encourage risk-taking and innovation. And it was essential to get very close to the customers, to be responsive and sensitive to their needs, not forcing them to fit bureaucratic needs.

Cultural change

These developments provided the framework for cultural change. In the old organization, the culture was inward-looking, bureaucratic, defensive and cautious. And we wanted one which was outward-looking, accountable to the public and customer focused. It is generally believed that culture change is a long and slow process. But we really had to make something change quickly – there had to be a marked shift in the first year.

The impetus was there – the need to adopt an entirely different approach as a Next Steps Agency. And if you have to achieve rapid cultural change, use any external threat or pressure to help make it happen.

We did not have the luxury of being able to spend four or five years on achieving change. We had to go for what we believed we could get, recognizing that we might not be able to achieve it all. We had to be absolutely clear about what needed to be done and what we were doing about it.

The key ingredients

Clear vision

Clarity of vision is one of the most important ingredients. With hindsight, we did not get that quite right at the outset but we began to when I launched my 'One Stop Shop', a holistic approach to the delivery of benefits.

Visibility

The new chief executive made a particular point of becoming highly visible to the staff. If you asked people in the old organization who led it, they would not have been able to tell you. The organization was too diffuse.

Values

We developed clear values for:

- Customer service, being responsive and flexible
- Caring for staff
- Value for money
- Bias for action – valuing people who achieve results.

It was not enough simply to state the core values. They had to be made to live not just by 'talking the talk' but also by 'walking the walk'. To achieve ownership of these values we put a premium on communications and we demonstrated their significance by the way we behaved.

Chapter 7
Clear thinking

Clear thinking is logical thinking. It is a process of reasoning by which one judgement is derived from another and correct conclusions are drawn from the evidence. Clear thinking is analytical: sifting information, selecting what is relevant, establishing and proving relationships.

If you say people are logical, you mean that they draw reasonable inferences – their conclusions can be proved by reference to the facts used to support them. They avoid ill-founded and tendentious arguments, generalizations and irrelevancies. Their chain of reasoning is clear, unemotional and based on relevant facts.

Clear thinking – a logical approach to problem-solving, decision-making and case presentation – is an essential attribute of an effective manager. This does not mean that it is the only way to think. Edward de Bono has made out an incontrovertible case for lateral, ie creative, thinking as a necessary process for innovative managers to use alongside the more traditional vertical or logical thinking pattern (see Chapter 17). But a logical approach is still an essential requirement.

A further attribute of a good manager is the ability to argue persuasively and to detect the flaws in other people's arguments. To think clearly and to argue well, you need to understand: first, how to develop a proposition or a case from basic principles; second, how to test your proposition; and third, how to avoid using fallacious arguments and how to expose the fallacies used by others.

Developing a proposition

The first rule is to 'get the facts'. It is the starting point for clear thinking. The facts must be relevant to the issue under consideration. If comparisons are being made, like must be compared with like. Trends must be related to an appropriate base date and, if trends are being compared, the same base should be used. Treat opinions with caution until they are supported by evidence. Avoid a superficial analysis of surface data. Dig deep. Take nothing for granted. Sift the evidence and discard what is irrelevant.

Your inferences should be derived *directly* from the facts. Where possible, the connection between the facts and the conclusion should be shown to be justified on the basis of verifiable and relevant experience or information on similar relationships occurring elsewhere.

If, as is likely, more than one inference can be deduced from the facts, you should test each inference to establish which one most clearly derives from the evidence as supported by experience. But it is no good saying 'it stands to reason' or 'it's common sense'. You have to produce the evidence which proves that the inference is reasonable and you have to pin down the vague concept of common sense to the data and experience upon which it is based. It was Descartes who wrote: 'Common sense is the best distributed commodity in the world, for every man is convinced that he is well supplied with it.'

Testing propositions

Susan Stebbing (53) in *Thinking to Some Purpose* wrote: 'We are content to accept without testing any belief that fits in with our prejudices and whose truth is necessary for the satisfaction of our desires.' Clear thinking must try to avoid this trap.

When we form a proposition or belief we generalize from what is observed – our own analysis or experience – and thence infer to what is not observed. We also refer to testimony – other people's observations and experience.

If your proposition or belief is derived from a generalization based upon particular instances you should test it by answering the following questions:

- Was the scope of the investigation sufficiently comprehensive?
- Are the instances representative or are they selected to support a point of view?
- Are there contradictory instances that have not been looked for?
- Does the proposition or belief in question conflict with other beliefs for which we have equally good grounds?
- If there are any conflicting beliefs or contradictory items of evidence, have they been put to the test against the original proposition?
- Could the evidence or testimony lead to other equally valid conclusions?
- Are there any other factors which have not been taken into account

which may have influenced the evidence and, therefore, the conclusion?

If your belief is based on testimony, you should test the reliability of the testimony, its relevance to the point, and whether or not your belief follows logically from the evidence, ie can reasonably be inferred from the facts.

Fallacious and misleading arguments

A fallacy is an unsound form of argument leading to a mistake in reasoning or a misleading impression. The main fallacies to avoid or to spot in other people's arguments are:

- Sweeping statements
- Potted thinking
- Special pleading
- Over-simplification
- Reaching false conclusions
- Begging the question
- False analogy
- Using words ambiguously
- Chop logic.

These are discussed briefly below.

Sweeping statements

In our desire for certainty and to carry the point we often indulge in sweeping statements. We sometimes then repeat them more and more loudly and angrily in order to convince our opponent. If we do it often enough and forcibly enough we can even deceive ourselves.

It has been said that 'it's never fair, it's never wise, it's never safe to generalize'. But that is a generalization in itself. Scientific method is based on generalizations. They can be valid if they are inferred properly from adequate, relevant and reliable evidence.

Generalizations are invalid when they have been produced by over-simplifying the facts or by selecting instances favourable to a contention while ignoring those that conflict with it. The classic form of a fallacious generalization is the contention that if some A is B then all A must be B. What frequently happens is that people say A is B when all they know is that *some* A is B or, at most, A *tends* to be B. The argument is misleading unless the word 'some' or 'tends' is admitted.

Many of the fallacies considered below are special cases of unsafe generalization, the most common symptom of unsound reasoning.

Potted thinking

Potted thinking happens when we argue using slogans and catch phrases, when we extend an assertion in an unwarrantable fashion.

It is natural to form confident beliefs about complicated matters when we are proposing or taking action. And it is equally natural to compress these beliefs into a single phrase or thought. But it is dangerous to accept compressed statements that save us the trouble of thinking. They are only acceptable if fresh thinking has preceded them.

Special pleading

If anyone says to you: 'everyone knows that', 'it's obvious that' or 'it's indisputably true that', you can be certain that he has taken for granted what he is about to assert.

We indulge in special pleading when we stress our own case and fail to see that there may be other points of view, other ways of looking at the question. Special pleading happens when we cannot detach ourselves from our own circumstances. We often blunder because we forget that what is true of one of us is also true of the other in the same situation.

A safeguard against this mistake is to change *you* into *I*. Thus, *I* feel that you can't see what is straight in front of your nose; *you* feel that I can't see what is on the other side of my blinkers. A rule that appears to be sound when I apply it to you may seem to be unsatisfactory when you ask me to apply it to myself.

Of course, thinking for too long about other points of view is a recipe for indecision. There are not necessarily two sides to every question and even if there are, you eventually – and often quickly – have to come down firmly on one side. But before you do this, check in case the other points of view or the alternative approaches are valid, and take them into account.

Over-simplification

Over-simplification is a special form of potted thinking or special pleading. It often arises in the form of what Susan Stebbing terms 'the fallacy of either black or white', the mistake of demanding that a sharp line should be drawn, when in fact no sharp line can be drawn. For example, we cannot ask for a clear distinction to be drawn between the sane and the insane, or between the intelligent and the unintelligent. Our readiness to make this mistake may be taken advantage of by a dishonest opponent, who insists that we define precisely that which does not permit such definition.

Reaching false conclusions

One of the most prevalent fallacies is that of forming the view that because *some* are or may be, *all* are. An assertion about several cases is twisted into an assertion about all cases. The conclusion does not follow the premise.

The most common form of this fallacy is what logicians call the 'undistributed middle', which refers to the traditional syllogism consisting of a premise, a middle term and a conclusion.

A valid syllogism takes the following form:

Premise	:	All cows are quadrupeds.
Middle term	:	All quadrupeds are vertebrates.
Conclusion	:	Therefore, all cows are vertebrates.

This may be represented as:

Premise	:	All A is B.
Middle term	:	All B is C.
Conclusion	:	Therefore, all A is C.

This is logical. The middle term is fully distributed. Everything that applies to A also applies to B, everything that applies to B also applies to C, therefore, everything that applies to A must apply to C.

An invalid syllogism would take the following form:

All cows are quadrupeds.
All mules are quadrupeds.
Therefore, all cows are mules.

This may be represented as:

All A is B.
All C is B.
Therefore, all A is C.

This is false because, although everything that applies to A and C also applies to B, there is nothing in their relationship to B which connects A and C together.

The difference between the true and false syllogism may be illustrated in Figure 7.1.

In the false syllogism, A and C could be quite distinct although still contained within B. To link them together goes beyond the original evidence. Because two things A and B are related to another thing, C, it

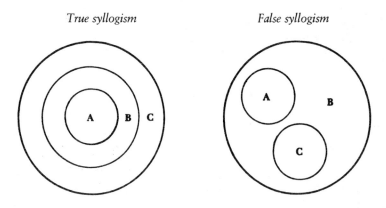

True syllogism   *False syllogism*

Figure 7.1: *The difference between true and false syllogisms*

does not *necessarily* mean that they are related together. In forming arguments, we too often jump to the conclusion that *some* means *all*.

Allowing the conclusion to go beyond the evidence can also take the form of assuming that because we are aware of the effect (the *consequent*), we also know the cause (the *antecedent*). But this assumption may be incorrect. An effect can have many different causes. This fallacy of the consequent, as it is termed, can be illustrated by the following example:

If he came up on the pools, he would go to the West Indies.
He has gone to the West Indies.
Therefore he has come up on the pools.

ie If P then Q,
Q
Therefore P.

But there are a number of other reasons why he could have gone to the West Indies besides coming up on the pools. A clear inference can only be drawn if the cause is directly related to the effect, thus:

If he comes up on the pools he will go to the West Indies.
He has come up on the pools.
Therefore he will go to the West Indies.
ie If P then Q,
P
Therefore Q.

A further danger in drawing conclusions from evidence is to forget that circumstances may alter cases. What has happened in the past will not necessarily happen again unless the circumstances are the same. You may be able to infer something from history but you cannot rely on that inference. Times change.

Begging the question

We beg the question when we take for granted what has yet to be proved. This can take the form of assuming the point in dispute without adequate reason; what the logicians call *petitio principii*.

If you spot someone taking for granted a premise which is not contained in his conclusion you must challenge the assumption and ask for information about the premises upon which the conclusion is based. You can then assess whether or not the conclusion follows logically from those premises.

Challenging assumptions is a necessary part of thinking clearly. You should challenge your own assumptions as well as those made by others.

False analogy

Analogy forms the basis of much of our thinking. We notice that two cases resemble each other in certain respects and then infer an extension of the resemblance. Analogies also aid understanding of an unfamiliar topic.

Analogies can be used falsely as vivid arguments without any real evidence. Just because A is B, where both are familiar matters of fact, does not mean that X is Y, where X and Y are unfamiliar or abstract. When we argue by analogy we claim that if:

x has properties of p1, p2, p3 and f, and
y has properties of p1, p2 and p3, therefore
y also has the property of f.

This could be true unless y has a property incompatible with f, in which case the argument is unsound.

Analogies may be used to suggest a conclusion but they cannot establish it. They can be carried too far. Sometimes their relevance is more apparent than real.

Use argument by analogy to help to support a case but do not rely upon it. Don't allow anyone else to get away with far-fetched analogies. They should be tested and their relevance should be proved.

Using words ambiguously

The Lewis Carroll approach – 'When I use a word it means just what I choose it to mean, neither more nor less' – is a favourite trick of those who aim to deceive. People use words that beg the question, that is, they define a word in a special way that supports their argument. They shift the meaning of words in different contexts. They may choose words which have the same meaning as each other but which show approval or disapproval. There is a well-known saying that the word 'firm' can be declined as follows: 'I am firm, You are obstinate, He is pigheaded.'

Chop logic

'Contrariwise,' continued Tweedledee, 'if it was so, it might be, and if it were so, it would be; but as it isn't, it ain't. That's logic.'

Chop logic is not quite as bad as that, but it can be equally misleading. It includes such debating tricks as:

- Selecting instances favourable to a contention while ignoring those that conflict with it
- Twisting an argument advanced by opponents to mean something quite different from what was intended – putting words in someone's mouth
- Diverting opponents by throwing on them the burden of proving something they have not maintained
- Deliberately ignoring the point in dispute
- Introducing irrelevant matter into the argument
- Reiterating what has been denied and ignoring what has been asserted.

Chapter 8
Coaching

Coaching is a personal (usually one-to-one), on-the-job approach used by managers and trainers to help people develop their skills and levels of competence. As a manager, you are there to get results through people; this means that you have a personal responsibility for ensuring that they acquire and develop the skills they need. Other people in the shape of training and management development specialists may help, but because by far the best way of learning is on the job, the onus is mainly on you.

The need for coaching may arise from formal or informal performance reviews but opportunities for coaching will emerge during normal day-to-day activities. Every time you delegate a new task to someone, a coaching opportunity is created to help the individual learn any new skills or techniques which are needed to do the job. Every time you provide feedback to an individual after a task has been completed, there is an opportunity to help that individual do better next time. Methods of giving feedback are described in Chapter 34.

The coaching process

Coaching consists of:

- Making people aware of how well they are performing by, for example, asking them questions to establish the extent to which they have thought through what they are doing
- Controlled delegation – ensuring that individuals not only know what is expected of them but also understand what they need to know and be able to do to complete the task satisfactorily. This gives you an opportunity to provide guidance at the outset – guidance at a later stage may be seen as interference

- Using whatever situations which may arise as opportunities to promote learning
- Encouraging people to look at higher-level problems and how they would tackle them.

Coaching skills

Coaching will be most effective when:

- The coach understands that his or her role is to help people to learn
- Individuals are motivated to learn – they should be aware that their present level of knowledge or skill, or their behaviour needs to be improved if they are going to perform their work to their own and to others' satisfaction
- Individuals are given guidance on what they should be learning and feedback on how they are doing
- Learning is an active, not a passive, process – individuals need to be actively involved with their coach
- The coach listens to individuals to understand what they want and need
- The coach adopts a constructive approach, building on strengths and experience.

Planned coaching

Coaching may be informal but it has to be planned. It is not simply checking from time to time on what people are doing and then advising them on how to do it better. Nor is it occasionally telling people where they have gone wrong and throwing in a lecture for good measure. As far as possible, coaching should take place within the framework of a general plan of the areas and direction in which individuals will benefit from further development. Coaching plans can and should be incorporated into the general development plans set out in a performance agreement as described in Chapter 34.

The manager as coach

Coaching enables you to provide motivation, structure and effective feedback as long as you have the required skills and commitment. As coaches, good managers believe that people can succeed and that they can contribute to their success. They can identify what people need to be able to do to improve their performance. They have to see this as an important part of the role – an enabling, empowering process which focuses on learning requirements.

Chapter 9
Communicating

People recognize the need to communicate but find it difficult. Like Schopenhauer's hedgehogs, they want to get together, it's only their prickles that keep them apart.

Words may sound or look precise, but they are not. All sorts of barriers exist between the communicator and the receiver. Unless these barriers are overcome the message will be distorted or will not get through.

Barriers to communication

Hearing what we want to hear

What we hear or understand when someone speaks to us is largely based on our own experience and background. Instead of hearing what people have told us, we hear what our minds tell us they have said. We have preconceptions about what people are going to say, and if what they say does not fit into our framework of reference we adjust it until it does. (Advice on how to listen is given later in this chapter.)

Ignoring conflicting information

We tend to ignore or reject communications that conflict with our own beliefs. If they are not rejected, some way is found of twisting and shaping their meaning to fit our preconceptions. When a message is inconsistent with existing beliefs, the receiver rejects its validity, avoids further exposure to it, easily forgets it and, in his or her memory, distorts what has been heard.

Perceptions about the communicator

It is difficult to separate what we hear from our feelings about the person who says it. Non-existent motives may be ascribed to the communicator. If we like people we are more likely to accept what they say – whether it is right or wrong – than if we dislike them.

Influence of the group

The group with which we identify influences our attitudes and feelings. What a group hears depends on its interests. Workers are more likely to listen to their colleagues, who share their experiences, than to outsiders such as managers or union officials.

Words mean different things to different people

Essentially, language is a method of using symbols to represent facts and feelings. Strictly speaking, we can't convey *meaning*, all we can do is to convey *words*. Do not assume that because something has a certain meaning to you, it will convey the same meaning to someone else.

Non-verbal communication

When we try to understand the meaning of what people say we listen to the words but we use other clues which convey meaning. We attend not only to *what* people say but to *how* they say it. We form impressions from what is called body language – eyes, shape of the mouth, the muscles of the face, even posture. We may feel that these tell us more about what someone is really saying than the words he or she uses. But there is enormous scope for misinterpretation.

Emotions

Our emotions colour our ability to convey or to receive the true message. When we are insecure or worried, what we hear seems more threatening than when we are secure and at peace with the world. When we are angry or depressed, we tend to reject what might otherwise seem like reasonable requests or good ideas. During heated argument, many things that are said may not be understood or may be badly distorted.

Noise

Any interference to communication is 'noise'. It can be literal noise which prevents the message being heard, or figurative in the shape of distracting or confused information which distorts or obscures the meaning.

Size

The larger and more complex the organization, the greater the problem of communication. The more levels of management and supervision through which a message has to pass, the greater the opportunity for distortion or misunderstanding.

Overcoming barriers to communication

Adjust to the world of the receiver

Try to predict the impact of what you are going to write or say on the receiver's feelings and attitudes. Tailor the message to fit the receiver's vocabulary, interests and values. Be aware of how the information might be misinterpreted because of prejudices, the influence of others and the tendency of people to reject what they do not want to hear.

Use feedback

Ensure that you get a message back from the receiver which tells you how much has been understood.

Use face-to-face communication

Whenever possible talk to people rather than write to them. That is how you get feedback. You can adjust or change your message according to reactions. You can also deliver it in a more human and understanding way – this can help to overcome prejudices. Verbal criticism can often be given in a more constructive manner than written reproof which always seems to be harsher.

Use reinforcement

You may have to present your message in a number of different ways to get it across. Re-emphasize the important points and follow up.

Use direct simple language

This seems obvious. But many people clutter up what they say with jargon, long words and elaborate sentences.

Suit the actions to the word

Communications have to be credible to be effective. There is nothing worse than promising the earth and then failing to deliver. When you say you are going to do something, do it. Next time you are more likely to be believed.

Use different channels

Some communications have to be in writing to put the message across promptly and without any variations in the way they are delivered. But, wherever possible, supplement written communications with the spoken word. Conversely, an oral briefing should be reinforced in writing.

Reduce problems of size

If you can, reduce the number of levels of management. Encourage a reasonable degree of informality in communications. Ensure that activities are grouped together to ease communication on matters of mutual concern.

Listening skills

There are many good writers and speakers but few good listeners. Most of us filter the spoken words addressed to us so that we absorb only some of them – frequently those we want to hear. Listening is an art which not many people cultivate. But it is a very necessary one, because a good listener will gather more information and achieve better rapport with the other person. And both these effects of good listening are essential to good communications.

People don't listen effectively because they are:

- Unable to concentrate, for whatever reason
- Too preoccupied with themselves
- Over-concerned with what they are going to say next
- Uncertain about what they are listening to or why they are listening to it
- Unable to follow the points or arguments made by the speaker
- Simply not interested in what is being said.

Effective listeners:

- Concentrate on the speaker, following not only words but also body language which, through the use of eyes or gestures, often underlines meaning and gives life to the message
- Respond quickly to points made by the speaker, if only in the shape of encouraging grunts
- Ask questions frequently to elucidate meaning and to give the speaker an opportunity to rephrase or underline a point
- Comment on the points made by the speaker, without interrupting the flow, in order to test understanding and demonstrate that the

speaker and listener are still on the same wavelength. These comments may reflect back or summarize something the speaker has said, thus giving an opportunity for him to reconsider or elucidate the point made

- Make notes on the key points – even if the notes are not referred to later they will help to concentrate the mind
- Are continuously evaluating the messages being delivered to check that they are understood and relevant to the purpose of the meeting
- Are alert at all times to the nuances of what the speaker is saying
- Do not slump in their chairs – they lean forward, show interest and maintain contact through their oral responses and by means of body language
- Are prepared to let the speaker go on with the minimum of interruption.

Chapter 10
Conflict management

Conflict is inevitable in organizations because the objectives, values and needs of groups and individuals do not always coincide. Conflict may be a sign of a healthy organization. Bland agreement on everything would be unnatural and enervating. There should be clashes of ideas about tasks and projects, and disagreements should not be suppressed. They should come out into the open because that is the only way to ensure that the issues are explored and conflicts are resolved.

There is such a thing as creative conflict – new or modified ideas, insights, approaches and solutions can be generated by a joint re-examination of the different points of view as long as this is based on an objective and rational exchange of information and ideas. But conflict becomes counter-productive when it is based on personality clashes, or when it is treated as an unseemly mess to be hurriedly cleared away, rather than as a problem to be worked through.

Conflict resolution can be concerned with conflict between groups or conflict between individuals.

Handling inter-group conflict

There are three principal ways of resolving inter-group conflict: peaceful coexistence, compromise and problem-solving.

Peaceful coexistence

The aim here is to smooth out differences and emphasize the common ground. People are encouraged to learn to live together; there is a good deal of information, contact and exchange of views, and individuals move freely between groups (for example, between headquarters and the field, or between sales and manufacturing).

This is a pleasant ideal, but it may not be practicable in many situations. There is much evidence that conflict is not necessarily resolved by bringing people together. Improved communications and techniques such as briefing groups may appear to be good ideas but are useless if management has nothing to say that people want to hear. There is also the danger that the real issues, submerged for the moment in an atmosphere of superficial bonhomie, will surface again later.

Compromise

The issue is resolved by negotiation or bargaining and neither party wins or loses. This concept of splitting the difference is essentially pessimistic. The hallmark of this approach is that there is no 'right' or 'best' answer. Agreements only accommodate differences. Real issues are not likely to be solved.

Problem-solving

An attempt is made to find a genuine solution to the problem rather than just accommodating different points of view. This is where the apparent paradox of 'creative conflict' comes in. Conflict situations can be used to advantage to create better solutions.

If solutions are to be developed by problem-solving, they have to be generated by those who share the responsibility for seeing that the solutions work. The sequence of actions is: first, those concerned work to define the problem and agree on the objectives to be attained in reaching a solution; second, the group develops alternative solutions and debates their merits; third, agreement is reached on the preferred course of action and how it should be implemented.

Handling conflict between individuals

Handling interpersonal conflict can be even more difficult than resolving conflicts between groups. Whether the conflict is openly hostile or subtly covert, strong personal feelings may be involved. Yet, as James Ware and Louis Barnes (58) say:

> The ability to productively manage such conflict is critical to managerial success. Interpersonal differences often become sharpest when the organizational stakes seem to be high, but almost all organizations include their share of small issues blown into major conflicts. The manager's problem is to build on human differences of opinion while not letting them jeopardize overall performance, satisfaction and growth.

71

Ware and Barnes go on to say that interpersonal conflict, like intergroup conflict, is an organizational reality which is neither good nor bad. It can be destructive, but it can also play a productive role. 'Problems usually arise when potential conflict is artificially suppressed, or when it escalates beyond the control of the adversaries or third-party intermediaries.'

The reaction to interpersonal conflict may be the withdrawal of either party, leaving the other one to hold the field. This is the classic win/lose situation. The problem has been resolved by force, but this may not be the best solution if it represents one person's point of view which has ignored counter-arguments, and has, in fact, steamrollered over them. The winner may be triumphant but the loser will be aggrieved and either demotivated or resolved to fight again another day. There will have been a lull in, but not an end to, the conflict.

Another approach is to smooth over differences and pretend that the conflict does not exist, although no attempt has been made to tackle the root causes. Again, this is an unsatisfactory approach. The issue is likely to re-emerge and the battle will recommence.

Yet another approach is bargaining to reach a compromise. This means that both sides are prepared to lose as well as win some points and the aim is to reach a solution acceptable to both sides. Bargaining, however, involves all sorts of tactical and often counter-productive games, and the parties are often more anxious to seek acceptable compromises than to achieve sound solutions.

Ware and Barnes identify two other approaches to managing interpersonal conflict: controlling, and constructive confrontation.

Controlling

Controlling can involve preventing interaction, or structuring the forms of interaction or reducing or changing external pressures.

Preventing interaction is a strategy for use when emotions are high. Conflict is controlled by keeping those apart in the hope that, although the differences still exist, the people involved have time to cool down and consider more constructive approaches. But this may only be a temporary expedient and the eventual confrontation could be even more explosive.

Structuring the forms of interaction can be a strategy when it is not possible to separate the parties. In these cases, ground rules can be developed to deal with the conflict concerning such behaviours as communicating information or dealing with specific issues. However, this may also be a temporary strategy if the strong underlying feelings are only suppressed rather than resolved.

Personal counselling is an approach which does not address the conflict itself but focuses on how the two people are reacting. Personal counselling gives people a chance to release pent-up tensions and may encourage them to think about new ways of resolving the conflict. But it does not address the essential nature of the conflict, which is the relationship between two people. That is why constructive confrontation offers the best hope of a long-term solution.

Constructive confrontation

Constructive confrontation is a method of bringing the individuals in conflict together, ideally with a third party whose function is to help build an exploratory and cooperative climate.

Constructive confrontation aims to get the parties involved to understand and explore the other's perceptions and feelings. It is a process of developing mutual understanding to produce a win/win situation. The issues will be confronted but on the basis of a joint analysis, with the help of the third party, of facts relating to the situation and the actual behaviour of those involved. Feelings will be expressed but they will be analysed by reference to specific events and behaviours rather than inferences or speculations about motives.

Third parties have a key role in this process, and it is not an easy one. They have to get agreement to the ground rules for discussions aimed at bringing out the facts and minimizing hostile behaviour. They must monitor the ways in which negative feelings are expressed and encourage the parties to produce new definitions of the problem and its cause or causes and new motives to reach a common solution. Third parties must avoid the temptation to support or appear to support either of those in contention. They should adopt a counselling approach, as follows:

- Listen actively
- Observe as well as listen
- Help people to understand and define the problem by asking pertinent, open-ended questions
- Recognize feelings and allow them to be expressed
- Help people to define problems for themselves
- Encourage people to explore alternative solutions
- Get people to develop their own implementation plans but provide advice and help if asked.

Conclusions

Conflict, as has been said, is in itself not to be deplored: it is an inevitable concomitant of progress and change. What is regrettable is the failure to use conflict constructively. Effective problem-solving and constructive confrontation both resolve conflicts and open up channels of discussion and cooperative action.

Many years ago one of the pioneering writers on management, Mary Parker Follett (19), wrote something on managing conflict which is as valid today as it was then:

> Differences can be made to contribute to the common cause if they are resolved by integration rather than domination or compromise.

Chapter 11
Continuous improvement

The concept of continuous improvement is based on the assumption that continually striving to reach ever higher standards in every part of the organization will provide a series of incremental gains that will build superior performance. In Japan the process is called *kaizen* which is a composite of the word *kai* meaning change, and *zen* meaning good or for the better. It consists of the organization creating an environment in which *all* employees can contribute to improving performance and overall effectiveness as a normal and continuing part of their job.

In an environment dedicated to continuous improvement, such as that developed at Nissan (61), the prime objective of managers and team leaders is to bring out new ideas and concepts from their staff. Their task is to create an environment in which new thinking is encouraged and welcomed. The management of Nissan believes that it is part of everyone's job to improve continually. This is embedded in the organization as a fundamental value not by exhortation but by practical steps such as workshops, where employees with ideas for new tooling or other changes can go to try them out.

The supervisor is expected to lead problem-solving and continuous improvement activities, but as experience develops, other team members will assume responsibility for improvement groups. It is accepted by managers and supervisors that they have no monopoly of wisdom on the best means of performing a task or making improvements. This is on the basis that the person actually doing the work is likely to know much more about the problem than they do.

By methods such as these and by constant emphasis at all levels on its importance, continuous improvement can become a way of life in an organization. It can, and should, be one of its key values, reflected in the way everyone behaves and underpinned by such processes as performance and reward management, where ability to stimulate and achieve improvements will be an important criterion for assessing and rewarding performance.

Implementing continuous improvement

The steps required to implement continuous improvement are:

1. Formulate and communicate the business strategy.
2. Define the key areas where a policy of continuous improvement will support the business strategy.
3. Appoint a member of the top management team to take charge.
4. Develop programmes for continuous improvement, with particular reference to process improvement, quality, and speeding up development, manufacturing and delivery times.
5. Provide facilities for identifying, reviewing and developing ideas for continuous improvement, eg improvement groups, team meetings, suggestion schemes.
6. Provide training in developing and implementing ideas.
7. Develop performance measures which enable progress to be monitored and assist in determining priorities for future developments.
8. Ensure that good ideas are recognized – the recognition need not necessarily be financial.
9. Communicate to everyone the aims of continuous improvement, how they are expected to contribute and what has been achieved.
10. Keep it simple. Avoid multiple initiatives and focus on developments which promise significant improvements.

The development of a culture of continuous improvement, however, is also fostered if the enterprise functions as a learning organization and implements continuous development policies.

The learning organization

A learning organization can be defined as an organization which facilitates the learning of all its members and continually transforms itself.

According to Alan Mumford (40), the characteristics of a learning organization are that it:

- Encourages managers and staff to identify their own learning needs
- Provides a regular review of performance and learning for the individual

- Encourages employees to set challenging learning goals for themselves
- Provides feedback at the time on both performance and achieved learning
- Reviews the performance of managers in helping to develop others
- Assists employees to see learning opportunities on the job
- Seeks to provide new experiences from which people can learn
- Provides or facilitates on-the-job training
- Tolerates some mistakes, provided people try to learn from them
- Encourages managers to review, conclude and plan learning activities
- Encourages people to challenge traditional ways of working.

Charles Handy (22) points out that a learning organization can and should mean two things: an organization which learns and/or an organization which encourages learning in its people. He believes that a learning organization needs a formal way of asking questions, seeking out theories, testing them and reflecting upon them. The learning organization constantly reframes the world and its part in it. Members of the organization are encouraged to suggest improvements. The organization has to find answers to questions about its strengths and talents, its weaknesses and what sort of organization it wants to be. It also has to cultivate its 'negative capability', ie its capacity to learn from its mistakes.

Explicit steps are taken by learning organizations to learn from experience. They provide various forums such as development centres, team meetings, 'away day' conferences and workshops to enable people to reflect on what they have learned and what they still need to learn. Such reflections provide a basis for formulating organizational and individual improvement plans.

A learning organization will be concerned with the development of skills and competences at all levels, emphasizing the importance of learning by informal means on the job with the help and guidance of managers and colleagues. The importance will be recognized of what Alan Mumford calls 'incidental learning' – the learning that can be built around incidents in everyone's day-to-day working life and career. Performance management, as described in Chapter 34, is a process which can systematize this incidental learning by providing for the review of achievements in relation to agreed objectives and the analysis of the behaviours which have contributed to success or failure.

Continuous improvement checklist

1. Does the culture of the organization support and encourage new

thinking and the involvement of employees at all levels in problem-solving and seeking improvements?

2. Is the capacity to involve people in seeking improvements and having new ideas accepted, recognized and rewarded appropriately?

3. Are people encouraged to challenge traditional ways of operating?

4. Are steps taken by the organization to ensure that the top management and employees at all levels have the 'space' and encouragement to reflect on their experiences and learn from them?

5. Are managers and individuals encouraged to identify their own learning needs and set learning goals for themselves?

6. Are managers and staff encouraged to see learning opportunities in their day-to-day work?

7. Are systematic efforts made by the organization and its managers to provide new experiences from which employees can learn?

8. Are people encouraged to learn from their mistakes as well as their successes?

9. Are forums (meetings, conferences, etc) provided for people to learn from their experiences and develop improvement plans?

10. Are managers encouraged to define and meet learning needs as they appear?

Chapter 12
Controlling

Basically, you are seeking to control two areas – input and output – and the relationship between them, which is productivity or performance. All managers will know Murphy's two laws: if anything can go wrong, it will; and of the things that can't go wrong, some will.

The aim of good control is to protect your plans from the operation of these laws as far as possible; to detect trouble spots before they erupt; to prevent those accidents which are just waiting to happen. Prevention is better than cure.

Essentials of control

Control is relative. It does not deal with absolutes, only with the difference between good and not-so-good performance.

The basis of control is measurement. It depends on accurate information about what is being achieved. This is then compared with what *should* have been achieved and with what has been achieved in the past. But that is only a starting point. Good control also identifies responsibility and points the way to action.

Effective control

If you want to exercise good control you need to:

1. *Plan* what you aim to achieve
2. *Measure* regularly what has been achieved
3. *Compare* actual achievements with the plan
4. *Take action* to exploit opportunities revealed by this information or to correct deviations from the plan.

Note that control is not only a matter of putting things right. It also has a positive side – getting more or better things done on the basis of information received.

Problems of control

A good control system is not easy to set up. There are two essentials:

- To set appropriate and fair targets, standards and budgets. (This may be difficult where the scope for quantification is limited or if circumstances make forecasts unreliable.)
- To decide what information is crucial for control purposes and design reports which clearly convey that information to the people who need it and can use it to point the way to action. This also produces problems. Too many control systems generate a surfeit of indigestible data which go to the wrong people and are not acted upon. You can have too little information, but there is also such a thing as information overkill. There is, moreover, a tendency for some people to report good results and cover up poor results. In any case, the figures may not tell the whole story.

Overcoming the problem

There are five steps to take if you want to achieve good control:

1. Decide what you want to control.
2. Decide how you are going to measure and review performance.
3. Use ratio analysis to make comparisons and to identify variations and problems.
4. Set up a control system.
5. Manage by exception.

Controlling inputs and outputs

In controlling input and output, and hence productivity, an overview is essential. It is no good concentrating on inputs, mainly expressed as costs, unless you look at the benefits arising from these expenditures and the effectiveness with which the costs have been incurred. Cost benefit and cost-effectiveness studies are an essential part of the control process.

Input control

When you control inputs you should aim to measure and assess the performance of:

- *Money* – its productivity, flow, liquidity and conservation.

You need to know what return you are getting on investments compared with the return you want.

You should ensure that you have the cash and working capital to run the business. Cash-flow analysis is vital. One of the golden rules of management, as stated by Robert Heller, is 'cash in must exceed cash out'.

You must conserve and provide the money needed to finance future trading and development projects and for capital investment.

Management has to know how effectively its financial resources are being used to produce goods, services and profits and this requires continuous and close attention to the control of direct and indirect costs and overheads generally.

- *People* – the effectiveness of the people you employ in terms of their quality and performance
- *Materials* – their availability, condition, convertibility and waste
- *Equipment* – machine utilization and capability.

Output control

- *Quantitative control measures* – the units produced or sold, the amount of services provided, the sales turnover obtained and the profits achieved. Key performance measures will vary between organizations. You need to determine through analysis which are the crucial indicators of success or failure.
- *Qualitative control measures* – the level of service provided by an organization (eg a public corporation) or by a non-productive department within an organization (eg personnel). It is more difficult to select valid performance measures in these areas, but the attempt should be made.

Productivity control

Productivity is the relationship between input and output. Cost benefit studies are productivity studies in that they assess how much benefit (output) is obtained from a given cost (input).

Productivity is expressed by ratios. A productivity index can be produced as follows:

$$\text{Productivity index} = \frac{\text{Output}}{\text{Input}} = \frac{\text{Performance achieved}}{\text{Resources consumed}} = \frac{\text{Effectiveness}}{\text{Efficiency}}$$

Ratio analysis

Expressing items as percentages or ratios of other items – ratio analysis – is the best way to measure and control inputs, outputs, productivity and the financial resources of the company generally. Ratios should not, however, be used in isolation. You should always take account of trends between present and past performance. And you should compare ratios within the business and between your business and other businesses. Most important, you should compare actual ratios with planned ratios.

It is essential to seek the *key* indicators in the form of ratios for your business. You will not want to collect sheets of ratios from every direction, but you should know when you look at a set of figures which one you have got to divide into the other to tell you what is really happening. It is no good just knowing how much sales have increased over the last period. You also need to know how the number of sales representatives has changed and the volume of sales per representative, this period compared with budget, the last period, and the same period last year.

The most important financial and productivity ratios are described below.

Return on capital employed

This is usually expressed as net profit as a percentage of capital. It tells you the extent to which an investment is paying off. It could apply to the whole business from the point of view of the shareholders, to part of the business, or to the specific return on an investment in capital equipment. When compared with the return you could get if you invested your money elsewhere, this ratio indicates the extent to which the investment is justified.

This can lead into an analysis of opportunity costs which are the costs as compared with the profit or loss expected from an alternative investment or course of action. In other words, if you failed to make a decision or take an opportunity that would have produced a better result than the decision you did make, that lost revenue is an 'opportunity cost'.

When analysing returns on capital employed, be careful to check the basis of the figures to ensure that like is compared with like. A common, but not universal, definition of capital employed includes share capital, reserves (excluding those for taxation), long-term loans and bank overdraft. The return figure is usually defined as net profit, excluding tax and interest on capital.

Tax is excluded because its varying nature makes it difficult to compare data from year to year. Interest on capital is omitted because its inclusion would mean that the return on capital would be measured *after* a return had been obtained on investment. Bear in mind that comparisons can be distorted when there are few fixed assets, for example, when plant is rented or leased by the company.

Profit to sales ratio

This is the fundamental measure of the profitability of the company as a trading concern. It is expressed as a ratio:

$$\frac{\text{Net trading profit (ie the difference between expenses and income from sales)}}{\text{Sales revenue}}$$

Solvency ratios

These measure the company's short-term financial liabilities – its ability to pay its current liabilities as they fall due.

The 'current' ratio is calculated as follows:

$$\frac{\text{Current assets (stock, debtors and cash)}}{\text{Current liabilities (creditors and accrued charges)}}$$

If the current ratio is more than 1:1, the company has more current assets than current liabilities and, if it were forced to pay out all its current liabilities, would have sufficient current assets to do so.

If a really strict appraisal of a company's solvency is required, however, it is best to leave stock out of the current assets, and to take only the liquid assets into consideration. This is because if a company were forced to realize its stock quickly, it is doubtful if it would even recover its cost value. The ratio then becomes:

$$\frac{\text{Current assets excluding stock}}{\text{Current liabilities}}$$

This is sometimes called the 'acid test'. Ideally, the ratio should be at least 1:1 but there are cases where a ratio of somewhat less than 1:1 is acceptable. Too high a ratio, on the other hand, would mean that the company is not making sufficient use of its finances – cash by itself does not generate much profit.

Stock ratios

If the company holds too much stock it will be wasting its financial resources in an unused asset. If it holds too little stock it will lose sales revenue through not being able to service its customers.

To measure how much is being tied up in stock use the ratio:

$$\frac{\text{Stock}}{\text{Current assets}}$$

To measure how quickly the stock is turned over (stock turn) the ratio is:

$$\frac{\text{Sales}}{\text{Stock}}$$

The greater the stock turnover figure the better for the company. If the goods are being sold at a profit, the more that are sold the better the profit at the year end.

Other financial ratios

There are a number of other financial ratios you can use. Perhaps the most important are:

$$\frac{\text{Debtors}}{\text{Average daily sales}}$$

This measures how well management is speeding the flow of cash through the business, ie how many days' credit is being allowed to customers.

$$\frac{\text{Debtors}}{\text{Creditors}}$$

If creditors begin to outweigh debtors this may be a sign that the company is over-trading. The bad debt ratio (bad debts/sales) is also revealing.

$$\frac{\text{Current liabilities} - (\text{current assets minus stock})}{\text{Profit before tax and interest}} \times 365$$

This is the current liquidity ratio. It shows how many days it would take at current profit levels to pay off the deficit between current liabilities and liquid assets.

Productivity ratios

The most useful productivity ratio is:

$$\frac{\text{Results}}{\text{Resources}} \quad \text{ie} \quad \frac{\text{Sales}}{\text{Employees}}$$

The other main ratios are:

$$\frac{\text{Units produced or processed}}{\text{Number of employees}}$$

$$\frac{\text{Added value (ie sales revenue minus cost of sales)}}{\text{Number of employees}}$$

$$\frac{\text{Profit after tax}}{\text{Number of employees}}$$

Cost ratios

The best way to look at costs is to express them as a percentage of sales. Thus the fundamental measure is:

$$\frac{\text{Overheads}}{\text{Sales}} \times 100$$

Other measures include:

$$\frac{\text{Payroll costs}}{\text{Sales}} \times 100$$

$$\frac{\text{Cost of materials and bought in parts}}{\text{Sales}} \times 100$$

$$\frac{\text{Selling costs}}{\text{Sales}} \times 100$$

Use of ratios

Use ratios as you would use any other figures. They are no more than indicators. In themselves, they will not tell the whole story. You have to dig. A ratio is no more than a symptom. You need to find out the real cause of a variation or problem.

Control systems

What you need from a control system

Your basic requirement is reports that clearly identify areas of good and bad performance so that appropriate action can be taken.

At higher levels 'exception reporting' should be adopted so that significant deviations, on which action should be taken, can be highlighted. Overall summaries of performance against plan and of trends will also be necessary at this level, but these may disguise significant underlying deviations which would be pointed out in an exception report.

The reports themselves should:

- Contain measurements which are accurate, valid and reliable. Permit a direct and easy comparison between planned and actual performance
- Analyse trends, comparing one period's performance with that of the previous period or of the same period the previous year and, where appropriate, summarizing the year to date position
- Be given to the person who is responsible for the activity concerned

- Arrive promptly, in time to allow the necessary action to be taken
- Provide succinct explanations of any deviations from plan.

Measurements

Measurement is a good thing, but all figures need to be treated with caution. They may conceal more than they reveal. The weaknesses to look for are:

- *Non-representative reporting* – data selected which do not cover the key issues, disguise unfavourable results or over-emphasize favourable performance.
- *Not comparing like with like* – the 'apples and pears syndrome'. For example, a trend or projection which does not take account of changing or new factors which have altered or will alter the situation since the base data were collected.
- *Not starting from a common base*. This is a variant on the 'like with like' problem. Trend comparisons should be related to a common base in terms both of the period and the elements covered by the information.
- *Misleading averages*. Averages do not always tell you the whole story. They may conceal extremes in performance, which are significant.
- *Unintentional errors* – simple mistakes in calculation, presentation or observation.
- *Measurements out of context*. Almost any single measure is influenced by, or inseparable from, other measures. Figures in isolation may not mean very much. You have to know about relationships and underlying influences.

Management by exception

Management by exception is a system which rings alarm bells only when the manager's attention is needed. The principle was invented by the father of scientific management, Frederick Taylor (55). In 1911 he wrote in *Principles of Scientific Management*:

> Under the exception principle the manager should receive only condensed, summarized and invariably comparative reports covering, however, all of the elements entering into the management and even these summaries should all be carefully gone over by an assistant before they reach the manager, and have all the exceptions to the past averages or standards pointed out, both the especially good and the especially bad exceptions, thus giving him in a few minutes a full view of progress which is being

made, or the reverse, and leaving him free to consider the broader lines of policy and to study the character and fitness of the important men under him.

Management by exception frees the boss to concentrate on the issues that matter. It gives the subordinate more scope to get on with his or her work while knowing that events out of the ordinary will be reported upwards.

Deciding what constitutes an exception is a useful exercise in itself. It means selecting the key events and measures which will show up good, bad or indifferent results and indicate whether or not performance is going according to plan.

The chosen indicators or ratios can be studied so that the significance of changes or trends is readily understood. More important, the possible causes of deviations can be analysed and kept in mind. Investigations will then be quickly launched in the right direction and swift remedial action can be taken.

Most of us have come across the boss or manager who seems to have the almost magic facility for studying a mass of figures and immediately spotting the one really important deviation or the item that does not ring true. It sometimes seems to be pure instinct, but of course it is not. Such managers are practising the art of management by exception, even if they never call it by that name. Their experience and analytical powers have told them what constitutes normal performance. But they can spot something out of the ordinary at a thousand paces. They *know* what the key indicators are and they look for them, hard. This is a skill that anyone can develop. And the effort of acquiring it is well worth while.

Chapter 13
Coordinating

Coordinating – 'achieving unity of effort' – is not a separate function of a manager. The concept of coordination does not describe a *particular* set of operations but *all* operations which lead to a certain result.

Coordination is required because individual actions need to be synchronized. Some activities must follow one another in sequence. Others must go on at the same time and in the same direction in order to finish together.

How to coordinate

Obviously, you can achieve good coordination if you get people to work well together. This means integrating their activities, communicating well, exercising leadership, and team building (all subjects covered in individual chapters). But you should also pay attention to the specific techniques discussed below.

Planning

Coordination should take place before the event rather than after it. Planning is the first step. This means deciding what should be done and when. It is a process of dividing the total task into a number of sequenced or related sub-tasks. Then you work out priorities and time-scales.

Organizing

You know what should be done. You then decide who does it. When you divide work between people you should avoid breaking apart those tasks which are linked together and which you cannot separate cleanly from each other.

Your biggest problem will be deciding where the boundaries between distinct but related activities should be. If the boundary is either too rigid or insufficiently well defined, you may have coordination problems. Don't rely too much upon the formal organization as defined in job descriptions, charts and manuals. If you do, you will induce inflexibility and set up communication barriers, and these are fatal to coordination.

The informal organization which exists in all companies can help coordination. When people work together they develop a system of social relationships which cut across formal organizational boundaries. They create a network of informal groups which tend to discipline themselves. This frees management from detailed supervision and control and leaves it more time for planning, problem-solving and the overall monitoring of performance.

Delegating

The informal organization can help, but you still need to delegate work to individuals in a way that ensures they know what is expected of them *and* are aware of the need to liaise with others to achieve a coordinated result.

The art is to make everyone concerned understand the points on which they must link up with other people and the time in which such actions have to be completed. You should not have to *tell* people to coordinate; they should coordinate almost automatically. This they will do if you delegate not only specific tasks but also the job of working with others.

Communicating

You should not only communicate clearly what you want done, you should also encourage people to communicate with one another.

Avoid situations in which people can say: 'Why didn't someone tell me about this? If they had, I could have told them how to get out of the difficulty.' Nobody should be allowed to resort to James Forsyte's excuse that 'no one tells me anything'. It is up to people to find out what they need to know and not wait to be told.

Controlling

If you use the processes described above, and they work, theoretically you will not have to worry any more about coordination. But of course, life is not like that. You must monitor actions and results, spot problems and take swift corrective action when necessary. Coordination doesn't just happen. It has to be worked at, but avoid getting too involved. Allow people as much freedom as possible to develop horizontal relationships. These can facilitate coordination far more effectively than rigid and authoritarian control from above.

A case study

There is no one right way of coordinating a number of activities. It all depends on the nature of those activities and the circumstances in which they are carried out; for example, the present organization structure, the existence of coordinating committees and the facility with which communication can take place between those involved. Ultimately, good coordination depends upon the will of everyone concerned – to coordinate or be coordinated. Mechanical devices such as committees will not necessarily do the trick.

An example of good coordination took place in a company which was developing a new product in a new market. Neither the product nor the market fitted conveniently into the existing divisional structure and it was therefore decided to appoint one man as project manager to get the product launched. He would have a staff of two – a brand manager and a secretary. The work of development, production, marketing, selling and customer servicing would be carried out by the relevant departments in various divisions of the company.

The project manager had the status and authority to get things done by each department. The board was right behind the project and had allocated the priorities and resources required. But the different activities had to be coordinated and only the project manager could do it.

The easy way out would have been to set up a massive coordinating committee and leave it at that. This would have failed. Projects of this complexity cannot be coordinated just by creating a committee.

The project manager developed a different approach which proved to be highly successful. His first objective was to make everyone concerned enthusiastic about the project. He wanted them to believe in its importance so that they would be committed to working closely with the other departments involved.

His next step was to hold separate discussions with departmental heads so that they completely understood the programme of work required in each area. With the help of a project planner he then drew up a chart showing the key events and activities, and the relationships between them and the sequence in which they needed to take place in order to complete the project. This chart was distributed to all the departmental heads supplemented by an explanatory brief on the work required at each stage of the programme. Only then did he call a meeting to iron out difficulties and to ensure that everyone knew what had to be done and when.

He set up a system of progress reports and held progress meetings with departmental heads. But these were only held as necessary and he did not rely upon them to achieve coordination. He depended much more on personal contacts with individual managers, reviewing problems, noting where adjustments to the programme were needed, and stimulating the managers to even greater efforts when required. It was time consuming, but it kept him closely in touch so that he could anticipate any likely delays, setbacks or failures in communication, and be in a position to take action. He used the chart as his main instrument for checking that the critical events took place as planned.

The successful coordination and completion of the project were not achieved by one method but by the judicious use of a combination of techniques relevant to the situation: motivating, team building, planning, integrating, monitoring and controlling.

Chapter 14

Corporate culture and how to manage it

What is corporate culture?

Corporate culture is the pattern of shared beliefs, attitudes, assumptions and values in an organization which may not have been articulated but, in the absence of direct instructions, shape the way people act and interact and strongly influence the ways in which work is carried out.

Corporate culture is a key component in the achievement of an organization's mission and strategies, the improvement of organizational effectiveness and the management of change.

The significance of culture arises because it is rooted in deeply held beliefs. It reflects what has worked in the past, being composed of responses which have been accepted because they have met with success.

Corporate culture can work for an organization by creating an environment which is conducive to performance improvement and the management of change. It can work against an organization by erecting barriers which prevent the attainment of corporate strategies. These barriers include resistance to change and lack of commitment.

Corporate culture can be described in terms of *values, norms and artifacts*. It will be perceived by members of the company as *organizational climate*, and it will influence and be expressed by *management style*.

Values

Values refer to what is regarded as important. They are expressed in beliefs of what is best or good for the organization and what sort of behaviour is desirable. The 'value set' of an organization may only be recognized at top level, or it may be shared throughout the organization so that it could be described as being 'value driven'.

Areas in which values can be expressed include:

- Care and consideration for people

- Care for customers
- Competitiveness
- Enterprise
- Equity in the treatment of employees
- Excellence
- Growth
- Innovation
- Market/customer orientation
- Priority given to organizational rather than to people needs
- Performance orientation
- Productivity
- Provision of equal opportunity for employees
- Quality
- Social responsibility
- Teamwork.

Norms

Norms are the unwritten rules of behaviour, the 'rules of the game', which provide informal guidelines on how to behave. Norms tell people what they are supposed to be doing, saying, believing, even wearing. They are never expressed in writing – if they were, they would be policies or procedures. They are passed on by word of mouth or behaviour and can be enforced by the reactions of people if they are violated. Norms can exert very powerful pressure on behaviour because of these reactions – we control others by the way we react to them.

Norms refer to such aspects of behaviour as:

- How managers treat subordinates and how subordinates relate to their subordinates
- The prevailing work ethic, eg 'Word hard, play hard', 'Come in early, stay late', 'If you cannot finish your work during business hours you are obviously inefficient', 'Look busy at all times', 'Look relaxed at all times'
- Status – how much importance is attached to it; the existence or lack of obvious status symbols
- Ambitions – naked ambition is expected and approved of, or a more subtle approach may be the norm
- Performance – exacting performance standards are general; the highest praise that can be given in the organization is to be referred to as very professional
- Power – recognized as a way of life; executed by political means, dependent on expertise and ability rather than position; concentrated

at the top; shared at different levels in different parts of the organization.

- Politics – rife throughout the organization and treated as normal behaviour; not accepted as overt behaviour
- Loyalty – expected, a cradle-to-grave approach to careers; discounted, the emphasis is on results and contribution in the short term
- Anger – openly expressed; hidden, but expressed through other, possibly political, means
- Approachability – managers are expected to be approachable and visible; everything happens behind closed doors
- Formality – a cool, formal approach is the norm; forenames are/are not used at all levels; there are unwritten but clearly understood rules about dress.

Artifacts

Artifacts are the visible and tangible aspects of an organization which people hear, see or feel. Artifacts can include the working environment, the tone and language used in letters or memoranda, the manner in which people address each other at meetings or over the telephone, the welcome (or lack of welcome) given to visitors and the way in which telephonists deal with outside calls. Artifacts can be very revealing.

Organizational climate

Organizational climate is how people perceive (see and feel about) the culture that has been created in their company or unit. It can be measured by the use of attitude surveys.

Management style

Management style describes the way in which managers set about achieving results through people. It is how managers behave as team leaders and how they exercise authority. Managers can be autocratic or democratic, tough or soft, demanding or easy-going, directive or laissez-faire, distant or accessible, destructive or supportive, task orientated or people orientated, rigid or flexible, considerate or unfeeling, friendly or cold, keyed up or relaxed. How they behave will depend partly on themselves – their natural inclinations – partly on the example given to them by their managers and partly on organizational values and norms.

Development of culture

The norms and values which are the basis of culture will be developed over time as a result of the influence of the organization's external environment and its internal processes, systems and technology.

The external environment covers economic, market, competitive and social trends, technological innovations and government interventions. Internally, culture is shaped by the purpose, strategy and technology of the organization and by particularly significant events or influences, such as a major crisis or the impact of a dynamic, visionary and inspirational chief executive. In fact, the philosophy and values of top management over the years will have played a dominant role.

Culture is developed and manifests itself in different ways in different organizations. It is not possible to say that one culture is better than another, only that it is dissimilar in certain ways. There is no such thing as an ideal culture, only an appropriate culture. This means that there can be no universal prescription for managing culture, although there are certain approaches which can be helpful, as described in the next section.

What is culture management?

Culture management is the process of developing or reinforcing an appropriate culture – that is, one which helps the organization to fulfil its purpose.

Culture management is concerned with:

- *Culture change*, the development of attitudes, beliefs and values which will be congruent with the organization's mission, strategies, environment and technologies. The aim is to achieve significant changes in organizational climate, management style and behaviour which positively support the achievement of the organization's objectives
- *Culture reinforcement*, which aims to preserve and reinforce what is good or functional about the present culture
- *Change management*, which is concerned with enabling the culture to adapt successfully to change and gaining acceptance for changes in organization, systems, procedures and methods of work (see Chapter 6)
- *Commitment gain*, which is concerned with the commitment of members of the organization to its mission, strategies and values.

Aims of culture management

The aims of culture management are to:

- Develop an ideology which guides management on the formulation and implementation of coherent strategies and policies for managing the organization and its members

- Create and maintain a positive climate within an organization which indicates the behaviour which is expected of its members in the course of their work
- Promote understanding of, and commitment to, the values of the organization.

Culture management does not, however, aim to impose a uniform, bland culture on an organization. It recognizes that different cultures may be appropriate to its different parts. Although there will be certain values which management believes are important, the process of disseminating them will show that members of the organization have their own sets of values which they will only modify if convinced that it is in their own interests as well as those of the organization.

The management of the organization's culture is a central activity for senior management with the advice and help of human resource management specialists in their increasingly important role as internal consultants.

Approaches to culture management

Culture management is about reinforcing or embedding an existing functional culture or changing a dysfunctional culture. It is a matter of analysis and diagnosis followed by the application of appropriate reinforcement or change levers.

The steps required in a culture management programme are:

1. Develop a vision of what the organization needs to become.
2. In the light of this vision, define and communicate the organization's mission.
3. Define and communicate the corporate or business strategies required to fulfil the mission.
4. Analyse the present culture of the organization – its values, norms, artifacts, management style and organization climate. The analysis can be conducted by attitude surveys, structured interviews or focus group discussions (a focus group is a group of people brought together to discuss a number of defined issues).
5. Prepare and implement a cultural change programme.

Managing cultural change

The process of managing cultural change can be modelled as three interlocking circles as shown in Figure 14.1.

The three key factors are:

- *Vision and commitment* – top management must articulate their vision of the culture they would like to have. They must then show their commitment by working within the articulated vision.
- *Communication* – people need to understand and work through the rationale for culture change, what it means for them and how they, the organization and its other stakeholders will benefit.
- *Supporting processes and systems*, eg education and training, performance management, reward systems.

The circles interlock because each of these elements must move forward together in harmony to achieve successful culture change.

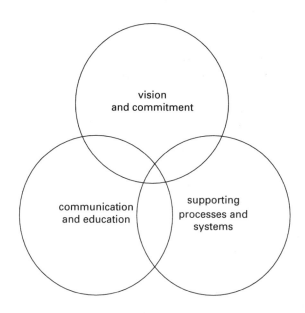

Figure 14.1: *The elements of cultural change*

Examples of cultural change programmes

British Airways

To quote what Dr Nicholas Georgiadis, formerly Director of Human Resources British Airways, said at the Management Centre Europe conference in Lisbon in 1987: 'British Airways has changed. Five years ago it was sick. It is now much healthier. At the root of that recovery (from losses of £11 million in 1981/82 to cumulative profits of £536 million over the last three years) is customer service.'

The dominant culture in British Airways, according to Georgiadis, had been militaristic and bureaucratic. And his comment on this was that: 'You cannot determine human behaviour by referring to paragraph 3(9)x. You cannot provide quality customer service by administrative fiat. What you have to have is an empowered workforce – a workforce which knows it has the power to take action and that its decisions will be backed by the bosses.'

The British Airways management decided that the main area for cultural change was customer service and that the key to successful customer service lies in ensuring that your people feel good about themselves and their company. In short, customer care demands caring, skilful management to support the caring skills for which British Airways managers were 'untrained, uninformed and unrewarded'.

The culture change programme was divided into three parts:

1. *Putting people first* – a two-day intensive workshop aimed at all customer contact staff, encouraging them to think about the importance of customer service. The workshop looked at issues such as the importance of helping other people to give good customer service, who owns a customer's problem, and the importance of body language in all human interaction. All 40,000 employees went through this programme.
2. *A day in the life* – a one-day event designed to help all staff to understand their mutual interdependence. Some 30,000 staff enjoyed this day.
3. *Managing people first* – a five-and-a-half-day event for managers which dealt with five themes:

   Urgency which should come from the leader, not from events – this means that managers must be pro-active rather than running just to stand still as they simply react to events.

   Vision which is 'having the image of a cathedral as we mix the cement' – managers must be able to work both in the here and now, as they mix the cement, and focus on the future as they plan the cathedral.

Motivation which is management by expectation – expect the best and catch them doing it right – because people who feel good about themselves and their manager produce good results.

Trust which gives confidence to the individual to act alone – and spirit to the group to act together – freeing people to own the problem and use their own judgement without fear.

Above all, *responsibility*, believing that I am in charge of my own behaviour which means that I can change the way I do things.

In addition to these courses, a new performance appraisal scheme was introduced, based on the mentor system, which focused on managerial behaviour, especially team management and the management of subordinates. Having been told how to do it in the 'managing people first' programme, appraisal tells them how they are doing, and 'pay for performance' rewards them for doing it.

ICL

The background to ICL's cultural change programme was provided by the new managing director who said:

I gradually realized that I lacked the levers to transfer my strategic insight into the hearts and minds of the organization so that they shared the imperative. They had to know *why*, not just *what*. An impressive programme of communication was not enough. I got immensely frustrated – thousands of bright people all working hard but not buying into the direction.

He is also reported as having used the well-worn Second World War saying of a US general: 'I have seen the enemy, and he is us.'

Mission statement
The approach was based on a new mission for the company implying significant changes in direction. This was defined as: ICL is an international company dedicated to applying information technology to provide profitable, high-value customer solutions for operational and management effectiveness.

Key strategies
Objectives were set which were designed to build strength as a major

European player in information technology, to focus on specific markets, and to be known as a systems integrator with a reputation for quality.

The key strategies were to be built around:

- High-value solutions to defined markets
- Commitment to open systems – providing customers with greater flexibility in the choice of manufacturer and with confidence for the future
- Collaborations – to gain market or technical leverage
- Organizational responsiveness – to react to the fast-changing market
- Focus on systems and solutions for customers and on providing real added value for them in running their business
- Changing the way that people thought, made their decisions and conducted their lives in the company. These can be summarized as follows:

From	To
technology-led	marketing-led
tactical, short-term	strategic, long-term
internal focus	external focus
try and do everything	specialized target markets
parochial	company commitment
procedure-bound	innovative and open-minded
UK expert	global competitor

Chapter 15
Cost cutting

Costs always need controlling. You should start with the assumption that costs are too high and can be reduced. This assumption is based on the knowledge that some companies have not only survived but flourished after drastic cost-cutting exercises. When you remove the fat that always exists, you are left with a leaner and more powerful organization.

Cost cutting requires these basic approaches:

- Decide where and what to cut.
- Plan to cut.
- Conduct the cost-reduction exercise.

What to cut

Your attack on costs should concentrate on these six areas:

- *Labour costs.* In labour-intensive companies manpower costs may exceed 50 per cent of income. Overmanning, especially in service and staff departments, is a major contributory cause of excessively high costs. Labour costs will include the direct costs of salaries, wages and benefits and the indirect cost of the personnel and training functions.
- *Manufacturing costs.* These are the actual costs incurred in making products; they reflect labour, material and operating costs but also, most important, the way in which the product has been designed.
- *Selling costs.* These may be largely accounted for by the sales force which is covered under labour costs. But the figure will also include advertising, promotions, public relations, packaging and display material.
- *Development costs.* These are the costs of developing new products, markets, processes and materials, and of acquiring new businesses.

- *Material and inventory costs.* The cost of buying materials and bought-in parts and of maintaining optimum stock levels.
- *Operating costs.* All the other costs incurred in operating the business. These will include space, computers, the provision of plant and equipment, paperwork systems and all the services required to keep the organization going.

Waste

Any examination of costs should aim to identify wasteful practices. The areas where they can occur need to be identified before conducting a cost-reduction exercise so that attention can be directed to likely trouble spots. Concentrate both on company practices or procedures which lead to waste or pointless costs and on areas where staff can waste time or incur unnecessary expenditure.

The company can be wasteful in any or all of the following ways:

- Unnecessary forms or over-complex paperwork procedures
- Too much checking and verifying of work
- Too many and/or too large committees
- Too many layers of management
- Bottlenecks and inefficient work flows or procurement procedures
- Delays in decision-making because authority is not delegated down the line
- Over-rigid adherence to rules and regulations
- Too much commitment to paper.

Time-wasting practices by staff include lateness or leaving early, prolonged tea or meal breaks, unnecessary breaks for any other reason, and dealing with personal matters in company time.

Cost-creating practices include absenteeism and frequent absence through illness (which may or may not be justified). Other wasteful practices include extravagant use of the company's facilities and equipment, such as photocopying machines, telephones and stationery.

Planning to cut costs

First, you build cost-effectiveness into your plans, using value analysis techniques when you can. Then you introduce or improve procedures which define what costs you can incur and, at a later stage, control expenditure against budget. Zero-base budgeting, as described in Chapter 4, is a useful technique for taking every expense and 'shaking it' to make sure that it is justified.

Plans

Plans should be based on cost/benefit studies which aim to find the best ratio between expenditure and results, ie to minimize costs and maximize benefits. The emphasis should be on realism. It is good to be forward looking and entrepreneurial. But if you are like that, you are always in danger of becoming euphoric about the future, overestimating the benefits and underestimating the costs. At the planning stage you must be realistic about costs. Don't accept averages and assumed overhead rates. Obtain actuals. Find out what you are really going to spend and add at least 10 per cent for contingencies. Allow for inflation too.

You should be equally realistic about likely benefits. Do some 'sensitivity analysis' to determine the effects on profits and costs of optimistic, realistic and pessimistic forecasts of performance.

Design

Ensure that when products, systems or services are designed, at every stage the costs of what you are going to do are evaluated. Use value analysis techniques for this purpose.

Value analysis

Value analysis takes each part of the product, service or system, and subjects it to detailed examination to see if there is any way in which its costs could be reduced without affecting quality. You start with the assumption that anything you use or do can be bought, made or operated at less cost.

Value analysis in manufacturing is often carried out by a committee using brainstorming techniques to consider alternative, less costly ways of achieving the functions for which the article is being manufactured. These functions cover the use to which the article is being put and, therefore, consideration has to be given to marketing and pricing considerations as well as manufacturing costs. But, given a definition of use, the main aim of value analysis is to reduce the costs of materials, processing and labour. The following is a checklist of points to be covered.

1. Does its use contribute to value?
2. Is its cost proportionate to its usefulness?
3. Does it need all its features?
4. Is there a better alternative which will meet its intended use?
5. Can a usable part be made by a less costly method?
6. Can a standard and less costly part be used instead?
7. Will another dependable supplier provide it at less cost?
8. Can alternative and cheaper materials or components be used?

9. Can it be manufactured with the use of less skilled labour or less expensive machinery or equipment?
10. Can it be manufactured in a way which will reduce the number of standard labour hours required?
11. Can its design be simplified to reduce manufacturing costs?
12. Can the tolerances specified be modified to ease manufacture and reduce reject rates?

Although value analysis was first developed as a design engineering technique, the approach is equally applicable to the design of any system or service where the component parts can be costed.

The cost-reduction exercise

A cost-reduction exercise is a planned campaign aimed at cutting costs by a specified amount. It requires three steps:

- *Setting targets*, either for immediate cuts in crisis conditions or for specific reductions in the short term (defined in weeks rather than months). Targets may be set in specific areas, eg a 10 per cent cut in staff; or they may be for a more comprehensive overhead reduction or a productivity increase.

  The significant impact of overheads on profits should be emphasized to everyone. It is interesting to note that in a company with a turnover of £200,000 where profits are 10 per cent of sales, a reduction in the ratio of labour costs to sales from 11 to 10 per cent would increase profits by 10 per cent. It all ends up on the bottom line, and that is what counts.

  Productivity targets expressed in financial terms, such as 'reduce costs per unit of output by 3 per cent', may be less immediate but they could usefully be incorporated in a set of cost-reduction targets as longer-term objectives. Increases in productivity can be achieved by reducing costs in relation to output, or by increasing output in relation to costs or, preferably, by both reducing costs and increasing output (see Chapter 41). The message must be put across that unit costs are there to be attacked at all times – after all, they aggregate into total costs. Wherever possible, get down to basics – the shop floor and the general office. That is where the main costs are incurred. Keep it simple. Look at specific items. Use value analysis. Compare and contrast to identify places where costs are excessive.
- *Deciding where to cut*, which will probably be in manpower costs or wasteful practices. It is remarkable how often departmental managers who scream with pain when they are told to cut their staff

by 10 per cent cope quite well afterwards. O & M specialists will claim and prove that they can always cut staff numbers by 15 per cent without reducing efficiency.

With regard to wasteful or unnecessary practices, Sir Derek Rayner's campaign in Marks & Spencer illustrated what can be done. A drive on paperwork eliminated 26 million forms in annual use and cut the number of staff by 25 per cent.

- *Deciding how to cut*: allocating responsibilities and then drawing up the programme and implementing it.

Responsibility for the cost-reduction exercise

The most important thing to do is to appoint as senior an executive as possible, preferably a full-time member of the board, to direct the cost-reduction exercise. He or she should have drive, energy, determination and, most important, the authority and courage to implement measures, however unpleasant some of them may be.

The question of who is to assist this executive then arises. You may consider using management consultants to help and give advice on specific problem areas. But do not ask consultants to carry out the main task. If your organization is not capable of taking action itself, however drastic, it does not deserve to survive.

Neither should you set up a committee to control the exercise. Committees are obstacles to action. You might set up a small (not more than three people) project team of senior executives, but do not let them function as a standing committee with agenda, minutes, and so on. Better still, give complete authority to one director to control the exercise, to use whom he wants when he wants and to call meetings as and when he thinks fit.

The director in charge of the exercise requires terms of reference by which to operate. These should normally take the form of a set of targets to be achieved by a given date or sequence of dates. If there are any constraints (eg don't sack the chairman's son-in-law) they should be mentioned now. The director should also be told the extent of his or her authority to make decisions and when and in what circumstances to report back. He or she can then proceed to solicit opinions about what needs to be done, gather the facts to support or refute the opinions, define the problem areas, decide what to do and draw up a programme for doing it.

Approach to the exercise

The highly successful cost-reduction exercises conducted by Marks & Spencer used the most simple of questioning techniques:

- What is done?
- Why is it done?
- Does it need to be done at all?
- If it needs to be done, can it be simplified or carried out more cheaply?

The basis of the approach, to paraphrase Wittgenstein, was 'if anything needs to be done at all it can be done more simply'.

A number of other principles emerged from the Marks & Spencer experience which are universally applicable. These were summarized by Sir Derek Rayner as follows:

- *Top managers must accept a revision of the administrator's task.* Top management has imposed on administration countless rules and regulations to ensure that the systems and methods used in the business are foolproof. These have apparently been 'written largely on the assumption that all employees fall into two categories: stupid or crooked'. As Sir Derek wrote: 'If you cast the role of the administrator as bureaucrat he will perform it superbly.' The paraphernalia of administrative systems drawn up under this type of regime can only be swept away by top management.
- *The price of perfection is prohibitive: sensible approximation costs less.* Or, in Voltaire's words, 'the best is the enemy of the good'. Aim towards perfection, but don't overstretch yourself in achieving it. Productivity applied to administration means one person trying to achieve 95 per cent efficiency and reaching it, rather than two people trying to achieve 100 per cent and reaching perhaps 90 per cent.
- *Most employees can be trusted.* If this principle is accepted, a wide range of checks and monitoring can be discarded and replaced by managers managing and supervisors supervising. Thorough spot checks can be used to supplement day-to-day management.
- *All staff can help to bring about the desired changes.* Most people, if encouraged, will bring forward ideas to simplify and rationalize their work.
- *Staff can become too specialized.* Too many specialists create unnecessary work and hinder flexibility. 'Specialists exist to serve and ease the running of the business, not to stifle initiative, become barriers to action, and create yet another paper chain.'
- *Never legislate for every eventuality* but instead leave as much as possible to the common sense of those who are trusted in managerial positions.
- *These is no substitute for personal probing into what really happens.* 'You will find your most cherished documents and reports conceal a multitude of inaccuracies and omissions. Do not be afraid of only a

sample first-hand investigation. It is often far more valuable than the all-embracing written one. And do not mistake for personal probing a meeting held in a private office.'

A case study

The policy pursued over a long period by Marks & Spencer is the best example of a company-wide programme for improving productivity by streamlining procedures and eliminating wasteful and unnecessary practices.

The main attack launched by Sir Derek Rayner in Marks & Spencer was on unnecessary paperwork, which generates unnecessary work and leads to the employment of superfluous labour.

The purpose was not to achieve economies for economy's sake, but to make more effective use of resources. The campaign eliminated 26 million forms in annual use and progressively reduced the number of staff from 27,000 to 20,000. Yet Marks & Spencer continued to grow rapidly.

An example of the improvements produced by the campaign was a complete change in the method of providing merchandizing information to the stores. There was a detailed system of recording sales, stocks and requirements which was theoretically sound. Unfortunately, it took many people a great deal of time to digest the information and to act upon it. They were tied to paper and could not see the merchandise for the figures. The system was completely swept away and members of the staff were invited to pay more attention to the goods themselves, which, of course, they then had time to do. Very short summaries were now sent to head office and many simple ways of giving the stores a reasonably balanced supply of goods were developed.

Another key change was the reduction in the extent to which staff in the stores had become specialized, largely because of the forms and systems used. For example, there were many stock room specialists and the stock rooms were virtually isolated from the sales floor. Sales personnel had to fill in a form if they required stock for their counters. The stock was sorted out by a stock room specialist and eventually delivered to the counters. This practice was abolished and the stock room was thrown open to all, so that sales staff could simply go and replenish their counters. This not only saved time and paper and speeded up the supply of goods, but also paid an unexpected dividend in that the sales staff quickly became far more interested in their jobs.

Simultaneously with this drive on unnecessary paperwork, Marks & Spencer stopped recruitment. It became apparent in the early stages of the exercise that each stage in simplification meant that the system could work with fewer people. As simplification proceeded, the staff numbers steadily ran down by natural wastage. At the same time, people were redeployed from unproductive to productive work.

To win one battle, however, does not mean that you have won the war. As Sir Derek Rayner wrote:

> Though our management believed it was alert to the dangers of excessive paperwork and over-complication, the familiar signs of trouble began to reappear; for instance, fast-rising administrative expenses and ever-increasing demands for more staff. So . . . we mounted a new campaign known as 'Good Housekeeping'. Again the results were outstanding. Millions of pieces of paper in the shape of reports, forms and returns were eliminated. Thousands of hours spent on needless detail were saved. We reduced the staff from 27,000 people to 26,000 by not hiring replacements as employees left . . . Most important, good housekeeping has freed our managers to spend more time on managing instead of interpreting the written word. It has enabled important staff members to get away more often from their desks and learn first hand what is going on in the stores and in supplier organizations.

This campaign saved 200,000 forms a year by simplifying control of cash in tills. Stock control was simplified and the information needed by headquarters was cut by half a million pages a year. The investigating team dispensed with the 13 million forms used each year to process returned goods before the customer got his or her money back: why not, they asked, meet legitimate claims at once from the till? The campaign reduced staff costs by 5 per cent, *and*, Sir Derek Rayner argues, it gave customers a better service.

Chapter 16
Counselling

Counselling has been described by the Institute of Personnel Management (26) as: 'Any activity in the workplace where one individual uses a set of skills and techniques to help another individual to take responsibility for and to manage their own decision-making whether it is work related or personal.'

Counselling is central to the management and development of people. All managers engage in some activity which could be termed as counselling during their normal working life. It is therefore a natural component of management – an everyday activity which can arise from immediate feedback or play an important part in a formal performance review session (see Chapter 34).

One important aim as a manager is to encourage individuals to accept much of the responsibility for their own self-development. What people seek out for themselves, with some guidance as necessary, is likely to make a greater impact than anything handed out to them by their managers or by a trainer. Of course, you still have to make clear what you expect individuals to achieve. It is also necessary to ensure that people have the required training and guidance to enable them to meet your expectations. There will be occasions when you have to spell out how you expect the job to be done. But you will make no progress in developing the skills and abilities of your staff if you only *tell* them how to do things or how they should solve their work problems. Your job is to do as much as you can to help them to help themselves, because that is the best way for them to learn.

The counselling process

The counselling process as described by the IPM consists of three stages:

- *Recognition and understanding* – recognizing the indicators of problems and issues.
- *Empowering* – enabling employees to recognize their own problem or situation and encouraging them to express it.
- *Resourcing* – managing the problem, which will include the decision on who is best able to act as counsellor: the manager, the specialist or an outside resource.

Counselling stages

Egan (17) has suggested that the stages to be followed in counselling are:

1. *Listening, understanding and communicating.* This focuses on understanding the perspective of the other person and communicating that understanding. It is non-judgemental and concentrates on ensuring that both parties have the same understanding of the situation.
2. *Changing the picture.* Talking through an issue can help to change the individual's perspective and indicate a solution to the problem. But this does not always happen and as a counsellor you may have to use the 'tougher' skills of challenging and confronting, sharing the other's different perceptions and providing a different framework. The initial listening phase should have established an atmosphere of acceptance and openness which enables this tougher stage to take the process forward into action.
3. *Implementing action.* In this stage you resource the individual to take action. You become a facilitator, helping the individual to formulate action plans, and providing expertise and guidance as necessary. But it is not your role as a counsellor to tell the individual what action to take. Individuals must be helped to work out for themselves what needs to be done and how it should be done, although you should provide the resources required in the shape of coaching, training or the provision of better working facilities or systems. You can also be available to provide any additional guidance or help each individual requires.

Counselling skills

The counselling skills you need to develop are:

- *Problem identification* – recognizing that the problem exists
- *Open questioning* – probing by open-ended, non-directive questions

to identify the real focus of the problem rather than concentrating on its symptoms

- *Listening* – the ability to listen actively to obtain the full story by probing, evaluating, interpreting and supporting
- *Sensitivity* – to individual beliefs and values, some of which may be based on culture or religion
- *Reflecting* – being able to restate the problem from the individual's point of view
- *Empathy* – having regard for the feelings and anxieties of the individual
- *Impartiality* – the ability to remain non-judgemental and to refrain from prescribing solutions
- *Sincerity* – having a genuine attitude of interest and openness to the individual's problems
- *Belief* – having the belief that individuals have the resources to solve their own problems, albeit with passive or active help.

Chapter 17
Creative thinking

Walter Bagehot wrote: 'It is often said that men are ruled by their imagination; but it would be truer to say that they are governed by the weakness of their imagination.'

Unimaginative management is a sure way to failure. Creative thinking aims to overcome the danger of being governed by this weakness.

Creative and logical thinking

Creative thinking is imaginative thinking. It produces new ideas, new ways of looking at things. It relates things or ideas which were previously unrelated. It is discontinuous and divergent. Edward de Bono (11) invented the phrase 'lateral thinking' for it and this term has stuck; it implies sideways leaps in the imagination rather than a continuous progression down a logical chain of reasoning.

Logical or analytical thinking is a step-by-step process. It is continuous, one step leading to the next until, ideally, you converge on the only possible solution. It is sometimes called 'convergent' thinking; de Bono refers to it as 'vertical thinking' because you go straight down the line from one state of information to another.

De Bono summed up the differences between vertical and lateral thinking as follows:

Vertical thinking	Lateral thinking
Chooses	Changes
Looks for what is right	Looks for what is different
One thing must follow directly from another	Makes deliberate jumps
Concentrates on relevance	Welcomes chance intrusions
Moves in the most likely directions	Explores the least likely

Creative thinking is not superior to logical thinking. It's just different. The best managers are both creative and logical. Eventually, however creative they have been, they have to make a decision. And logical thinking is necessary to ensure that it is the right decision.

The process of creativity

In *The Act of Creation*, Arthur Koestler (32) described the process of creativity as one of 'bisociation'; putting together two unconnected facts or ideas to form a single idea. The establishment of the relationship or bisociation is usually accompanied by a release of tension. There is a flash of illumination leading to a shout of 'Eureka!' or at least 'Aha!' As Koestler remarks, it is like the release of tension after the unexpected punch line of a joke – the 'haha' reaction. Or even the less dramatic release of tension when confronting a work of art.

If we assume that it is desirable to increase our capacity for creative thinking, there are three steps to take:

1. Understand the barriers to creative thinking.
2. Develop individual capacity for creative thinking.
3. Use the collective capacities of groups of people to develop new ideas by brainstorming.

Barriers to creative thinking

The main barriers to creative thinking are:

- Allowing your mind to be conditioned into following a dominant pattern – the mind is a patterning system and this means you can be trapped into a fixed way of looking at things, what de Bono calls a 'concept prison', or a 'tethering factor'
- Restricting the free growth of your ideas within rigidly drawn boundaries which are treated as limiting conditions
- Failure to identify and examine the assumptions you are making to ensure that they are not restricting the development of new ideas
- Polarizing alternatives – reducing every decision to an 'either/or' when there may be other ways of looking at things
- Being conditioned to think sequentially rather than laterally and looking for the 'best' idea, not different ideas. As de Bono says: 'It is better to have enough ideas for some of them to be wrong than always to be right by having no ideas at all.'

- Lack of effort in challenging the obvious – it is tempting to slip into the easy solution
- Evaluating too quickly – jumping to conclusions and not giving yourself enough time to allow your imagination to range freely over other possible ways of looking at things
- A tendency to conform – to give the answer expected
- Fear of looking foolish or being put down.

How to develop your ability to think creatively

If you want to think more creatively, the first thing to do is to analyse yourself. Go through the list of barriers to creativity and ask yourself the question, 'Is this me?' If it is, think about ways in which you can overcome the difficulty, concentrating on:

- Breaking away from any restrictions
- Opening up your mind to generate new ideas
- Delaying judgement until you have thoroughly explored the alternative ideas.

Breaking away

To break away from the constraints on your ability to generate new ideas you should:

- Identify the dominant ideas influencing your thinking
- Define the boundaries (ie past experience, precedents, policies, procedures, rules) within which you are working and try to get outside them by asking questions such as:

  - Are the constraints reasonable?
  - Is past experience reliable?
  - What's new about the present situation?
  - Is there another way?

- Bring your assumptions out into the open and challenge any which restrict your freedom to develop new ideas
- Reject 'either/or' propositions – ask, 'Is there really a simple choice between alternatives?'
- Keep on asking 'Why?' (But bear in mind that if you do this too bluntly to other people you can antagonize them.)

Generating new ideas

To generate new ideas you have to open up your mind. If you have removed some of the constraints as suggested above you will be in a better position to:

- Look at the situation differently, exploring all possible angles
- List as many alternative approaches as possible without seeking the 'one best way' (there is no such thing) and without indulging in premature evaluation (which can only lead to partial satisfaction)
- In de Bono's words, 'arrange discontinuity', deliberately set out to break the mould. The techniques for triggering off new ideas include:

  - Free thinking, allowing your mind to wander over alternative and in many cases apparently irrelevant ways of looking at the situation
  - Deliberately exposing yourself to new influences in the form of people, articles, books, indeed anything which might give you a different insight, even though it might not be immediately relevant
  - Switching yourself or other people from problem to problem
  - Arranging for the cross-fertilization of ideas with other people
  - Using analogies to spark off ideas. The analogy should be suggested by the problem but should then be allowed to exist in its own right to indicate a different way of looking at the problem.

Delaying judgement

Your aim in creative thinking should be to separate the evaluation of ideas from their generation. The worst mistake you can make is to kill off new ideas too quickly. It is always easy to find ten ways of saying 'no' to anything. For example:

- It won't work.
- We're already doing it.
- It's been tried before without success.
- It's not practical.
- It won't solve the problem.
- It's too risky.
- It's based on pure theory.
- It will cost too much.
- It will antagonize the customers/the boss/the union/the workers/ the shareholders, etc.
- It will create more problems than it solves.

Some of these objections may be valid. But they should be held back until you have generated as many ideas as possible. Allow ideas to grow a little. Don't strangle them at birth.

It is too easy to say 'no', too easy to ridicule anything new or different. In creative thinking it is the end result that counts, and if you want it to be original you must not worry too much about the route you follow to get there. It doesn't matter if you stumble sometimes or take the wrong turning, as long as delays are not protracted and you arrive in the right place at the end.

As de Bono (11) says:

> In vertical thinking one has to be right at every step. So, no matter how many steps are taken, the end point (idea, solution, conclusion) is automatically right if all the intervening steps have been right . . . In lateral thinking one does not *have* to be right at each step, but one must be right at the *end*.

Delaying judgement is difficult. It goes against the grain. You have to make a conscious effort to hold back until the right moment arrives, which is when you feel that you have collected as many new ideas as you can in the time available.

Our training, our inhibitions, our reluctance to look foolish or to go out on a limb all work against us. We should certainly try to do it ourselves and persuade other people to go along with us. But we can help the processes of opening up, introducing discontinuity and releasing new ideas by the technique of brainstorming.

Brainstorming

Brainstorming has been defined as a means of getting a large number of ideas from a group of people in a short time. It is essentially a group activity which uses a formal setting to generate as many ideas as possible without pausing to evaluate them.

The main features of a brainstorming session are as follows:

1. A group of between six and twelve people is assembled. Some will be directly involved with the problem, some should be drawn from other areas from which they can bring different ideas and experience to bear on the problem. There is a chairman and a note-taker.

2. The chairman defines the rules, emphasizing that:

   - The aim is to get as many ideas as possible
   - No attempt will be made to evaluate any ideas
   - No one should feel inhibited about coming up with suggestions.

3. If necessary there is a warm-up session to familiarize the group with the procedure. For example, they could be asked to suggest how many uses they can think of for a paper clip.

4. The chairman states the problem, avoiding the trap of defining it too narrowly.

5. The chairman opens the session by a phrase such as 'In how many ways can we . . .?'

6. The chairman encourages people to contribute and prevents any attempt to evaluate ideas. From time to time he or she may restate the problem.

7. The note-taker condenses the ideas suggested and lists them on flip charts, not attempting to act as an editor or worrying about duplications at this stage. The session should not be tape recorded as this may inhibit ideas.

8. The chairman keeps on encouraging the group to contribute, trying to get people to freewheel and produce as many ideas as possible – good, bad, indifferent, sensible or silly. He or she keeps the pace going and never comments or allows anyone else to comment on a contribution. Every idea is treated as relevant.

9. The chairman closes the meeting after 30 minutes or so – 45 minutes at most. The session must not be allowed to drag on.

10. Evaluation takes place later, possibly with a different group. At this session the aim is to:

   – Select ideas for immediate use
   – Identify ideas for further exploration
   – Review any different approaches which have been revealed by the session.

Brainstorming is a useful technique for releasing ideas, overcoming inhibitions, cross-fertilizing ideas and getting away from patterned thinking. It needs to be planned and executed carefully and proper evaluation is essential.

Use it selectively, where there seems to be ample scope for different ideas. It will not solve all your problems but can help you to crash through the barriers erected by the traditional approaches to decision-making.

Remember that however creative you are, what you finally decide on has to work. Brainstorming and other techniques for increasing creativity will help you to break new ground, but eventually you will have to think clearly and analytically about the pros and cons of the preferred solution before making your final decision.

Chapter 18
Crisis management

What is crisis management?

The phrase 'crisis management' was coined by Robert Macnamara at the time of the Cuban missile crisis when he said: 'There is no longer any such thing as strategy, only crisis management.'

Crisis management is a phrase used most commonly in diplomatic circles but it is something that happens in any organization where the pressure of events – external or internal – forces management into making urgent decisions. These arise because a crisis is a turning-point or a time of danger and suspense, and, in this turbulent age, turning-points and dangerous moments are always with us.

Crisis management can be defined as:

> The process of dealing with a pressurized situation in a way which plans, organizes, directs and controls a number of interrelated operations and guides the decision-making process of those in charge to a rapid but unhurried resolution of the acute problem faced by the organization.

Causes of crises

Crises are caused either by the actions of human beings or by natural disasters – fire, flood, earthquake, etc. If people are at the root of the crisis they may be deliberately inflicting harm on the organization from outside or, also externally, they may have taken actions which indirectly create a major problem. Internally, crises can be caused deliberately by people attempting to enforce their point of view or accidentally by some colossal misjudgement or a long history of compounded errors.

Crises may, however, be no more than sudden, unforeseen events which perhaps could have been anticipated. To dismiss strategy, as Macnamara did, is perhaps going too far, but Robert Burns did suggest that: 'The best laid schemes o' mice an' men gang aft a-gley', and this is as true today as when he wrote it in the eighteenth century.

In an ideal world, crises would not happen. You would know where you want to go and you would get there, with only minor deviations along the way. Problems would have been foreseen and contingency plans made to deal with them. This, of course, is not the way things are in real life. Murphy's law is always ready to strike again – if anything can go wrong it will.

Crises may appear to come suddenly, but this does not mean that they are unforeseeable. The Garcia Márquez novella, *Chronicle of a Death Foretold*, was written about a crisis, the murder of a young man, but, as the title implies, everyone knew it was going to happen only no one seemed able to stop it. Prior to a crisis there are often warning signs that disaster is about to strike. Even a volcanic explosion can be predicted.

There is a phenomenon which can be described as 'crisis slide'. Gradually, imperceptibly but inevitably, there is a build-up of events. Rain falls in ever-increasing volumes; the overflowing river is joined by equally overflowing streams, and the pressure increases. The force becomes progressively more irresistible until, under overwhelming pressure, the dam breaks. The crisis management process should, of course, have started as soon as observers had noticed the unusually heavy rainfall. Human error, however, creeps in and dams burst.

Steady slides down the slippery slope to an outright crisis can also happen, not because of human error, but because of human cussedness. If crisis management techniques are used coolly to assess potentially dangerous situations and bring the parties together in good time to discuss how to resolve the problems before they become critical, the dire effects of cussedness can be avoided. This can happen on the international scene as well as within organizations. Before Cuba, President Kennedy had been made aware of 60 nuclear near-disasters, including the launching of two missiles with nuclear warheads. He took steps not only to improve the US system of accident proofing but also to exchange information with the Russians. The Falklands crisis, however, was a sad story of a complete failure of the British both to understand how strongly the Argentines felt about the Malvinas and to appreciate that Galtieri was liable to go off the rails.

Management crises

In management all sorts of crises can happen: a takeover bid, a collapse in the foreign exchange rate, a drug which has disastrous side-effects, a competitive product which suddenly appears on the market and wipes the floor with a market leader brand, an innovation which renders a product obsolete, a sudden damaging strike, a dishonest senior executive who gets the company into the headlines, a fire or a flood, the departure of key members of the management team to competitors, and so on. The list is endless.

Tolstoy said of marriages: 'All happy families resemble one another, but each unhappy family is unhappy in its own way.' The same can be said of crises. Each crisis is a unique event and has to be dealt with accordingly. However, there are certain types of behaviour which are appropriate in all critical situations and there are some general principles that can be followed in crises involving negotiation or conflict. There are also a number of crisis management techniques that are generally applicable, subject to modification to suit particular circumstances.

Crisis management behaviour

The most important thing to do in a crisis is to keep cool. As Kipling put it:

> If you can keep your head when all about you
> Are losing theirs and blaming it on you . . .
> Yours is the Earth and everything that's in it
> And – which is more – you'll be a Man, my son.

Perhaps the best exponent of this approach was Harold Macmillan who said at London Airport of a political crisis in his Cabinet: 'I thought the best thing to do was to settle up these little local difficulties, and then turn to the wider vision of the Commonwealth.' But another Prime Minister, James Callaghan, went too far when he said, also at London Airport (a great place for aphorisms), 'Crisis, what crisis?'

Statesmen, of course, have to give the impression of playing it cool. Henry Kissinger, who spent his whole diplomatic career in crisis management, said once: 'There cannot be a crisis next week. My schedule is already full.' But managers should play it cool too.

One of the arts of dealing with a crisis is to maintain the confidence of everyone around that you *are* managing it. Insouciance like Macmillan's, but not like Callaghan's, is one way of doing this. Another way is deliberately to give the impression that you are taking it easy – relaxing almost – when in actual fact you are working at top speed. Good crisis managers, in situations where all hell is let loose, and people and pieces of paper are being thrown about in all directions, and three telephones are ringing at once, will, from time to time, lean back in their chair, sip a cup of coffee, and idly gossip about last night's football game. They then resume work with redoubled energy. Robert Townsend (56) described this approach well in *Up the Organization* when he wrote: 'There is a time for engagement and a time for withdrawal. A time to contemplate it, and a time just to laugh at it.'

And in *The Right Stuff*, Tom Wolfe, in describing how Chuck Yeager (the man who broke the sound barrier for the first time with two broken ribs) influenced the crisis management style of airline pilots, wrote this about their approach:

> Anyone who travels very much on airlines in the United States soon gets to know the voice of the airline pilot . . . coming over the intercom . . . with a particular drawl, a particular folksiness, a particular down-home calmness that is so exaggerated it begins to parody itself (nevertheless! – it's reassuring) . . . the voice that tells you, as the airliner is caught in thunderheads and goes bolting up and down a thousand feet at a single gulp, to check your seat belt because 'it might get a little choppy'.

Negotiating situations

Crises concerning takeovers, industrial relations, legal disputes and other problems where the crunch has come because two sides have radically different views, will often involve negotiations. The normal negotiating tactics described in Chapter 31 will apply, although they may have to be speeded up.

In tense situations, special ploys may have to be used. For example, you can use the 'Trollope' ploy, which is the acceptance of an offer that has not been made in order to induce the adversary to accept the acceptance. Robert Kennedy coined this term, naming it after those Victorian heroines in the novels of Anthony Trollope who interpret a squeeze of the hand on the hero's part as a proposal of marriage and succeed in making this interpretation stick. It was used in the Cuban missile crisis where the ambiguity arose in communications from Mr Krushchev. He sent two letters, one implying a hard line about the American blockade, the other a mild and even yielding one. To deepen the confusion, it was not clear whether the 'hawklike' letter (which was received second) had been written before or after the 'dovelike' one. The American decision (the Trollope ploy) was to treat the dovelike letter as the true communication, ignoring the other hawklike one which was probably written second as the Russian's final position. As reported by Robert Kennedy, it was this creative use of ambiguity which enabled the settlement to be reached.

In negotiations it can indeed be said that a shadow of ambiguity over a situation may be as effective as real strength. It gives you more room to manoeuvre and more scope to vary your tactics.

When to fight

In a crisis, the decision about when and how hard to fight is a matter of judgement. You can go in for aggressive brinkmanship or progressive appeasement, but either of these approaches will be inadequate if taken to an extreme.

At this stage it might be a good idea to remember Krushchev's message to Kennedy during the Cuban missile crisis: 'If people do not show wisdom, then in the final analysis they will come to a clash, like blind moles, and then reciprocal extermination will begin.'

The decision on tactics is never an easy one. It was said by Clausewitz that: 'War is nothing but the continuation of politics with the admixture of other means', and you should normally wait to launch an attack until you are certain that the normal process of peaceful negotiation is not going to get you anywhere.

The decision will also be affected by your ability to understand your opponent's strategy and tactics so that you can take pre-emptive action. Crisis management is very much about analysing other people's motives, intentions and ploys, and responding accordingly. Another adage from Clausewitz is worth bearing in mind: 'Despise the enemy strategically, respect him tactically.' In other words you may be quite certain that in the longer term your opponent will come to grief, but in the short term he may fight hard and you may have to fight back equally hard. Losing one battle may not lose the war but a succession of defeats must prejudice your chances, however just your cause and however superior your strategy.

Thomas Schelling (51), a leading commentator on crisis management, commented wisely on the fight or flight decision as follows:

> What is in dispute is usually not the momentary right of way, but everyone's expectations about how a participant will behave in the future. To yield is a signal that one can be expected to yield. To yield often or continuously may communicate an acknowledgement that that is one's role. To yield readily up to some limit, and then say 'enough', may guarantee that the first show of obduracy loses the game for both sides.

Crisis management may or may not take place within a well-defined strategy but, whatever happens, the tactics have got to be worked out on the basis of a complete understanding of the situation, especially those aspects of it which concern other people's intentions. If you yield, then, as Schelling says, take care to ensure that, because you have misunderstood or underestimated your opponent, he will not take advantage of it. Beware also of the possibility that both of you might lose in the end.

If you decide to fight, remember the following precepts of St Augustine and St Thomas Aquinas on what is a just war:

1. Just cause.
2. Right intention.
3. A reasonable chance of success.
4. If successful, a better situation than would prevail in the absence of action.
5. Force used (or threatened) should be proportional to the objective sought (or the evil repressed).
6. The intention should be to spare non-combatants or at least have a reasonable prospect of doing so.

Crisis management techniques

In *The Conventions of Crisis*, Coral Bell (8) wrote:

> Looking back over the history of the postwar crises as a whole, one is struck by a sense of how often the decision-makers seem to have been 'playing it off the cuff', acting on the promptings of intuition or temperament rather than plan or logic.

This highlights the biggest pitfall crisis managers can walk into in industry and commerce as well as in international affairs. All too easily they feel that instant and decisive action is required. Under acute pressure they do not look before they leap and they fall into the elephant trap.

Crisis management starts with avoiding action, keeping your finger on the pulse so that as soon as the pace hots up – at the first signs of the beginning of a crisis slide – you can take pre-emptive action. At this stage you have time to think, to consider contingency plans and to put them into effect.

If, however, in spite of all your efforts, you are faced with a crisis, the following is a checklist of the ten steps you should take:

1. Sit back as coolly as you can and assess the situation. You may have to go through the analytical and thinking process five times as fast as usual, but do it. You need to establish:

   - What exactly is happening
   - Why it is happening
   - What is likely to happen unless something is done about it
   - How quickly you *have* to act to prevent further damage

- Who else is involved
- Who is likely to be involved
- What resources you have got – people, equipment, finance, back-up from other organizations, access to people with influence.

2. Draw up your preliminary plan of action – set it out step by step and prepare other contingency plans to deal with eventualities.
3. Line up a crisis management team to deal with the situation. Allocate roles and tasks and authorities to act (you may have to give emergency authority to some people).
4. Set up a crisis management centre (your office, the board room).
5. Set up a communications system so that you receive instant intelligence on what is happening and can put your messages across to the members of your team and anyone else whom you want to take action.
6. 'Load shed' when you can on the principle of the electrical system which sheds part of the load when the total load rises above a certain point. This means getting rid of any peripheral problems as quickly as possible.
7. But items on the 'back burner', ie relegate problems to a non-crisis area where they can be dealt with at leisure.
8. Prepare your detailed plans, which will include:

- time-scales – act now or later
- scope for a cooling-off period
- longer-term solutions to be prepared and implemented at the right time
- contingency plans to deal with new developments or emergencies.

9. Monitor continuously exactly what is happening. Ensure that you get the information you need fast so that you can react quickly but without panicking.
10. Evaluate actions and reactions continuously so that you can modify the plan and swiftly take corrective or pre-emptive steps.

Qualities of a crisis manager

Good crisis managers are decisive. They can react swiftly but their great skill is in being able to speed up the decision-making process. They will not miss out any steps in the standard problem-solving, decision-making sequence:

- Define the situation
- Specify objectives
- Develop hypotheses
- Gather the facts
- Analyse the facts
- Consider possible courses of action
- Evaluate possible courses of action
- Decide and implement
- Monitor implementation.

Effective crisis managers will get through these stages more quickly, using their own experience and intelligence and that of their team.

Crisis managers buy time by putting issues on the back burner but, like all good managers, they can make things happen fast when they want to. They are good leaders – providing inspiration to their team, encouraging their efforts and giving them confidence in the successful outcome of the crisis management process.

Finally, and most important, they keep cool. They do not panic, they do not over-react, they do not lose their heads. In fact, they deliberately slow down the pace, when they can, to give the impression that everything is under control and it is all going according to plan.

To sum up, crisis management is no more than good management under pressure. The adrenalin may flow faster but this concentrates the mind wonderfully. Good managers thrive under pressure and they are the good crisis managers.

Chapter 19
Delegating

You can't do everything yourself, so you have to delegate. At first sight delegation looks simple. Just tell people what you want them to do and then let them do it. But there is more to it than that.

It may be that you would wish to delegate everything except what your subordinate cannot do. But you cannot then withdraw. You have arranged for someone else to do the job, but you have not passed on the responsibility for it. You are always accountable to your superior for what your subordinate does. Hence, as is often said, you can't delegate responsibility.

Delegation is difficult. It is perhaps the hardest task that managers have to do. The problem is achieving the right balance between delegating too much or too little and between over- or under-supervision. When you give people a job to do you have to make sure that it is done. And you have to do that without breathing down their neck, wasting your time and theirs, and getting in the way. There has to be trust as well as guidance and supervision.

Advantages of delegation

- It relieves you of routine and less critical tasks.
- It frees you for more important work – planning, organizing, motivating and controlling.
- It extends your capacity to manage.
- It reduces delay in decision-making – as long as authority is delegated close to the point of action.
- It allows decisions to be taken at the level where the details are known.
- It develops the capacity of staff to make decisions, achieve objectives and take responsibility.

When to delegate

You should delegate when:

- You have more work than you can effectively carry out yourself
- You cannot allocate sufficient time to your priority tasks
- You want to develop your subordinate
- The job can be done adequately by your subordinate.

How to delegate

When you delegate you have to decide:

- What to delegate
- To whom you delegate – choosing who does the work
- How to inform or brief your subordinate – giving out the work
- How you will guide and develop your subordinate
- How you will monitor his or her performance.

What to delegate

You delegate tasks that you don't need to do yourself. You are not just ridding yourself of the difficult, tedious or unrewarding tasks. Neither are you trying to win for yourself an easier life. Delegation will, in fact, make your life more difficult, but also more rewarding.

Clearly, you delegate routine and repetitive tasks which you cannot reasonably be expected to do yourself – as long as you use the time you have won productively.

You also delegate specialist tasks to those who have the skills and know-how to do them. You cannot do it all yourself. Nor can you be expected to know it all yourself. You have to know how to select and use expertise. There will be no problem as long as you make it clear what you want from the experts and ask – if necessary force – them to present it to you in a usable way. As a manager you must know what specialists can do for you and you should be knowledgeable enough about the subject to understand whether or not what they produce is worth having.

Choosing who does the work

Ideally, the person you choose to do the work should have the knowledge, skills, motivation and time needed to get it done to your complete satisfaction. Frequently, however, you will have to use someone who has less than ideal experience, knowledge or skills. In these cases you should try to select an individual who has intelligence, natural aptitude and, above all, willingness to learn how to do the job with help and guidance. This is how people develop, and the development of your staff should be your conscious aim whenever you delegate.

You are looking for someone you can trust. You don't want to over-supervise, so you have to believe that the person you select will get on with it and have the sense to come to you when stuck or before making a bad mistake.

How do you know whom you can trust? The best way is to try people out first on smaller and less important tasks, increasingly giving them more scope so that they learn how far they can go and you can observe how they do it. If they get on well, their sense of responsibility and powers of judgement will increase and improve and you will be able to trust them with more demanding and responsible tasks.

Giving out the work

When you delegate you should ensure that your subordinates understand:

- Why the work needs to be done
- What they are expected to do
- The date by which they are expected to do it
- The authority they have to make decisions
- The problems they must refer back
- The progress or completion reports they should submit
- How you propose to guide and monitor them
- The resources and help they will have to complete the work.

Subordinates may need guidance on how the work should be done. The extent to which you spell it out will clearly depend on how much they already know about how to do the work. You don't want to give directions in such laborious detail that you run the risk of stifling initiative. As long as you are sure they will do the job without breaking the law, exceeding the budget, embarrassing you or seriously upsetting people, let them get on with it. Follow Robert Heller's golden rule: 'If you can't do something yourself, find someone who can – and then let him do it in his own sweet way.'

You can make a distinction between *hard* and *soft* delegation. Hard delegation takes place when you tell someone exactly what to do, how to do it and when you want the results. You spell it out, confirm it in writing and make a note in your diary of the date when you expect the job to be completed. And then you follow up regularly.

Soft delegation takes place when you agree generally what has to be achieved and leave your subordinate to get on with it. You should still agree limits of authority, define the decisions to be referred to you, say what exception reports you want (see Chapter 12), and indicate when and how you will review progress. Then you sit back until the results are due and observe from afar, only coming closer for periodical progress meetings, or when the exception reports suggest that something needs looking into, or when a problem or decision is referred to you.

You should always delegate by the results you expect. Even if you do not need to specify *exactly* how the results should be achieved, it is a good idea when delegating a problem to ask your subordinates how they propose to solve it. You then have the opportunity to provide guidance at the outset; guidance at a later stage may be seen as interference.

Guidance and development

Delegation not only helps you to get your work done; it can be used to improve your subordinates' performance and therefore your trust in their ability to carry out more responsible work. Instruction, training and development are part of the process of delegation.

Monitoring performance

At first you may have to monitor your subordinates' performance carefully. But the sooner you can relax and watch progress informally the better.

You will have set target dates, and you should keep a reminder of these in your diary so that you can ensure they are achieved. Don't allow your subordinates to become careless about meeting deadlines.

Without being oppressive, you should ensure that progress reports are made when required and that you discuss deviations from the original plan in good time. You will have clearly indicated to your subordinates the extent of their authority to act without further reference to you. They must therefore expect to be reprimanded if on any occasion they exceed their brief or fail to keep you informed. You don't want any surprises and your subordinates must understand that you will not tolerate being kept in the dark.

Try to restrain yourself from undue interference in the way the work is being done. It is, after all, the results that count. Of course, you must step in if there is any danger of things going off the rails. The Nelson touch is all right if your subordinate is a Nelson, but how many Nelsons have you got? Rash decisions, over-expenditure and ignoring defined and reasonable constraints and rules must be prevented.

There is a delicate balance to be achieved between hedging people around with restrictions which may appear petty and allowing them licence to do what they like. You must use your knowledge of your subordinates and the circumstances to decide where the balance should be struck. The best delegators are those who have a comprehensive understanding of the strengths and weaknesses of their staff and the situation in which they are working.

Above all, avoid 'river banking'. This happens when a boss gives a subordinate a task which is more or less impossible to do. As the subordinate is 'going down' for the third time the boss is observed in a remote and safe position on the river bank saying: 'It's easy really, all you need to do is to try a bit harder.'

The thoughts of some successful delegators

John H Johnson, editor and publisher of Johnson Publishing Company, chief executive officer of Supreme Life Insurance Company and on the board of many large US corporations, said of his delegation techniques: 'I want to be big and I want to be bigger and I can't do it all by myself. So I try to do only those things that I can't get anyone else to do.'

Franklin D Roosevelt used a particularly ruthless technique based on competition, when he requested his aides to find some information. One of his aides told the story as follows: 'He would call you in, and he'd ask you to get the story on some complicated business and you'd come back after a couple of days of hard labour and present the juicy morsel you'd uncovered under a stone somewhere and *then* you'd find out he knew all about it, along with something else you *didn't* know. Where he got this information from he wouldn't mention, usually, but after he had done this to you once or twice you got damn careful about your information.'

Robert Townsend's approach to delegation when he was chairman of Avis was to emphasize the need to delegate 'as many important matters as you can because that creates a climate in which people grow'.

Robert Magaven, when he started as the head of Safeway Food Stores, told his division managers: 'I don't know anything about the grocery business but you fellows do. From now on, you're running your division as if it were your own business. You don't take orders from anyone but me and I'm not going to give you orders. I'm going to hold you responsible.'

Franklin Moore related the following example of strong delegation: Ralf Cordiner, the head of General Electric in the US for ten years, had a vice president who wanted to see him urgently about a problem. The vice president explained his problem, and the choices he thought he had. 'Now, Mr Cordiner,' he said, 'What should I do?' 'Do?' Cordiner answered, 'You'd damn well better get on an airplane and get back to your office and decide. And if you can't decide we'd better get someone who can.'

Peter Drucker (15), writing about responsibility, referred to a newspaper interview with a young American infantry captain in the Vietnam jungle. The reporter asked: 'How in this confused situation can you retain command?' The captain replied: 'Around here, I am the only guy who is responsible. If these men don't know what to do when they run into an enemy in the jungle, I'm too far away to tell them. My job is to make sure they know. What they do depends on the situation which only they can judge. The responsibility is always mine, but the decision lies with whoever is on the spot.'

A case study

A group of researchers studying how managers delegate found that the following was happening in one of the companies they were studying:

In the situations in which the men we were interviewing found themselves, the boss was usually a hurried, and sometimes a harried, man. He gave out broad, briefly stated assignments, expecting his subordinates to make sense out of them. He also expected them to decide what information they needed, to obtain that information and then to go ahead and carry out their assignments. In the case of repetitive tasks, the typical boss assumed that after a few trials his subordinates would know for themselves when a job needed doing.

Frequently the boss wasn't sure himself about which issues needed attention in his department. And although he knew what eventually had to be accomplished, often he had less idea than his subordinates about the approaches to take. It wasn't unusual, therefore, for the boss to be vague or even impatient when approached with questions about the job while it was going on. Usually he was much more assertive in describing what he wanted after a job was done than while it was in progress.

The production director came out of the board of directors' meeting where he had been roundly criticized for not getting the most out of his organization. He immediately called a meeting of his subordinates and told them: 'I don't intend to subject myself to such humiliation again. You men are paid to do your jobs; it's not up to me to do them for you. I don't know how you spend your time and I don't intend to try to find out. You know your responsibilities, and these figures bear out that you haven't discharged them properly. If the next report doesn't show a marked improvement, there will be some new faces around here.'

Chapter 20
Developing people

Investing in people

The chairman of an advertising firm once said that his 'inventory goes up and down in the lift'. His prime resource – his working capital – was people. The same applies in any other sort of organization. Money matters, but the human beings who work there matter even more.

If you want to take a pragmatic view of people, regard them as an investment. They cost money to acquire and maintain and they should provide a return on that outlay; their value increases as they become more effective in their jobs and capable of taking on greater responsibility. In accounting terms, people may be treated like any other asset on the balance sheet, taking into account acquisition costs and their increasing value as they gain experience.

The manager's contribution to effective training

The following are ten ways in which you can contribute to the effective training of your staff:

1. Determine the standards of performance required for each of the jobs you control.
2. Analyse the competences (knowledge and skills) relevant to the achievement of these standards. If necessary, seek help from specialized trainers to carry out this analysis.
3. Agree with the individuals concerned what these standards and competences are.
4. Review with these individuals their performance so that agreement can be reached on any gaps to be filled between what they can do and what they should be able to do.

5. Every time you give someone an instruction, treat it as a training opportunity. Encourage individuals to tell you how they would do the job. If they get it wrong, help them to work out the best way for themselves, progressively giving them less guidance so that they learn to stand on their own feet.

6. Allow for the learning curve. Don't expect too much, but do require trainees to improve at a pace which matches their natural aptitudes. Only bear down hard on people if they are clearly not trying – without any excuse.

7. Train and develop by example. Give people the opportunity to learn from the way you do things. Remember the truth of the saying that managers learn best how to manage by managing under a good manager. This principle applies equally well to other categories of job holders.

8. Remember that the prime responsibility for training and developing your staff rests with you. Your results depend on their competence. You neglect your training responsibilities at your peril. And you must not rely on the training department to do it for you. They can provide advice and help but cannot replace your capacity to train on the job.

9. Plan the training for your staff in accordance with a regular review of their training needs.

10. Remember to use a variety of training techniques such as job instruction, assignments, coaching, guided reading and computer-based training.

Management development

Management development is about improving the performance of existing managers, giving them opportunities for growth and development, and ensuring, as far as possible, that management succession is provided for.

Managers need to be given the opportunity to develop themselves. As Peter Drucker (14) wrote in *The Practice of Management*:

> Development is always self-development. Nothing could be more absurd than for the enterprise to assume responsibility for the development of a man. The responsibility rests with the individual, his abilities, his efforts ... Every manager in a business has the opportunity to encourage self-development or to stifle it, to direct it or to misdirect it. He should be specifically assigned the responsibility for helping all men working with him to focus, direct and apply their self-development efforts productively. And every company can provide systematic development changes to its managers.

In Douglas McGregor's phrase, managers are grown – they are neither born nor made. And your role is to provide conditions favourable to faster growth. As McGregor (36) wrote in *The Human Side of Enterprise*:

> The job environment of the individual is the most important variable affecting his development. Unless that environment is conducive to his growth, none of the other things we do to him or for him will be effective. That is why the 'agricultural' approach to management development is preferable to the 'manufacturing' approach. The latter leads, among other things, to the unrealistic expectations that we can create and develop managers in the classroom.

There are two main activities in management development – performance management, discussed in Chapter 34, and planned experience, discussed below.

Planned experience

People learn mainly through experience. Surely, therefore, it is worth spending a little of your time planning the experience of anyone with potential for development.

Planning people's experience means giving them extra tasks to do which provide a challenge or extend them into a new area. It could be a project which they have to complete themselves or they could be included in a project team looking at a new development or problem which cuts across organizational boundaries. Projects which enlarge experience in unfamiliar areas, for example, a marketing executive in finance or vice versa, are particularly useful. Planned experience will work better if it is accompanied by coaching so that those undergoing it can receive the maximum benefit from expert advice.

Coaching

The best way to learn how to manage is to manage, under the guidance of a good manager. Coaching is an informal but deliberate way of providing this guidance. It should be linked to performance appraisal and the counselling that takes place as part of the appraisal procedure.

But coaching is a more continuous process. Every time you delegate a task to someone and discuss the outcome you are presented with a coaching opportunity. When you delegate you can provide guidance on how the job should be done. When you discuss progress with your subordinates or when they report back to you, you can ask questions on how well they have thought through what they are doing, suggest alternative ways of looking at a problem (do not provide the solution), and provide constructive criticism if things are not going right.

You can help to develop people by discussing higher-level problems with them, involving them in your decisions and increasing their understanding of how to tackle a job senior to the areas for which they are responsible. (See also Chapter 8.)

Chapter 21
Empowerment

What is empowerment?

Empowerment is the process of giving people more scope or 'power' to exercise control over, and take responsibility for, their work. It means getting people to use their own judgement in the interests of the organization and its customers. Jan Carlson, Chief Executive of Scandinavian Airline Systems, as quoted by Jane Pickard (48) says that: 'The purpose of empowerment is to free someone from rigorous control by instructions and orders and give them freedom to take responsibility for their ideas and actions, to release hidden resources which would otherwise remain inaccessible.'

Empowerment provides greater 'space' for individuals to use their abilities by enabling and encouraging them to take decisions close to the point of impact.

Basis

The basis for the belief that empowerment is a valid approach to improving organizational effectiveness is that people who are nearest to the problem are best able to judge its solution, provided they have a framework within which to make their decisions.

Assumptions about the empowered organization

Charles Handy (22) has suggested that the assumptions behind the concept of the empowered organization are:

- *Competence* – the belief that individual employees can be expected to perform to the limit of their competence with the minimum of supervision

- *Trust* – it is necessary not only to believe in people's competence but also to trust them to get on with the job
- *Teamwork* – few organizational problems can be solved by one person acting alone. The sheer rate of change and turbulence means that as new challenges and problems appear, people must naturally group together in flexible teams without barriers of status or hierarchy, to solve the problems within the framework of the organization's goals and values. The organization is held together by these beliefs and values – by people who are committed to one another and to common goals.

But Handy has more recently made an interesting distinction between empowerment and subsidiarity: 'Empowerment implies that someone on high is giving away power. Subsidiarity on the other hand, implies that the power belongs, in the first place, lower down or further out. You take it away as a last resort.' (23).

Reasons for empowerment

The reasons for empowerment are that it:

- Can speed up decision-making processes and reaction times
- Releases the creative and innovative capacities of employees
- Provides for greater job satisfaction, motivation and commitment
- Gives people more responsibility
- Enables employees to gain a greater sense of achievement from their work
- Reduces operational costs by eliminating unnecessary layers of management, staff functions and quality control and checking operations.

Replacing the command organization

A 'command' organization is one in which decision-making is centralized, reliance is placed on the authority of managers to 'get things done', management believes it always knows best (however far away it is from the scene of action – the client or the customer), and the contributions of staff are taken for granted rather than welcomed.

In contrast, the empowered organization makes much better use of the ability and enthusiasm of its employees. It has the potential to improve continuously by a series of small and large steps, day after day, and at all levels, feeding the learning from its experience back, to make it work better.

The command organization can be likened to a dinosaur with its tiny brain impotently issuing instructions to its massive body. The empowered organization is more like a shoal of fish, moving rapidly and consistently and adjusting through instantly understood signals.

The process of empowerment

Empowerment can be achieved through:

- Structural means – organizational and work grouping
- The behaviour or style of individual managers
- Enlisting the support of employees in tackling immediate organizational issues
- Gaining the 'hearts and minds' of people.

Structural empowerment – organizational

An empowered organization is likely to have a flat structure with the minimum number of management layers. A multi-layered structure filters the two-way flow of information and hinders decision-making from penetrating as far down the organization as it should.

Structural empowerment – work group

As suggested by Christian Schumacher (51) of *Small is Beautiful* fame, empowerment can be achieved at the work group level by applying the following principles:

1. Work should be organized around basic operations to form 'whole tasks'.
2. The basic organizational unit should be the primary work group (ie 4–20 people).
3. Each work group should include a designated leader.
4. Each work group and its leader should, as far as possible, plan and organize its own work.
5. Each work group should be able fully to evaluate its performance against agreed standards of excellence.
6. Jobs should be structured so that work group members can personally plan, execute and evaluate at least one operation in the process.
7. All work group members should have the opportunity to participate in the group's processes of planning, problem-solving and evaluation.

Management style

Managers empower the members of their teams, not by giving up control but by changing the way control is exercised. They have to learn to delegate more and to allow individuals and teams more scope to plan, act and monitor their own performance.

But they still have the responsibility to provide guidance and support to their staff as required. They must also help them to develop the skills and competences they need to function effectively in an empowered organization.

Involvement in issues

Empowerment can be achieved by involving people in developing their own solutions to specific issues. This can be done by expecting teams not simply to propose ways forward or to hope that someone else will do something, but actually to solve the problem in their part of the organization, in accordance with the resources they have and the constraints within which they work.

At General Electric, the Chief Executive, Jack Welch, arranged for employees at all levels to get together and work out how to improve the ways in which work was carried out. His aim was 'to give people a voice, give them a say, give them a chance to participate'. In describing these 'work-outs' he also said that:

> Ultimately, we're talking about redefining the relationship between boss and subordinate. I want to get to the point where people challenge their bosses every day: 'Why do you require me to do wasteful things? Why don't you let me do things you shouldn't be doing so you can move on and create? That's the job of the leader – to create, not to control. Trust me to do my job and don't make me waste all my time trying to deal with you on control issues' (60).

Hearts and minds

Empowerment is about engaging both the hearts and minds of people so that they can take the opportunities made available to them for increased responsibility.

At management level this is achieved by sharing strategic vision and corporate values throughout the organization, creating the assumption of competence and furthering the trust without which an empowered organization cannot operate.

Case studies

Ciba-Geigy

As described by Jane Pickard (48), the approach to empowerment at Ciba-Geigy UK was to cascade a general philosophy of empowerment from the centre, with policy details being left to each business. At the Clayton Aniline factory in Manchester, for example, work teams no longer take orders which filter down the hierarchy from manager to superintendent to supervisor to worker. Instead, they receive questions and challenges to which they supply the answers. They also frequently supply the questions as well. There are no targets only a policy of continuous improvement. People are expected to keep a written record of their own or their team's productivity and the line, while it may dip as well as rise, is expected to maintain a general, upward curve.

Neither are there any new titles or accountabilities; everyone is responsible. There are still 'workers' and 'supervisors', but their relationship has changed. As in other empowered workplaces, the supervisor no longer commands and checks; he or she coaches, discusses and assesses training needs.

Nuclear Electric (a Kinsley Lord Ltd case)

Each week that one of the reactors at Nuclear Electric's top performing Wylfa power station in Anglesey is closed for maintenance, £2.5 million of electricity is lost. Last year, staff at all levels worked together to plan how to reduce this 'outrage' from eight weeks to, at most, seven, making even more output possible. The complexity of such a change in a nuclear power station, with its stringent safety requirements, is immense. But the teams identified new procedures, new ways of working together and new skills which in fact achieved the result in just over six weeks. The annual revenue gain will be some £4 million.

Chapter 22
Getting on

Getting on is first about knowing what you can do – your strengths and weaknesses. Then you can decide what you want to do and set out to do it.

You can start in the right direction, therefore, by trying to analyse yourself and the situation which you are in.

Beyond that there are certain actions you can take which will help you to get on. Some are obvious, others less so. How you apply them must depend on your assessment of where you are and what you can do. With due acknowledgement to the two men who have written the most sense on this subject – Peter Drucker and Robert Townsend – the list of steps to take is set out below under four main headings:

- Knowing yourself.
- Knowing what you want.
- Developing and deploying the skills required to get what you want.
- Displaying the personal qualities and behaving in the ways that will contribute to your success.

Knowing yourself

Carlyle once described the saying 'know thyself' as an impossible precept. He felt that to 'know what thou canst work at' would be better advice. Therefore, the starting point in career management is what you can do – your strengths and your weaknesses. This means developing self-awareness by analysing your achievements, skills and knowledge and by assessing your own performance.

Achievement, skills and knowledge

The questions to ask yourself are:

1. *What have I achieved so far?* Answer this question by looking back on your life and list the key events, happenings, incidents and turning points that have taken place. Whenever you have succeeded in doing something new or better than ever before, analyse the factors which contributed to that success. Was it initiative, hard work, determination, the correct application of skills and knowledge based on a searching analysis of the situation, the ability to work in a team, the exercise of leadership, the capacity to seize an opportunity (another and better word for luck) and exploit it, the ability to articulate a need and get into action to satisfy it, the ability to make things happen – or any other factor you can think of?

2. *When have I failed to achieve what I wanted?* You do not want to dwell too much on failure but it can be treated positively, as long as you analyse dispassionately where you went wrong and assess what you might have been able to do to put it right.

3. *What am I good or bad at doing?* What are your distinctive competences? Consider these in terms of professional, technical or managerial know-how as well as the exercise of such skills as communicating, decision-making, problem-solving, teamworking, exercising leadership, delegating, coordinating, meeting deadlines, managing time, planning, organizing and controlling work, dealing with crises.

4. *How well do I know my chosen area of expertise?* Have you got the right qualifications? Have you acquired the right know-how through study, training and relevant experience?

5. *What sort of person am I?* (This is the most difficult question of all to answer truthfully.) The following is a checklist of the points you should consider, based on Cattell's classification of primary personality factors. In each case, assess the extent to which either of the paired descriptions applies to you:

   - *Outgoing* – warm-hearted, easy-going, participating, extroverted; or
   - *Reserved* – detached, critical, cool, introverted.

   - *Intellectual* – good at abstract thinking; or
   - *Non-intellectual* – better at concrete thinking.

   - *Emotionally stable* – calm, able to face reality; or
   - *Affected by feelings* – emotionally unstable, easily upset.

   - *Assertive* – independent, aggressive, stubborn; or
   - *Submissive* – mild, obedient, conforming.

   - *Enthusiastic* – lively, happy-go-lucky, heedless, talkative; or

- *Sober* – prudent, serious, taciturn.

- *Conscientious* – persevering, staid, rule-bound; or
- *Expedient* – 'a law unto yourself', bypasses obligations.

- *Venturesome* – bold, uninhibited, spontaneous; or
- *Shy* – restrained, diffident, timid.

- *Tender-minded* – dependent, over-protected, sensitive; or
- *Tough-minded* – self-reliant, realistic, a no-nonsense approach.

- *Suspicious* – self-opinionated, distrustful, hard to fool; or
- *Trusting* – free of suspicion or jealously, adaptable, easy to get on with.

- *Imaginative* – speculative, careless of practical matters, wrapped up in inner urgencies; or
- *Practical* – inclined to action rather than speculation, regulated by external realities, careful, conventional.

- *Shrewd* – calculating, penetrating, worldly; or
- *Artless* – guileless, ingenuous, natural.

- *Apprehensive* – a worrier, depressive, troubled; or
- *Confident* – self-assured, serene, placid.

- *Experimenting* – critical, liberal, analytical, free-thinking; or
- *Conservative* – respecter of established ideas, tolerant of traditional practices.

- *Self-sufficient* – resilient, resourceful, prefers own decisions; or
- *Group-dependent* – a 'joiner', happiest in a group, reliant on the support of others.

- *Controlled* – socially precise, self-disciplined, compulsive; or
- *Casual* – careless of protocol, untidy, follows own inclinations.

- *Tense* – driven, overwrought, fretful; or
- *Relaxed* – tranquil, unfrustrated, calm.

Assess your managerial competences

While self-awareness is the basis for a more specific assessment of your strengths and weaknesses as a manager, you need also to consider your basic managerial qualities and the competences required to operate effectively.

In analysing your effectiveness as a manager it is useful to look at the criteria used by major organizations in measuring the competence of their managers at their assessment or development centres (two- to three-day affairs where managers are subjected to a number of tests and undertake various exercises to demonstrate their skills). The headings used by two organizations in their assessment centres are set out below:

1. *The National Westminster Bank*
Effective managers:

- *Are achievement orientated* – they are strongly motivated by achievement, recognition and reward, and possess internal drive that continually urges them forward to higher levels
- *Have a positive outlook* – they are energetic, enthusiastic and want to make a unique personal contribution to every job they do
- *Are reliable* – they are noted for always doing a job properly with attention to relevant detail
- *Are adaptable* – they are flexible, self-organized and self-monitoring
- *Are good organizers* – they are able to organize themselves and those around them to meet targets effectively and on time
- *Have a natural affinity with people* – they possess well-developed leadership skills and a high degree of maturity in dealing with others
- *Are good team builders* – they understand that their progress can be enhanced by building up the performance of their teams. They are therefore keen to advance the interests of others as well as themselves
- *Are good communicators* – both face to face and on paper.

2. *W H Smith*
The performance areas used in W H Smith's general management assessment centre are:

- *Self-management* – the ability to organize, plan and manage time.
- *Interactive management and leadership* – the ability to work constructively with peers and seniors.
- *Financial management* – financial knowledge and the ability to make sound financial judgements.
- *Marketing management* – the ability to consider and approve strategic marketing issues, recognizing and responding to strengths and opportunities.
- *Strategic planning* – the ability to think and act at a strategic level and to define clear, longer-range, business-related objectives.
- *Situation assessment* – the ability to make an analysis of a business situation, to identify its key variables and to generate appropriate objectives and courses of action.
- *Staff management* – the ability to work successfully with subordinates and/or experts to obtain information and understanding of unfamiliar subjects.

- *Manpower planning* – the ability to determine future requirements against available resources, identifying training and development needs.
- *Oral communications* – the ability to speak clearly and present or argue a situation in a logical and positive manner which gains commitment and support.
- *Written communications* – the ability to create business-like correspondence and, where appropriate, present well-argued proposals supported by relevant data.

You can assess your competence as a manager against these criteria giving yourself marks between 1 and 10 for each item relating to a classification along these lines:

A = outstanding   (9–10 points)
B = very effective   (7–8 points)
C = satisfactory   (5–6 points)
D = barely satisfactory (3–4 points)
E = unsatisfactory   (0–2 points)

On completing this assessment, note the particularly high and low scores in each list and draw up a schedule of your strengths and weaknesses as a manager. You can complete this 'SWOT' analysis (Strengths and Weaknesses, Opportunities and Threats) by considering your opportunities for advancement in your present organization (or elsewhere) and assessing any threats that might prevent you from realizing your ambitions.

Knowing what you want

1. Find out what you are good at doing and then do it.
2. Analyse not only your strengths but also your weaknesses: 'There is nothing that helps a man in his conduct through life more than a knowledge of his own characteristic weaknesses' (William Hazlitt).
3. Decide what you want to do and then go for it. Believe that if you really want something you can get it, and act accordingly.
4. Set demanding targets and deadlines for yourself. 'People grow according to the demands they make on themselves' (Drucker). But don't over-commit yourself. Be realistic about what you can achieve.
5. Pursue excellence. 'If you can't do it excellently don't do it at all' (Townsend).

6. Focus on what *you* can contribute. 'To ask "what can I contribute?" is to look for the unused potential in a job' (Drucker).
7. Get your priorities right. Adapt Drucker's rules for identifying them:

   - pick the future as against the past
   - focus on opportunities rather than on problems
   - choose your own direction – rather than climb on the bandwagon
   - aim high, aim for something that will make a difference rather than something that is 'safe' and easy to do.

8. Be specific about what you want to do yourself and what you want others to do for you.
9. Keep it simple. Concentrate. Consider all your tasks and eliminate the irrelevant ones. Slough off old activities before you start new ones. 'Concentration is the key to economic results . . . no other principle of effectiveness is violated as constantly today as the basic principle of concentration . . . Our motto seems to be: "let's do a little bit of everything"' (Drucker).
10. Take the broad view but don't ignore the significant detail: 'Ill can he rule the great, that cannot reach the small' (Spenser). It is sometimes necessary to penetrate beneath the surface to find out what is really happening – on the shop floor or in the field. But do this selectively.
11. Adapt to changing demands. 'The executive who keeps on doing what he has done successfully before is almost bound to fail' (Drucker).

Develop skills

Every chapter in this book refers to an area of management skill that you need to develop if you want to get on. The key areas are:

- Communicating – express yourself clearly, concisely and persuasively
- Problem-solving – adopt a logical approach to problem-solving but don't forget that lateral thinking can be very productive of new ideas
- Decision-making – develop the analytical skills and confidence in yourself to enable you to make incisive judgements
- Listening – listen to ideas and act on the good ones. Hear what is said, let the other person know that you have heard, show an interest, let him feel important
- Motivating – understand what your people can do and what makes

them tick, make clear what you expect them to do, setting standards which are grounded on the requirement of the task and not personal, reward them or otherwise according to their contribution

- Staffing – select people for their strengths, accept that everyone has some weakness or other, don't go for mediocrity
- Managing yourself – achieve control over your work day. Separate the essentials from the inessentials that litter your desk. Know how to simplify your workload – where appropriate cut corners.

Personal qualities and behaviour

- Be enthusiastic and show it.
- Innovate and create – come up with new ideas and react positively to other people's ideas. Don't sulk if your ideas are not accepted. Try again another way.
- Show willing – there is nothing worse than the person who always moans when he is given something to do. Don't say: 'How can I possibly do that?' Instead, respond immediately with something like this: 'Right, this is what I propose to do – is that what you want?'
- Be positive – in the words of the old Bing Crosby song: 'accentuate the positive and eliminate the negative'.
- Work hard – people who get on are hard workers. But they don't work for work's sake. Effectiveness is never a function of how late you stay in the office. It's what you do while you are there that counts.
- Present yourself well – life is not all about making a good impression but you might as well make sure that your achievements are known and appreciated. And if people are impressed by executives who are decisive, punctual and answer promptly, why not impress them that way? More good than harm will come of it.
- Be ambitious – 'A man's reach should exceed his grasp, or what's a heaven for?' (Robert Browning). But don't overdo it. Don't appear to be more concerned about your future status than with present effectiveness.
- Be courageous – take calculated risks, believe in what you are doing and stick to your guns.
- Be assertive but not aggressive.
- Put your points across firmly and succinctly.
- Don't talk too much. Never over-commit yourself. Save up what you want to say until the right moment. Keep your powder dry. Don't shoot your mouth off. 'Whereoff one cannot speak, thereon one must remain silent' (Wittgenstein).

- Learn to cope with stress. You won't avoid it and you have to live with it. If problems are coming at you thick and fast, try to slow down. Relax. Take a little time off. Give yourself a chance to put the situation into perspective. (See also Chapter 46.)
- If things go wrong, bounce back. Accept reverses calmly. Think about what you need to do and then get into action – fast. There is nothing like purposeful activity in these circumstances.
- Get people to trust you – you will do this if you never lie or even shade the truth, if you avoid playing politics and if you always deliver what you promise.
- Accept constructive criticism.
- 'Admit your own mistakes openly, even joyfully' (Townsend, 56). Never make an excuse. Accept the responsibility *and* the blame if you make a mistake.

Chapter 23
How things go wrong and how to put them right

Theodore Roosevelt once said: 'Do what you can, with what you have, where you are.' The trouble is, people don't always take this advice. Things go wrong because people do less than they are capable of, misuse their resources or choose an inappropriate time or place in which to do it. Situations are misjudged and the wrong action is taken.

There have been two interesting analyses of incompetence which, if studied, will give you some clues about how to avoid or at least minimize mistakes. The first of these is *The Peter Principle* by Dr Lawrence J Peter (44); the second is *On the Psychology of Military Incompetence* by Norman F Dixon (13).

The Peter Principle

In *The Peter Principle*, Dr Lawrence Peter suggested that in a hierarchy, individuals tend to rise to the level of their own incompetence. This somewhat pessimistic view was based on his experience that the system encourages this to happen because people are told that if they are doing their job efficiently and with ease, the job lacks challenge and they should move up. However, as Peter says: 'The problem is that when you find something you can't do very well, that is where you stay, bungling your job, frustrating your co-workers, and eroding the effectiveness of the organization.'

The Peter Principle has only been accepted as common parlance because it reflects a fundamental problem when assessing potential. We know, or we think we know, that someone is good at his or her present job. But does this predicate success in the next one up? Perhaps yes, perhaps no; however, we cannot be sure because the skills needed by, for example, a first-rate research scientist are quite different from those required by the leader of a research team. Technical competence does not necessarily indicate managerial competence.

Beating the Peter Principle – for yourself

Can the Peter Principle be beaten? The answer is yes, but with difficulty. People don't usually refuse promotion. If they do, they become suspect. It is thought that they should be made of sterner stuff. It is, however, perfectly reasonable to check on what is involved if you are promoted. You should obtain precise answers to questions on what you will be expected to achieve, the resources you will be given to achieve it and the problems you will meet. If you think these demands are unreasonable, discuss the job to see if they can be modified.

Don't take a job unless you are satisfied that you can do it, or at least that you can learn how to do it within an acceptable period of time. You can quite properly ask what training and help you will be given in the early stages. If your predecessor failed, you can ask what went wrong so that you can avoid making the same mistakes.

Beating the Peter Principle – for others

If you are in a position of offering promotion or a new job, you have to be aware of the Peter Principle and how to circumvent it. You need to match the capacities of the candidate to the demands of the job, and your starting point for this process should be an analysis in depth of the skills required. These should be classified under the headings of MATCH:

1. *Managerial* – making things happen, leading, inspiring and motivating people, team building and maintaining morale, coordinating and directing effort, using resources productively, and controlling events to achieve the required results.
2. *Analytical* – dissecting problems and coming up with the right conclusions about what is happening and what should happen.
3. *Technical/professional* – an understanding not only of all the tricks of the trade but also of how to use other people's knowledge effectively.
4. *Communications* – putting the message across.
5. *Human resource management/personal* – the ability to persuade, enthuse and motivate, trustworthiness, integrity, dedication.

When you have drawn up the specifications, measure the candidate against each of these criteria. Obtain whatever evidence you can about his or her performance in the present job which gives any indication of potential competence in these areas. Ask for information on successes and failures and why they occurred.

This matching process should identify any potential weaknesses. You can then discuss these and decide on any help the individual needs in the shape of coaching, training or further experience.

Monitor the progress of the individual carefully in the initial months. Your aim should be to spot dangerous tendencies in good time so that swift remedial action can be taken.

Military incompetence

Norman Dixon suggests that there are two basic types of military incompetence. The first group includes Generals Elphinstone (first Afghan war), Raglan (the Crimean War), Butler (Boer War) and Percival (Singapore). These were all mild, courteous and peaceful men, paralysed by the burden of decision-making under fire. The second group includes people like Haig, Joffre, and a number of the other First World War generals. They are characterized by overweening ambition coupled with a terrifying insensitivity to the suffering of others. Far from being paralysed by decisions, they were active, but active in vain, devious, scheming and dishonest ways. Alastair Mant in *Leaders We Deserve* quotes the example of the catastrophic results achieved in the Crimean War when an incompetent in the first group (Raglan) has authority over someone in the second group (the Earl of Cardigan, reputed by one contemporary to possess the 'brains of a horse').

The elements of military incompetence are listed by Norman Dixon as:

- Serious wastage of human resources
- Fundamental conservatism and clinging to outworn tradition or to past successes
- Tendency to reject or ignore information which is unpalatable or which conflicts with preconceptions (eg, company yes men)
- Tendency to underestimate the enemy
- Indecisiveness and a tendency to abdicate from the role of decision-maker
- Obstinate persistence in a given task despite strong contrary evidence
- Failure to exploit a situation gained and a tendency to 'pull punches'
- Failure to make adequate reconnaissance
- A predilection for frontal assaults, often against the enemy's strongest point (reference the gross overcrowding of once profitable markets)
- Belief in brute force rather than the clever ruse
- Failure to make use of surprise or deception
- Undue readiness to find scapegoats

- Suppression or distortion of news from the Front, usually deemed necessary for morale or security
- Belief in mystical forces – fate, bad luck, etc.

Examples of all these can be found in the actions or inactions of business leaders and managers.

1. *Wasting resources.* Most factories and offices are overstaffed, to the tune of 10 per cent or more.
2. *Conservatism.* 'That's the way it has always worked.' We have been market leaders for the last 20 years, why change?
3. *Rejecting unpalatable information.* 'What did you say about our losing market share? I don't believe it; these desk surveys are always inaccurate.'
4. *Underestimating the enemy.* 'What's this? Bloggs & Co have introduced a new product in our range. And you think it will compete? Forget it. They're useless. They couldn't run a winkle stall.'
5. *Indecisiveness.* 'We need to think a bit more about this.' 'I need more information.' 'I sometimes think that if you put problems like this in the "too difficult" section of your pending tray, they will go away.' 'It seems to me that we have several alternative routes (*sic*) ahead of us. Let's call a meeting next week or sometime to look at the pros and cons.' 'This is something for the Board.'
6. *Obstinate persistence.* 'Don't confuse me with the facts.' 'That's the way it's going to be.'
7. *Failure to exploit a situation.* 'Okay, you think we're going to exceed budget on our launch and you want to accelerate the programme. But let's not get too excited, we mustn't overstretch ourselves.'
8. *Failure to reconnoitre.* 'I don't believe in market research.'
9. *A predilection for frontal assaults.* 'Bloggs are doing particularly well in widgets. Yes, I appreciate we know nothing about widgets, but we can soon find out. Let's get in there fast and topple them from their perch.'
10. *A belief in brute force.* 'Tell the union they can either take 5 per cent or do the other thing . . . What's this about a productivity package? I don't believe in messing about. It's a straight offer or nothing . . . They'll come out? I don't believe it, not with unemployment levels round here topping 15 per cent.'
11. *A failure to make use of surprise.* 'I don't like playing about. Let's get this show on the road . . . You think we'll get off to a better start if we keep the competition guessing? Forget it, we're miles better than they are!'

12. *Scapegoating.* 'It's not us, it's the rate of exchange.' 'This xxxx government has screwed us up!' 'Why am I surrounded by incompetent fools?'
13. *Suppression of news.* 'Don't tell them about how well we're doing. They'll only ask for more money.'
14. *A belief in mystical forces.* 'I just *feel* in my bones we must do this thing.'

Why things go wrong – a summary

The main reasons for things going wrong are:

- Inability to learn from mistakes
- Sheer incompetence through over-promotion
- Poor selection, inadequate training
- Over-confidence
- Under-confidence
- Laziness
- Lack of foresight.

What can you do about it?

Inability to learn from mistakes

Remember Murphy's Law, which states that if anything can go wrong it will. Mistakes will happen. The unforgivable thing is to make the same mistake twice. You learn from your mistakes by analysing what went wrong – no excuses, no alibis – and making notes of what to do and what not to do next time.

Incompetence

This is something you should minimize in your subordinates by a constant drive to improve selection and performance standards and by training and coaching aimed at correcting specified weaknesses.

If you have doubts about your own ability, analyse your own strengths and weaknesses and grab every opportunity you can to get extra training and advice from people you believe in. If that still does not work, get out in good time.

Over-confidence

This is the most difficult problem to eradicate. It is always said in the

Royal Air Force that the most accident-prone pilots are the over-confident ones. You need confidence in yourself and your staff. How can it be controlled from going over the edge?

It takes time to understand or demonstrate that misjudgements occur because you are so certain that you know all the answers that no attempt is made to foresee or take care of the unexpected. Over-confident people tend to have tunnel vision – they can see quite clearly to the end but they take no notice of what is happening on either side or beyond. And if they see the light at the end of the tunnel they may not appreciate that it is the light of the oncoming train.

Under-confidence

This can be overcome as long as the individual is fundamentally competent. People who lack confidence often need help from someone who can underline achievements and provide encouragement to do more of the same. Mentors can help, as can a deliberate policy of extending people steadily so that they are not suddenly faced with a daunting leap in the level of work they have to do. Start by giving the under-confident tasks that are well within their capabilities and progressively increase demands, but only in achievable steps.

Carelessness

This is a universal problem. It can happen through over-confidence, but we all make mistakes under pressure or because we think the task is easier than it is. Sadly, reputations can be damaged, even destroyed by relatively minor mistakes. If you submit a report to your board with a glaring arithmetical error in it, the credibility of your whole report may be damaged, even if the mistake, although obvious, was not significant. Never submit a report or write a key letter without checking every figure and every fact at least once. If possible, ask someone else to do it as well.

Laziness

No one would ever admit to being lazy. But lazy people do exist, either because they are naturally indolent or they have not been given sufficient leadership and a well-defined role in the organization. If one of your staff is lazy, put the boot in. It cannot be tolerated.

Lack of foresight

This is a common reason for errors. As a manager, one of your prime responsibilities is to think ahead. You must try to anticipate all the eventualities and make contingency plans accordingly. You won't get it right every time and you may find yourself occasionally in a crisis-management situation. But you will at least be better prepared if thought has been given to some of the eventualities, even if you could not anticipate them all.

Chapter 24
Improving organizational effectiveness

An effective organization can broadly be defined as one that makes the best use of its resources to attain high levels of performance, thus successfully achieving its purpose and objectives while also meeting its responsibilities to its stakeholders. These stakeholders consist of:

- The owners, shareholders, public authorities or trustees who direct or fund the organization
- The employees who run the organization and carry out the activities required to achieve targets and standards of performance and delivery
- The customers, clients or members of the public for whom the organization provides goods or services
- The third parties such as suppliers or providers through or with whom the organization does business
- The community in which the organization operates.

Factors contributing to organizational effectiveness

There is no single factor or mix of factors which will guarantee organizational effectiveness, but the following is a selection of factors which, in one way or other, will contribute to success:

- A clear and well-articulated vision of the future of the organization
- A well-defined mission and goals, and strategies to accomplish them
- A value system which emphasizes performance, productivity, quality, customer service, teamwork and flexibility
- Strong visionary leadership from the top
- A powerful management team
- A well-motivated, committed, skilled and flexible workforce
- Effective teamwork throughout the organization, with win/lose conflict well under control

- Continuous pressure to innovate and grow
- The ability to respond fast to opportunities and threats
- The capacity to manage, indeed thrive, on change
- A sound financial base and good systems for management accounting and cost control.

Prescriptions from the gurus

Richard Beckhard

Richard Beckhard (5) defined a healthy organization from a behavioural scientist's point of view as having the following characteristics:

- The total organization, the significant subparts and individual employees manage their work against goals and plans for the achievement of goals.
- Form follows function – the problem, task or project determines how human resources are organized.
- Decisions are made by or near the sources of information.
- Managers and supervisors are rewarded not only in relation to short-term profit or production performance, but also for developing their subordinates and creating an effective working group.
- Communication laterally and vertically is relatively undistorted.
- People are open and confronting.
- There is a minimum amount of win/lose activity between individuals and groups.
- Conflict (clash of ideas) may exist about tasks and projects but relatively little energy is wasted on interpersonal difficulties.

Peter Drucker

Management by objectives
Peter Drucker (14) achieved fame many years ago by inventing the concept of management by objectives. He emphasized that objectives in a business enterprise enable management to explain, predict and control activities in a way which single ideas like profit maximization do not. He identifies five key characteristics of objectives:

1. They enable the organization to explain the whole range of business phenomena in a small number of general statements.
2. They allow the testing of these statements in actual experience.
3. They enable behaviour to be predicted.

4. They facilitate the examination of the soundness of decisions while they are still being made rather than after they fail.
5. They provide for performance in the future to be improved as a result of the analysis of past experience.

Efficiency and effectiveness

In a later book, Drucker (15) pointed out that to concentrate on efficiency rather than effectiveness could be limiting and therefore dangerous. It can result in:

- Doing things right rather than doing right things
- Solving problems rather than producing creative alternatives
- Safeguarding resources rather than optimizing resource utilization
- Lowering costs rather than increasing profit
- Minimizing risk rather than maximizing opportunities.

Organization

In 'The coming of the new organization', Peter Drucker (16) has suggested that the typical organization of the future will be knowledge-based, composed largely of specialists who direct and discipline their own performance through organized feedback from colleagues, customers and headquarters.

The information-based organization of 20 years hence will have fewer than half the levels of management of its counterpart today, and no more than a third of the managers. He noted that in many organizations, 'whole layers of management neither make decisions nor lead. Instead, their main, if not their only function is to serve as "relays" – human boosters for the faint, unfocused signals that pass for communication in the traditional pre-information organization.'

This creates a number of critical problems, namely:

- Developing rewards, recognition and career opportunities for specialists
- Creating unified vision in an organization of specialists
- Devising the management structure for an organization of task forces
- Ensuring the supply, preparation and testing of top management people.

Charles Handy

Charles Handy (22) has suggested that an effective organization is a learning organization, which has a formal way of asking questions, seeking out theories, testing them and reflecting upon them. The questions include:

- What are its strengths, talents and weaknesses?
- What sort of organization does it want to be?
- What does it want to be known for?
- How does it plan to achieve it?

On organization structure, Charles Handy believes the trend is for there to be not one workforce but three: the core, the contractual fringe and the flexible labour force. Businesses, he says, are trying to have the best of both worlds: size, to give them clout in the marketplace and economies of scale, and small units to give them the flexibility they need as well as the 'sense of community for which individuals increasingly hanker'.

He has also forecast the growth of the federal organization. This takes the process of decentralization one stage further by establishing each key operational, manufacturing or service provision activity as a distinct, federated unit. Each federal entity runs its own affairs, although they are linked together by the overall strategy of the organization and, if it is a public company, are expected to make an appropriate contribution to corporate profitability in order to provide the required return on their shareholders' investments and to keep external predators at bay.

The centre in a federal organization maintains a low profile. The federated activities are expected to provide the required initiative, drive and energy. The centre is at the middle of things, not at the top. It is not just a banker but it does provide resources. Its main role is to coordinate, advise, influence, suggest and help to develop integrated corporate strategies.

John Harvey-Jones

John Harvey-Jones (24) has made the following suggestions – among many others – on the approaches adopted by successful businesses:

- Nothing will happen unless everyone down the line knows what they are trying to achieve and gives of their best to achieve it.
- The whole of business is about taking an acceptable risk.
- The process of deciding where you are taking the business is an opportunity to involve others, which actually forms the motive power that will eventually make it happen.

Rosabeth Moss Kanter

Rosabeth Moss Kanter (29) has emphasized the importance of managing change. She believes that managers must become 'change masters, helping and guiding the organization, its management and all who work in it to manage and, indeed, to exploit and triumph over change'. Kanter also recorded how Apple Computers devised a three-pronged approach to improving organizational effectiveness as follows:

1. Develop an organizational structure that produces synergies, not conflict.
2. Create more cooperative alliances with suppliers and customers.
3. Find ways to maintain a flow of new ideas towards new products and new ventures.

She notes (30) that American corporations are being pushed in ever less bureaucratic and ever more entrepreneurial directions, cutting out unnecessary layers of the hierarchy and forging closer ties with employees. She emphasizes, however, that the pursuit of excellence has multiplied the number of demands on executives and managers.

Rosabeth Moss Kanter has described this as the 'post-entrepreneurial corporation'. This represents a triumph of process over structure. She suggests that relationships and communication, and the flexibility temporarily to combine resources, are more important than the formal channels and reporting relationships represented in an organization chart: 'What is important is not how responsibilities are divided but how people can pull together to pursue new opportunities.'

J Katzenbach and D Smith

In *The Wisdom of Teams*, Katzenbach and Smith (31) suggested that high performing organizations have the following characteristics:

- The primary purpose of top management is to focus on performance and the teams that will deliver it.
- There is a strong and balanced performance ethic which creates and pursues the performance challenges that create effective teams.
- To sustain a balanced performance ethic they provide superior value to their customers. This, in turn, generates both attractive returns for the company's owners and personal growth opportunities and attractive earnings for employees, who, of course, are responsible for providing superior value to customers.

Richard Pascale and Anthony Athos

The analysis of the art of Japanese management conducted by Richard Pascale and Anthony Athos (41) suggested that there are seven Ss for success:

- *Strategy* – the plan to reach identified goals.
- *Structure* – the characteristics of the organization's structure: functional, decentralized, etc.

- *Systems* – the routines for processing and communicating information.
- *Staff* – the categories of people employed.
- *Style* – how managers behave in achieving the organization's goals.
- *Skills* – the capabilities of key people.
- *Superordinate goals* – the significant meanings of guiding concepts with which an organization imbues its members (ie its values).

They also made the following perceptive comment on the clash between idealism and reality in organizations:

> The inherent preferences of organizations are clarity, certainty and perfection. The inherent nature of human relationships involves ambiguity, uncertainty and imperfection.

Richard Pascale

In *Managing on the Edge*, Richard Pascale (42) suggested a new 'paradigm' for organizations in which they:

- Place increased emphasis on the 'soft' dimensions of style and shared values
- Operate as networks rather than hierarchies
- Move from the status-driven view that managers think and workers do as they are told, to a belief in managers as 'facilitators' with workers empowered to initiate improvements and change
- Place less emphasis on vertical tasks within functional units and more on horizontal tasks and collaboration across units
- Focus less on content and the prescribed use of specific tools and techniques and more on 'process' and a holistic synthesis of techniques
- Change the military model to a commitment model.

Tom Peters and Robert Waterman

From their research into 75 highly regarded enterprises, Tom Peters and Robert Waterman (45) identified the following eight attributes which characterize the excellent companies:

1. *A bias for action.* The excellent companies get on with it. They are analytical in their decision-making but this does not paralyse them, as it does some companies.
2. *Close to the customer.* They get to know their customers and provide them with quality, reliability and service.
3. *Autonomy and entrepreneurship.* Leaders and innovators are fostered and given scope.

4. *Productivity through people.* They really believe that the basis for quality and productivity gain is in the rank and file. They do not just pay lip service to the slogan 'people are our most important asset'. They do something about it by encouraging commitment and involving everyone.
5. *Hands-on, value-driven.* The people who run the organization get close to those who work for them and ensure that the organization's values are understood and acted upon.
6. *Stick to the knitting.* The successful organizations stay reasonably close to the businesses they know.
7. *Simple form, lean staff.* The organization structure is simple and corporate staff are kept to a minimum.
8. *Simultaneous loose–tight properties.* They are both decentralized and centralized. They push decisions and autonomy as far down the organization as they can into individual units and profit centres. But, as Peters and Waterman say, 'they are fanatic centralists around the few core values they hold dear'.

However, some of the 'excellent' companies included in this study have not done so well subsequently.

Tom Peters

In *Thriving on Chaos* Tom Peters (46) commented that although many organizations have nominally decentralized (on paper) they have become re-centralized because of such factors as the dominance of finance staff with their complex, centralized control systems and the demand for the central coordination of advertising budgets. More layers of management were added and expert central staffs made '(1) more requests to the line for reports, and (2) more requests that this or that report be coordinated with numerous others'. At the same time, Peters comments, the 'matrix' organization on NASA lines became popular: 'yet another form of de facto centralization which attempted to gain synergies that would come from coordinating everything and everyone with everything else and anyone else'.

Against this background, he proposes the following approaches:

- Break organizations into the smallest possible independent units
- Give every employee a business person's strong sense of revenue, cost and profit
- Ever-closer involvement with the customer
- Minimize management layers – no more than five in very complex organizations; three in smaller, less complex organizations with, at supervisor level, spans of control from 25 to 75 people

- Achieve flexibility by empowering people
- Learn to love change by a new view of leadership at all levels
- Pursue fast-paced innovation.

The visible presence of 'new, flexible competitors', the need to respond to change, challenge and uncertainty, and the impact of new technology, have all combined to emphasize the need for flexibility and teamwork. The processes of federalizing and flattening organizations (stripping out layers of middle management) have added to this emphasis.

Peters also suggests that new, flexible manufacturing systems and the decentralized availability of the information needed for fast product changeover are leading to the wholesale adoption of cellular manufacturing, 'which eventually concentrates all the physical assets needed for making a product in a self-contained configuration which is tailor-made for team organization'. His prescription for the new model organization is:

- The creation of self-managing teams, responsible for their own support activities such as budgeting and planning
- Managers who act as 'on call' experts, spending most of their time helping teams
- Managers who encourage constant front-line contact among functions
- The use of small units – 'small within big' configurations everywhere.

Peter Wickens

Peter Wickens (61) describes the three components of the Nissan 'tripod' for success as being:

- Flexibility
- Quality consciousness
- Teamwork.

Case studies

In an insurance company the 'efficiency' of inspectors (ie sales representatives) was measured by the number of policies they sold and the volume of premium income they generated. Naturally, they concentrated on selling the easiest forms of policy and generated lots of income. But volume, while a measure of efficiency, did not indicate effectiveness, which could only be assessed by the relative profitability of the different policies. Without guidance on which policies were most profitable the inspectors were efficient in volume terms but ineffective in terms of the only true measure of performance – profitability.

The accounts department prided itself on the efficiency with which it delivered voluminous printouts analysing costs incurred against budget for each cost centre within two weeks of the end of the month. But the information was not effective in that it did not help cost centre managers to control some of their crucial costs. This was because so many items were accrued (ie assumptions were made about expenditure because invoices had not yet been processed) that many of the figures in key expenditure areas were meaningless. As a result, cost centre managers maintained their own sets of duplicate accounts.

The chairman of an Industrial Training Board, which collected training levies from firms in the industry and redistributed them in the form of grants for approved training, was concerned because levy income was exceeding grant expenditure. Many of the firms in the industry complained bitterly that the Training Board was accumulating vast useless reserves at their expense. The chairman therefore launched a nationwide campaign under the slogan 'Get your whack back Jack', encouraging firms to do training and claim levy. With great efficiency the firms in the industry completed forms by the dozen, making grant claims for all sorts of training. But much of the training was irrelevant and for show.

A direct mail company decided to set up a 'party plan' type of operation to sell its products. It had no previous experience in this activity. Demonstrators had to be recruited, and it was decided that the current mailing list of people who had already shown some interest in the products would prove to be the best source of recruits. This seemed a less haphazard approach than advertising for demonstrators. The recruitment campaign was planned meticulously and executed with the utmost efficiency. Everything was thought of and everything happened as planned *except* that hardly anyone responded. The method proved to be totally ineffective because it was based on an incorrect assumption. The only ways to get good party plan demonstrators are by direct contact and classified advertising in the local press. An enquiry into why the mailing list members had not responded showed that the written approach through the mail failed to overcome their natural suspicions about party plan.

A government agency responsible for the recruitment of large numbers of staff had its procedures examined by an organization and methods team. It was noted that there were a number of directors of recruitment, each responsible for particular 'competitions' to get different categories of staff. Each director had a group of staff to administer the various stages of a competition. But there was duplication of work, such as the sifting and acknowledgement of applications, between the various directorates. The O & M team therefore hit on the 'efficient' solution, which was to have a number of units dealing with different activities; sifting, acknowledging, obtaining references, etc. Each of these units provided a service to all directors of recruitment but was controlled separately by a director of administration. This solution was certainly efficient in that it grouped associated activities together and saved staff. But it was also ineffective. Because there was no one person responsible for the control and coordination of individual competitions (the directors of recruitment sat on the sidelines as far as administration was concerned), delays took place at each stage. Competitions took much longer to complete and good recruits were being lost because they got tired of waiting.

An engineering firm ran into hard times and decided that a general cut of 20 per cent in all indirect staff was required. A senior manager was appointed to implement the cut. He conducted the assignment with great efficiency. Everyone was quite clear about what they had to do, the programme was implemented exactly as planned, and documentation was precise and complete. But the decision to make an all round 20 per cent cut had repercussions which had not been fully appreciated when the plans were made. A number of key research departments employing only indirect staff found that they had to dismiss key employees to achieve their targets. Their ability to provide for the longer-term development of the business was therefore seriously affected. The assignment was conducted efficiently but led to a significant decline in effectiveness where it really mattered – the future.

Chapter 25
Innovating

Innovation is the life-blood of an organization. There is nothing so stultifying to a company – or the people in it – as a belief that the old ways must be the best ways. An organization which tries to stand still will not survive.

Innovation requires a blend of creativity, clear thinking and the ability to get things done. It requires thinkers and doers to work closely together. Top management must create a climate in which managers have the scope to develop new ideas and the resources to implement them.

The success of innovative projects, therefore, can be seen to depend on two issues: the characteristics of the individual manager and the climate of the organization.

Individual characteristics

To be an effective innovator you need:

- To have a clear initial view of the results you want to achieve – you should not worry too much to begin with about the ways of achieving them
- To define clearly the aims and benefits of the project
- To argue the case for the project persuasively
- To elicit support not only from your boss but also from your colleagues and subordinates – you need to build a coalition in which everyone shares equally in the belief that the project is worth while
- Courage – to take calculated risks and to weather the storm when the inevitable setbacks occur
- To be good at getting people to act – mobilizing people to contribute fully to the project means using a participative management style
- Power to mobilize support and resources and to achieve results

- The ability to handle interference or opposition to the project – resistance can be open, but it often takes a passive or covert form: criticism of the plan's details, foot-dragging, late responses to requests, or arguments over allocation of time and resources among projects. Covert resistance can be the most dangerous
- The force of character to maintain momentum, especially after the initial enthusiasm for the project has waned and the team is involved in more tedious work.

Organizational characteristics

The organizational characteristics which encourage innovation are:

- A free flow of information which allows executives to find ideas in unexpected places and pushes them to combine fragments of information
- Close and frequent contact between departments, and an emphasis on lateral as well as vertical relationships providing resources, information and support
- A tradition of working in teams and sharing credit
- Senior executives who believe in innovation and will make the necessary resources available
- Managers with the ability and desire to seize opportunities and to make time available for innovation.

Case studies

Float glass

The development at Pilkington's is sometimes described as a one-man campaign by Alistair Pilkington. This is not entirely correct. Alistair Pilkington did indeed have and deploy the qualities of a successful innovator. He knew what he wanted, he knew it was worth while and he was quite ruthless in getting his own way against opposition. But he had the advantage of working in a company where the climate was conducive to innovation. One of the most impressive research establishments in the world was there to provide the skills and facilities required for the enormous development programme. And of equal importance was the tradition at Pilkingtons of management by committee. Often considered to act as a brake on innovation and achievement, the committee system did in fact work well for research and development. Because all relevant departments were represented – research, development, production and sales – the float glass project was a fully integrated affair from the very beginning. The problems of cooperation and the misunderstandings that are inevitable in any major new project did not get a chance to flare up. The traditional rivalries between research, development and production did not, of course, vanish overnight, but the will and the machinery were there to minimize tension. The project was a triumph.

Innovation in management development

John Raimes was personnel manager in the Filton division of the British Aircraft Corporation. He successfully introduced project and do-it-yourself training a dozen years before various management development pundits announced this approach as a major new discovery.

Raimes was dissatisfied with the traditional type of management training course. He believed that managers would get much more out of being involved in a project which dealt with a real issue of immediate concern to the company. If the right group of managers were brought together they could benefit the company with their ideas as well as learning from and about each other, extending their understanding of how a firm is managed and testing their ability to analyse problems and think through new ideas. A do-it-yourself element could be introduced by giving the managers taking part in a project the scope to attend courses, call for outside advice (within limits) and extend their reading on the subject.

Raimes had to sell his idea to top management. He had to exercise all his considerable powers of persuasion to convince them that his concept would be much more beneficial to the company and its managers than conventional training. He had no proof that this would be the case. He could only carry his point by demonstrating his total conviction that he was right. Which he did.

Raimes' own belief in what he was doing was the main reason why he succeeded. But he was helped by the climate in the firm which, as part of the aerospace industry, lived by innovation and creativity. There were people on the board who recognized that the needs of management in this type of industry were different and had to be catered for in an original way.

Chapter 26
Interviewing

We all believe that we are good interviewers. Just as we all believe we are good drivers. But bad drivers abound, as road accident statistics prove. And the record of job failures in most organizations can often be attributed to poor selection in the first place. Many research studies have shown that predictions made at interviews often fail because of bias, failure to get the information required, or inability to interpret the information. To minimize these problems you need to adopt a systematic approach, based on a job description and a specification of the sort of person you need to fill the job. You then need to consider the method of interviewing you use, how to conduct the interview and how to evaluate the results.

Approach to the interview

An interview has been described as a conversation with a purpose. It is a conversation in which candidates should be drawn out to talk freely about themselves and their career. Apart from when talking about the job and the company, the interviewer should restrict him or herself to asking questions and making encouraging grunts. Open-ended questions will produce the most informative answers; 'yes or no' questions should be avoided as far as possible. If you simply say 'tell me about your present job' you will get most of what you want to know. Gaps can be filled in by asking follow-up questions. Avoid leading questions which indicate the answer you are expecting.

The interview's principal purpose is to provide evidence upon which a prediction can be made of a candidate's suitability for the job. It does, however, have two other aims: to provide the candidate with information about the job and the company, and to give him or her a favourable impression of the company. This should encourage the good candidate to join and should leave the rejected candidate without any ill-feelings.

Conducting the interview

The interview must be planned to elicit information from the candidate which will enable his experience, qualifications and personal qualities to be measured against the requirements set out in the job specification. There is no one best way of sequencing an interview. A fairly typical approach would be:

1. Put the candidate at his ease – he will be nervous and you want him to relax so that he will express himself freely.
2. Explain how you are going to handle the interview.
3. Start with a brief description of the job and the company. Do not spend too long over this, especially if the candidate is a marginal one. You can elaborate at the end of the interview.
4. Use a biographical approach, inviting the candidate to describe in his own words his education and career to date. Do not delve too deeply into the distant past – spend most time on the current job. Probe if necessary to ensure that the candidate is giving you the full picture. He will naturally try to gloss over any less successful episodes in his career. Get him to tell you not only what he did but why he did it. This is particularly relevant when discussing choice of career and reasons for leaving jobs. It will give you a chance to assess how well he is motivated.
5. Give him the opportunity to talk about his achievements and to explain any setbacks.
6. Allow time at the end of the interview for him to ask questions.

The information-gathering part of the interview should last between 20 and 40 minutes, depending on the level of the job.

For key jobs, a second interview by a more senior person is desirable.

Evaluating the interview

The only questions you need to answer at the end of the interview are:

- Does this candidate measure up to the job?
- How does this candidate compare with other candidates?

Qualifications are relatively easy to assess unless they have been obtained from some obscure institution. Experience should not be too difficult to evaluate once you have taken steps to assure yourself that the candidate has really done what he claims. Job titles are misleading; you must have information on the actual level of responsibility and compare this with what he will be expected to do in each of the key areas of the job for which he is being considered. Information on specific tasks and achievements is helpful.

His progress to date will give you some indication of how he will perform in the future. A steady progression in line with his ambitions is obviously what you are looking for. Anyone can fail once for reasons which are not particularly blameworthy. A pattern of failure, characterized by short stays in jobs, is highly suspect. If any gaps in the candidate's career emerge, find out where he was and what he was doing.

A candidate's personal qualities are difficult to assess at an interview. You may be able to decide quickly whether you like his manner or not, but it is much harder to assess qualities such as drive, ability to work with others and leadership.

Interviewers are always warned about the 'halo effect' which means allowing a favourable impression of, for instance, a candidate's appearance or manner to override judgement on other aspects of his character and ability. Equally dangerous is the 'horns effect' by which too much attention is paid to one unattractive feature. A balanced view must be achieved, which means looking at all aspects of the candidate's career as well as the initial impression he makes, even though this may be a very important part of the job itself.

Information on personality strengths and weaknesses can be obtained by analysing the applicant's career and interests. Someone with high aspirations who has consistently achieved what he set out to do is clearly well motivated. Someone from a poor background who has triumphed over early setbacks has obviously more drive than someone who has not made the most of the opportunities given to him. The candidate's interests may indicate the extent to which he likes mixing with people and taking up leadership positions. An indication of a person's drive and determination can be seen by how energetically he pursues his spare-time activities. Stamp collecting may sound pretty pedestrian but, if the candidate reveals that by sheer application he has become the leading authority in Britain on colonial stamps in the mid-nineteenth century, this will tell you about his ability to achieve something.

Candidates can make revealing statements about themselves if you allow them to talk – they may indeed talk themselves out of a job. If, for example, someone says that he left his last three jobs because his boss didn't appreciate him, this suggests an inability to get on with superiors or a tendency towards paranoia or both. He has drawn attention to a pattern which could well be repeated.

The final assessment

The evidence required to make an assessment of the candidate comes from various aspects of the interview and from the letter of application or application form. It needs to be looked at against the specification and summarized on an assessment form, especially if there are a number of candidates.

Dos and don'ts of interviewing

DO	DON'T
Plan the interview	Start the interview unprepared
Establish an easy and informal relationship	Plunge too quickly into demanding questions
Encourage the candidate to talk	Ask leading questions
Cover the ground as planned	Jump to conclusions on inadequate evidence
Probe as necessary	
Analyse career and interests to reveal strengths, weaknesses and patterns of behaviour	Pay too much attention to isolated strengths or weaknesses
Maintain control over the direction and time taken by the interview	Allow the candidate to gloss over important facts
	Talk too much

Chapter 27
Leadership

Leaders have a key role to play in developing effective organizations. They set people in the right direction, gain commitment to achieving the organization's mission and motivate them to achieve their goals.

As John Kotter (33) has written:

> The direction-setting aspect of leadership does not produce plans; it creates visions and strategies. These describe a business, technology or corporate culture in terms of what it should become over the long term and articulate a feasible way of achieving this goal.

And as Warren Bennis and Burt Nanus (9) conclude:

> Leaders articulate and define what has been previously implicit or unsaid; then they invent images, metaphors and models that provide a focus for new attention. By so doing, they consolidate or challenge prevailing wisdom. In short, an essential factor in leadership is the capacity to influence and organize meaning for members of the organization.

What is leadership?

Leadership is achieving results through people. It happens when there is an objective to be reached or a task to be carried out, and when more than one person is needed to do it. All managers are, by definition, leaders: they can only do their job with the support of their team, who must be inspired or persuaded to follow them. Leadership is therefore about encouraging and inspiring individuals and teams to give of their best to achieve a desired result.

The overall aim of leaders is to achieve the task with the help of their group. To meet this overall aim leaders have three main objectives:

1. To gain the commitment and cooperation of their team.

2. To get the group into action to achieve agreed objectives.
3. To make the best use of the skills, energies and talents of the team.

Leaders aim to get people to do what they think is necessary by obtaining willing cooperation, not grudging submission. They build up the morale of their groups, which will be high when the group is productive and works well together. The members of the group do not need to be made comfortable; in fact, they will often be under pressure to do more than they would if left to their own devices. But if they achieve something worth while together they will gain satisfaction from that.

Leadership qualities

Effective leaders focus on a fairly small range of key issues, have a very clear idea of what they want to do about those issues, and have the ability to set the direction and take people with them.

Successful leadership sometimes seems to depend on having the right qualities at the right time. But what are the factors that influence and develop these qualities? A study of chief executives in the UK produced the following ranked list of influences on success:

		Rating out of 100
1.	Ability to work with people	78
2.	Early responsibility for important tasks	75
3.	A need to achieve results	75
4.	Leadership experiences early in career	74
5.	Wide experience in many functions	68
6.	Ability to make deals and negotiate	66
7.	Willingness to take risks	63
8.	Ability to have better ideas than colleagues	62
9.	Having talents 'stretched' by immediate bosses	60
10.	Ability to change managerial style to suit the occasion	58

This list is a mix of abilities or skills (1, 3, 6, 7, 8 and 10) and the types of experience which have developed those abilities (2, 4, 5 and 9). It highlights the fact that natural abilities are only part of the picture. They are nurtured by experience and the situations in which potential and existing leaders have found themselves.

Leadership is largely an acquired skill. To start with, a leader needs intelligence, a positive attitude and a combination of the qualities of courage, shrewdness and common sense. Successful leaders build on these natural talents as they gain experience and develop the wide range of skills they need.

Visionary leadership

Visionary leaders have the capacity or the gift to create or reorientate organizations towards success. They are able to envision what the organization should become and what it should achieve and to ensure that their vision is realized. In the words of Tom Peters (46): 'The vision and managers' consistent, daily actions in support of it, is the sea anchor, the basis for keeping people from running around as the waves of change toss them to and fro.'

Visionary leaders can be mavericks, people who see and do things differently. They are often outsiders, recruited into an organization, or unconventional insiders – people from within the organization who clearly hold different views from the mainstream about how the organization should operate. Examples include Jan Carlzon of SAS, Sir John Harvey-Jones of ICI, Lord King and Sir Colin Marshall of British Airways, Barry Sullivan of First Chicago, and Jack Welch of General Electric.

Bill Richardson (51) suggests that visionary leaders are:

- Relatively comfortable in situations of ambiguity and can live without hard-and-fast answers until trends and solutions emerge
- Seldom original – their visions are formed by listening and observing; their new approaches are based on making connections between what is happening somewhere else and how it might be applied to their own area
- Seekers of excellence, seeing mismatches between how things are done now and how they could be improved
- Orientated towards action – they prefer to talk rather than to write or plan
- Good communicators, capable of ensuring that the meaning and implications of their vision are shared throughout the organization
- Calculated risk-takers
- Fixers, in the sense that Tom Peters (46) expressed it: 'fix what's been wrong in every place you've been'
- Independent – they listen but they make up their own minds
- Achievement orientated – they are determined to obtain results and to find ways around the obstacles which inevitably confront the visionary as new ideas are pushed to fruition
- Reward orientated – they want rewards, financial and non-financial, which recognize their achievements
- Optimistic – they believe the world is full of opportunities and that most things are possible.

Types of leader

Leaders can be defined in terms of characteristics, success factors and personality traits. To answer the question 'Who is a leader?' it is also helpful to explore how these combine to produce different types of leader.

Leadership types can be classified in a number of ways and the following are some of the most typical categorizations:

1. *Charismatic/non-charismatic.* Charismatic leaders rely on their aura, their personality and their inspirational qualities. These are natural characteristics, although experience may have taught them how best to project themselves. Non-charismatic leaders rely mainly on their know-how, their ability to give an impression of quiet confidence, and their cool, analytical approach to dealing with problems.
2. *Autocratic/democratic.* Autocratic leaders impose their decisions and tend to surround themselves with yes-men. They use their position to force people to do what they are told. Democratic leaders encourage people to participate and involve themselves in decision-taking. They will exert their authority to achieve results but will rely more on know-how and persuasive ability than the use of position power.
3. *The visionary/enabler or the controller/manipulator.* The visionary/enablers inspire people with their vision of the future. Controller/manipulators are concerned mainly with operating the internal system.
4. Transactional or transformational. Burns (10) distinguishes between transactional leaders who exchange money, jobs and security for compliance, and transformational leaders who motivate others to strive for higher-order goals rather than merely short-term interest.

The role of the leader

Leaders have two essential roles. They have to:

1. *Achieve the task* – that is why their group exists. The leader's role is to ensure that the group's purpose is fulfilled. If it is not, the result is frustration, disharmony, criticism and, eventually perhaps, disintegration of the group.
2. *Maintain effective relationships* – between themselves and the members of the group, and within the group. These relationships are effective if they are conducive to achieving the task. They can be divided into those concerned with the team and its morale and sense

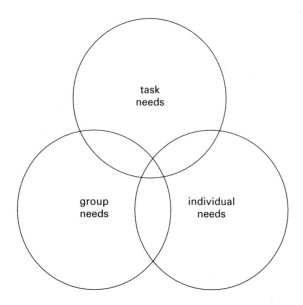

Figure 27.1: *Leadership needs*

of common purpose, and those concerned with individuals and how they are motivated.

John Adair (1) has suggested that these demands are best expressed as three areas of need which leaders are there to satisfy. These are:

1. *Task needs* – to get the job done
2. *Group needs* – to build up and maintain team spirit
3. *Individual needs* – to harmonize the needs of the individual with the needs of the task and the group.

These three needs are interdependent and are best expressed as three overlapping circles.

The law of the situation

The type of leadership exercised and success as a leader depend to a large extent on the situation and the leader's ability to understand it and act accordingly. The situation comprises the nature of the task, the impact of the organization – its policies, culture and environment, the degree to which the situation is structured or ambiguous, the sort of people in the working group, and the type of authority the leader has – given or assumed.

The performance of a group, as Fiedler (18) pointed out, is related to both the leadership style and the degree to which the situation provides the leader with the opportunity to exert influence. His research indicated that a task-orientated approach worked best for leaders in the favourable conditions when the leader has power, formal backing and a relatively well-structured task. In these circumstances the group is ready to be directed and told what to do.

In emergency or crisis conditions the task-orientated leader is likely to be more effective than the considerate leader who is concerned with interpersonal relationships. The latter will do better in a somewhat unstructured or ambiguous situation, or where his or her power as a leader is restricted.

Fiedler called this his contingency theory of leadership and emphasized the situational aspects of being a leader:

> Leadership performance then depends as much on the organization as on the leader's own attributes. Except perhaps for the unusual case, it is simply not meaningful to speak of an effective leader or an ineffective leader, we can only speak of a leader who tends to be effective in one situation and ineffective in another.

Not only does the situation affect the type of leadership required but it will also create conditions under which new and different types of leader will emerge who are appropriately qualified to meet changing demands.

Leadership checklist

The task

1. What needs to be done and why?
2. What results have to be achieved?
3. What problems have to be overcome?
4. Is the solution to these problems straightforward or is there a measure of ambiguity?
5. Is this a crisis situation?
6. What is the time-scale for completing the task?
7. What pressures are going to be exerted on the leader?

The team

8. What is the composition of the team?

9. How well is the team organized?
10. Do the members of the team work well together?
11. What will they want to get out of this?
12. How can the commitment of this particular team be achieved?
13. How are results to be obtained by satisfying their needs?
14. How are they likely to respond to the various leadership styles or approaches which may be adopted?

The individuals in the team

15. What are the strengths and weaknesses of each member of the team?
16. What sort of issues are likely to motivate them?
17. How are they likely to respond individually to the various leadership techniques or styles the leader may adopt?

Case studies

The following are descriptions of the leadership style deployed by three highly effective managers. In each case the style was influenced by three factors: the environment, the people involved, and the personality of the manager.

Edward Smith

Ted Smith was the planning manager in a large engineering works. He had some 200 people working in the departments under his control who dealt with process planning, shop loading and production control. It was a highly responsible job and his staff included highly qualified engineers as well as large numbers of clerks doing routine work.

Ted's job was to make sure that his departments ran like clockwork. Everyone had to know exactly what to do and when they had to do it. Close cooperation between the three areas under his control was essential. Charismatic-type leadership was out. He had to be cool, calm, measured and a little bit distant. Everyone in the department had to believe he knew what he was doing and what he wanted.

He therefore held regular meetings with all his subordinates at which he quickly and efficiently reviewed progress, gave instructions and, as and when necessary, discussed problems. At these meetings he was prepared to switch quickly from being someone who knew exactly what he wanted and who expected people to do exactly as they were told (because it was sensible and right for them to do so) to someone who was prepared to listen to different views, weigh them up and decide. Sometimes he would

179

deliberately throw his managers a problem and tell them to go away and solve it, and let him know the outcome of their actions.

Ted also ensured that his managers transmitted the content of these meetings down to first line supervisor level. And the latter were encouraged to meet their sections regularly. He emphasized throughout the need for teamwork and demonstrated his commitment by ensuring that at inter-departmental meetings problems of lack of cooperation or poor communications were given priority. The only time he was ever seen to express anger was when work suffered because of feuds between departments.

Elwyn Jones

Elwyn Jones was the personnel director of a large conglomerate in the food industry with over 80,000 employees. The firm had grown fast by acquisition and was highly decentralized. Staff were deliberately kept to a minimum at headquarters and Jones had only four executives responsible directly to him. He was, however, also responsible for the implementation of group personnel policies in each of the divisions and on these matters the divisional personnel directors were responsible to him.

Jones was not in a position to dictate to divisions what he wanted them to do. He could only influence them, and he felt that he had to get genuine acceptance for new policies before they could be introduced. He therefore had to consult on any changes or innovations he wished to introduce and, in most cases, he had to solicit cooperation on the testing of new ideas.

With his headquarters staff, Jones adopted a highly informal, almost permissive approach. He gave them broad guidelines on how they should develop their ideas in the divisions but encouraged them to think and act for themselves. He never called a formal meeting. He was more likely to withdraw to the local pub where, under the watchful eyes of 'big fat Nellie' behind the bar, he consumed pink gins with his colleagues and discussed strategies on entirely equal terms. He adopted precisely the same approach with the divisional personnel directors, although once or twice a year they all got together in a country hotel (one recommended by the *Good Food Guide*, of course) and spent a pleasant couple of days talking generally about their mutual interests.

James Robinson

Jim Robinson was the managing director of a medium-sized business (1000 employees) in the fast-moving consumer goods sector of industry. He had come up the hard way and his experience had always been in similar firms. Business was highly competitive and the pressures on maintaining, never mind increasing, market share were considerable. Tough decisions about products, markets and people had to be made often and quickly. There was a non-executive chairman and three outside non-executive directors on the board, but they let Robinson get on with it as long as he delivered the results they wanted – which he did.

Robinson was a despot, although a benevolent one. He knew much more about the business as a whole than any of the other four executive directors, and the chairman and the key institutions (who were represented by the non-executive directors on the board) relied implicitly on his judgement.

Robinson's management style was rumbustious. He did not suffer fools gladly and he cracked down on any repeated inefficiencies or mistakes. He made the key decisions himself. At meetings of the executive directors he would sometimes say that he wanted the views of those present but stated quite clearly that he had already made up his mind and would need a lot of convincing to change it.

But his deep understanding of the business and his ability to think faster on his feet than anyone else meant that, while his autocratic behaviour was sometimes resented at the time, those subjected to it would say on almost every occasion 'you've got to give it to the old so-and-so – he knows his stuff and he's right'. He led, they followed. This was simply because they knew he could accomplish whatever was required in the volatile environment in which they worked.

Chapter 28
Managing your boss

If you want to achieve results, innovate and get on, you have to learn how to manage your boss. The word 'manage' is defined in the *Oxford English Dictionary* as:

- To conduct affairs
- To control; cause to submit to one's rule
- To bring (a person) to consent to one's wishes by artifice, flattery, or judicious suggestion of motives
- To operate upon, manipulate for a purpose
- To bring to pass by contrivance; to succeed in accomplishing
- To deal with or treat carefully.

Although such concepts as artifice, flattery and manipulation would not normally play any part, all these definitions provide clues as to the various aspects of managing one's boss.

If you really believe that something needs to be done and you cannot do it without the consent of your boss, you have to work out how you are going to manage him. And it is worth careful and continuous thought. It is too easy to neglect this essential part of the art of management.

To manage your boss you need to know how to:

- Get agreement from him on what you want to do
- Deal with him over problems
- Impress him, so that he is more likely to accept your proposals and to place his trust in you.

Getting agreement

Getting agreement from your boss is in many ways like getting agreement from anyone else. You need to be good at case presentation and at persuasion. More specifically you need to do the following things:

1. Find out what he expects.
2. Learn about his likes and dislikes, his quirks and his prejudices.
3. Establish how he likes things presented to him. Does he like long, carefully worked out, written reports? Or does he prefer a succinct proposal on one side of one sheet of paper? Perhaps he is more likely to be persuaded if he is introduced gradually to a proposal – a softening-up process, as it were. It is often advisable to test the water before plunging straight in. Some people prefer to start by talking all the way round a problem before getting down to its essential elements. They don't like surprises.
4. Get to know how he likes things done – by observation and by asking other people. If something goes wrong, choose the right moment and ask his advice on how to do it better next time (most people love being asked for their advice).
5. Find out the right time to approach him. Some people are at their best first thing. Others take time to warm up. It is obviously inadvisable to spring surprises if he is at the end of a long hard day. Check on his mood in advance. His secretary can help. And it is always worthwhile having her on your side. Secretaries can be good friends but bad enemies.
6. Work out the best circumstances in which to tackle him. Alone in his office, or over lunch, or driving him at speed along a motorway (there is a lot to be said for making him a captive audience). Getting away from the office may be an advantage: there will be no interruptions and your boss is less likely to call in his henchman, and you will not then have to persuade two people at once. (Picking them off one at a time is much more likely to be successful.) Beware of the 'abominable no-man'. Most organizations have at least one – often the head of finance. He no doubt performs a useful role but keep him out of your way if you can.
7. Decide whether you want support. You may be able to make a better case on a one-for-one basis. There is a lot to be said for standing firmly on your own two feet.
8. Don't go in for open confrontation if you cannot get your own way at first. Get your boss to agree with what he is prepared to agree and then turn to the problem areas. Impress upon him that you want the two of you to cover every possible angle. Emphasize joint responsibility.
9. Leave him an escape route – a way open to consent without his

having to climb down. Don't beat him into the ground – you might win this one but what about the next time?

10. Don't overwhelm him with your ideas. Don't expect to achieve everything at once. Tackle one important thing at a time. Keep it simple. If you come up against a strong objection don't fight it for too long. Survive to fight another day. This does not mean that you should not argue your case strongly, but that you should avoid giving the impression of being pig-headed.

11. Keep in reserve alternative proposals or modifications to your original idea to use if you are getting nowhere.

12. If your boss comes up with a better idea than yours, recognize and accept it. Everybody likes recognition. There is no need to flatter him. You are only reacting to him the way you would like him to react to you.

13. If you can't convince him first time remember that he's the boss. He makes the ultimate decisions. If he says 'that's the way it's going to be' you *may* have to accept it. In the end he could say to you 'we're in a two-horse race and only one can win and that's going to be me'. But you don't have to give up completely. Watch for any signs that he might be prepared to change his mind – given time and a revision to your argument or proposal. Don't nag. If you press too hard he will become stubborn and begin to think that you are challenging his authority and his position. Retire in good order and re-open your campaign at the right moment.

Dealing with problems

Things are going wrong. You've made a mistake. You need your boss's help in sorting out a problem. How do you tackle him? You should adopt the following approach.

1. Keep him informed. Never let him be taken by surprise. Prepare him in advance for the bad news. If 'troubles come not in single spies but in battalions', don't let him have it all at once. Let him down as gently as possible. Don't use the 'first the good news then the bad news' line too crudely, but don't be too gloomy. Give him hope.

2. If something has gone wrong, explain what has happened, why it has happened (no excuses) and what you would like to do about it. Don't dump the problem in his lap in a 'take it or leave it' spirit.

3. Emphasize that you are seeking his views on what you propose, as well as his agreement.

4. If you think he is to blame, never say 'I told you so'. If you do, you will make an enemy for life.

5. If you admit responsibility, try to stop your boss keeping on at you. Steer him away from recriminations into a positive attitude on what you can *jointly* do to solve the problem.

Impressing your boss

Your purpose as a manager is not solely to impress your boss. Nor is it to make him like you. But you will get more done and get on better if you impress him. And why make an enemy of your boss when you can have him as a friend?

Your boss needs to trust you, to rely upon you and to believe in your capacity to come up with good ideas and to make things happen. He doesn't want to wet-nurse you or to spend his time correcting your mistakes or covering up.

To succeed in impressing your boss without really trying – it's fatal to push too much – you should:

1. Always be frank and open. Admit mistakes. Never lie or even shade the truth. If there is the faintest suspicion that you are not perfectly straightforward, your boss will never trust you again.

2. Aim to help your boss to be right. This does not mean being subservient or time-serving. Recognize, however, that you exist to give him support – in the right direction.

3. Respond fast to his requests on a can do/will do basis.

4. Don't trouble him unnecessarily with your problems.

5. Provide him with protection where required. Loyalty is an old-fashioned virtue, but you owe it to your boss. If you cannot be loyal to him then you should get out from under as quick as you can.

6. Provide your boss with what the army calls 'completed staff work'. This means that if you are asked to do something you should do it thoroughly. Come up with solutions, not problems. Test your ideas in draft form if you like but, having done so, present a complete proposal with whatever supporting arguments or evidence you need. Avoid half-baked suggestions. Your boss wants answers not questions. When you have finished your report and studied your conclusions and recommendations, ask yourself the question: 'If I were my boss would I stake my reputation on this piece of work and put my name to it?' If the answer is 'No', tear up your report and do it again. It's not completed staff work.

Chapter 29
Meetings

Down with meetings

Meetings bloody meetings, the title of a well-known training film, strikes a familiar chord with us all. When you think how many committees exist and how many meetings are held in any organization, it is remarkable how hard it is to find anyone who has a good word to say for them.

It has been said that committees are made up of the unfit appointed by the incompetent to do the unnecessary, and, again, that a camel is a horse designed by a committee. Experience of badly organized and pointless meetings is so widespread that, for many people, these cynical comments come very close to the truth.

What's wrong with meetings?

Meetings are criticized because they:

- Waste time – too many people talk too much
- Fail to produce decisions and can be slow, exasperating and frustrating – they legitimize procrastination and indecisiveness
- Tend to be dominated by a few people with strong personalities
- Make lowest common denominator recommendations
- Encourage political decisions where vested interests can prevail by means of lobbying and pressure
- Dilute responsibility
- Are costly in time and money
- Concentrate on trivialities they can grasp rather than big issues beyond their scope. Northcote Parkinson cited as an example of this a committee which approved a £1 million capital development

project (which it couldn't properly understand) in ten minutes flat yet spent two hours arguing about a new cycle shed costing £800.

What's right with meetings?

Meetings tend to incite such criticism because they are not properly organized. Many of the criticisms levelled at meetings are really criticisms of their misuse, not their proper use. A well-organized meeting held at the right time for the right reasons can bring a number of benefits. It can:

- Ensure that important matters receive proper consideration from all involved
- Clarify thinking in that members have to justify their positions before the others present
- Ensure that different viewpoints are aired
- Act as a medium for the exchange of information
- Save time by getting a number of people together
- Promote coordination
- Create something as a group which the individuals could not have achieved working separately – this is the process of synergy, where the whole is greater than the parts.

To make meetings work there are three things that must happen:

- They should be set up properly
- There should be a good chairman
- The members should be able to participate effectively.

Dos and don'ts of meetings

DO	DON'T
Use a meeting if the information or the judgement is too great for one person	Use a meeting if one person can do the job better
Set up committees only when it is essential to assemble people with different viewpoints in one place at one time	Set up a committee if you want sharp, clear responsibility
	Use a committee to administrate anything
Appoint a chairman who is going to be able to control the meeting and get the best out of it	Use a meeting or committee if you need speedy action
	Appoint a bigger committee than you need – over ten people can become unwieldy

DO	DON'T
Put people with different backgrounds who can contribute ideas on the committee	Hold unnecessary meetings – it may be good to meet regularly on the first Friday of every month but it may be even better to meet only when you have something to discuss.
Tell committees what they are to do and what their authority is	
Be explicit about when you want the meeting to report back	
Use meetings where they work best – reviewing or developing policies, coordinating decisions, ensuring that all concerned with a programme are consulted and kept informed	
Wind up committees as soon as they have served their purpose.	

Chairmanship

The success or failure of a meeting largely depends on the chairman. If you are chairing a meeting this is what you must do:

Prior to the meeting

Before the meeting starts ensure that it has proper terms of reference and that the members are briefed on what to expect and what they should be prepared to contribute. Plan the agenda to provide for a structured meeting, covering all the issues in a logical order. Prepare and issue briefing papers which will structure the meeting and spell out the background, thus saving time going into detail or reviewing purely factual information during the meeting.

During the meeting

1. Start by clearly defining the objective of the meeting, setting a time-scale which you intend to keep.
2. Go through each item of the agenda in turn ensuring that a firm conclusion is reached and recorded.
3. Initiate the discussion on each item by setting the scene very briefly and asking for contributions – ask for answers to specific questions (which you should have prepared in advance) or you may refer the matter first to a member of the meeting who can make the best

initial contribution (ideally, you should have briefed that individual in advance).

4. Invite contributions from other members of the meeting, taking care not to allow anyone to dominate the discussions.
5. Bring people back to order if they drift from the point.
6. If there is too much talk, remind members that they are there to make progress.
7. Encourage the expression of different points of view and avoid crushing anyone too obviously if he or she has not made a sensible comment.
8. Allow disagreement between members of the meeting but step in smartly if the atmosphere becomes too contentious.
9. Chip in with questions or brief comments from time to time, but do not dominate the discussion.
10. At appropriate moments during the meeting summarize the discussion, express views on where the committee has got to and outline your perception of the interim or final decision that has been made. Then check that the meeting agrees, amending the conclusion as necessary, and ensure that the decision is recorded exactly as made.
11. Summarize what has been achieved at the end of the meeting, indicating who has to do what by when.
12. If a further meeting is needed, agree the purpose of the meeting and what has to be done by those present before it takes place.

Members

If you are a member of a meeting you should:

1. Prepare thoroughly – have all the facts at your fingertips, with any supporting data you need
2. Make your points clearly, succinctly and positively – try to resist the temptation of talking too much
3. Remain silent if you have nothing to say
4. Keep your powder dry if you are not leading the discussion or if it is a subject you are not knowledgeable about. Listen, observe and save your arguments until you can make a really telling point. Don't plunge in too quickly or comprehensively – there may be other compelling arguments
5. If you are not too sure of your ground, avoid making statements such as 'I think we must do this'. Instead, pose a question to the chairman

or other member of the meeting such as, 'Do you think there is a case for doing this?'

6. Be prepared to argue your case firmly, but don't persist in fighting for a lost cause. Don't retire in a sulk because you cannot get your own way; accept defeat gracefully

7. Remember that if you are defeated in committee, there may still be a chance for you to fight another day in a different setting.

Chapter 30
Motivating

Motivating is the process of getting people to move in the direction you want them to.

The organization as a whole can provide the context within which high levels of motivation can be achieved through reward systems and the provision of opportunities for learning and development. But individual managers still have a major part to play in deploying their own motivating skills to get individual members of their team to give of their best, and to make good use of the motivational systems and processes provided by the company.

To do this it is necessary to understand:

- The process of motivation
- The different types of motivation
- The basic concepts of motivation
- The implications of motivation theory
- Approaches to motivation
- The roles of financial and non-financial rewards as motivators.

The process of motivation

Motivation is concerned with goal-directed behaviour. People are motivated to do something if they think it will be worth their while.

The process of motivation is initiated by someone recognizing an unsatisfied need. A goal is then established which, it is thought, will satisfy that need, and a course of action is determined which is expected to lead towards the attainment of that goal.

Basically, therefore, management and managers motivate people by providing means for them to satisfy their unsatisfied needs. This can be done by offering incentives and rewards for achievement and effort. But the needs of individuals and the goals associated with them vary so widely that it is difficult, if not impossible, to predict precisely how a particular incentive or reward will affect individual behaviour.

Types of motivation

Motivation at work can take place in two ways. First, people can motivate themselves by seeking, finding and carrying out work which satisfies their needs or at least leads them to expect that their goals will be achieved. Second, people can be motivated by management through such methods as pay, promotion, praise, etc.

These two types of motivation are described as:

- *Intrinsic motivation* – the self-generated factors which influence people to behave in a particular way or to move in a particular direction. These factors include responsibility (feeling the work is important and having control over one's own resources), freedom to act, scope to use and develop skills and abilities, interesting and challenging work and opportunities for advancement.
- *Extrinsic motivation* – what is done to or for people to motivate them. This includes rewards such as increased pay, praise or promotion; and punishments, such as disciplinary action, withholding pay or criticism.

The extrinsic motivators can have an immediate and powerful effect, but this will not necessarily last for long. The intrinsic motivators, which are concerned with the quality of working life, are likely to have a deeper and longer-term effect because they are inherent in individuals and not imposed from outside.

Basic concepts of motivation

The basic concepts of motivation are concerned with needs, goals, reinforcement and expectations (expectancy theory).

Needs

Needs theory states that behaviour is motivated by unsatisfied needs. The key needs associated with work are those for achievement, recognition, responsibility, influence and personal growth.

Goals

Goal theory states that motivation will be increased if goal-setting techniques are used with the following characteristics:

- The goals should be specific.
- They should be challenging but reachable.
- They should be seen as fair and reasonable.
- Individuals should participate fully in goal-setting.
- Feedback ensures that people feel pride and satisfaction from the experience of achieving a challenging but fair goal.
- Feedback is used to gain commitment to even higher goals.

Reinforcement

Reinforcement theory suggests that successes in achieving goals and rewards act as positive incentives and reinforce the successful behaviour, which is repeated the next time a similar need arises.

Expectancy theory

Expectancy theory states that motivation only happens when individuals:

- Feel able to change their behaviour
- Feel confident that a change in their behaviour will produce a reward
- Value the reward sufficiently to justify the change in behaviour.

The theory indicates that motivation is only likely when a clearly perceived and usable relationship exists between performance and outcome and the outcome is seen as a means of satisfying needs. This applies just as much to non-financial as to financial rewards. For example, if people want personal growth they will only be motivated by the opportunities available to them if they know what they are, if they know what they need to do to benefit from them (and can do it) and if the opportunities are worth striving for.

Expectancy theory explains why extrinsic motivation – for example, an incentive or bonus scheme – works only if the link between effort and reward is clear and the value of the reward is worth the effort. It also explains why intrinsic motivation arising from the work itself can sometimes be more powerful than extrinsic motivation. Intrinsic motivation outcomes are more under the control of individuals, who can place greater reliance on their past experiences to indicate the extent to which positive and advantageous results are likely to be obtained by their behaviour.

Implications of motivation theory

Motivation theory conveys two important messages. First, there are no simplistic solutions to increasing motivation. No single lever such as performance-related pay exists which is guaranteed to act as an effective motivator. This is because motivation is a complex process. It depends on:

- *Individual needs and aspirations* which are almost infinitely variable
- Both *intrinsic and extrinsic motivating factors*, and it is impossible to generalize on what the best mix of these is likely to be
- *Expectations* about rewards which will vary greatly among individuals according to their previous experiences and perceptions of the reward system
- *The social context* where the influences of the organization culture, managers and co-workers can produce a wide variety of motivational forces which are difficult to predict and therefore to manage.

The second key message provided by motivation theory is the significance of expectations, goal-setting, feedback and reinforcement as motivating factors.

The implications of these messages are considered below.

Approaches to motivation

Creating the right climate

It is necessary, in general, to create a climate which will enable high motivation to flourish. This is a matter of managing the culture. The aims would be, first, to reinforce values concerning performance and competence; second, to emphasize norms (accepted ways of behaviour) relating to the ways in which people are managed and rewarded; and third, to demonstrate the organization's belief in empowerment – providing people with the scope and 'space' to exercise responsibility and use their abilities to the full (see also Chapter 21). Without the right climate, quick fixes designed to improve motivation, such as performance-related pay, are unlikely to have much of an impact on overall organizational effectiveness, although they may work with some individuals.

Goal-setting, feedback and reinforcement

Goal-setting, feedback and reinforcement can all contribute to high motivation and they are all within your control.

Managing expectations

It is necessary to manage expectations. No reward offered through an incentive, bonus or performance-related pay scheme will be effective as a motivator unless individuals believe it is worth while and can reasonably expect to obtain it through their own efforts. Similarly, people are more likely to be motivated if they know that their achievements will be recognised.

The implications of these approaches as they affect financial and non-financial reward policies and practices are set out below.

Financial rewards

Financial rewards need to be considered from three points of view:

● The effectiveness of money as a motivator.
● The reasons why people are satisfied or dissatisfied with their rewards.
● The criteria which should be used when developing a financial reward system.

Money and motivation

Money is important to people because it is instrumental in satisfying a number of their most pressing needs. It is significant not only because of what they can buy with it but also as a highly tangible method of recognizing their worth, thus improving their self-esteem and gaining the esteem of others.

Pay is the key to attracting people to join an organization, although job interest, career opportunities and the reputation of the organization will also be factors. Satisfaction with pay among existing employees is mainly related to feelings about equity and fairness. External and internal comparisons will form the basis of these feelings, which will influence their desire to stay with the organization.

Pay can motivate. As a tangible means of recognizing achievement, pay can reinforce desirable behaviour. Pay can also deliver messages on what the organization believes to be important. But to be effective, a pay-for-performance system has to meet the following stringent conditions:

● There must be a clear link between performance and reward.
● The methods used to measure performance should be perceived to be fair and consistent.
● The reward should be worth striving for.

- Individuals should expect to receive a worthwhile reward if they behave appropriately.

As a manager you can make sure that the company's reward system is applied in your part of the organization in accordance with these principles.

Non-financial rewards

Non-financial rewards can be focused on the needs most people have, in varying degrees, for achievement, recognition, responsibility, influence and personal growth. You will be in a position to provide or withhold these rewards for those of your staff who are doing well or badly.

Achievement

The need for achievement is defined as the need for competitive success measured against a personal standard of excellence.

Achievement motivation can take place by providing people with the opportunity to perform and the scope in their jobs to use their skills and abilities.

Recognition

Recognition is one of the most powerful motivators. People need to know not only how well they have achieved their objectives or carried out their work but also that their achievements are appreciated.

Praise, however, should be given judiciously – it must be related to real achievements. And it is not the only form of recognition. Financial rewards, especially achievement bonuses awarded immediately after the event, are clear symbols of recognition to which tangible benefits are attached, and this is an important way in which mutually reinforcing processes of financial and non-financial rewards can operate. There are other forms of recognition such as long service awards, status symbols of one kind or another, sabbaticals and trips abroad, all of which can be part of the total reward process.

Recognition is also provided by managers who listen to and act upon the suggestions of their team members and, importantly, acknowledge their contribution. Other actions which provide recognition include promotion, allocation to a high-profile project, enlargement of the job to provide scope for more interesting and rewarding work, and various forms of status or esteem symbols.

Responsibility

People can be motivated by being given more responsibility for their own work. This is essentially what empowerment is about and is in line with the concept of intrinsic motivation based on the content of the job. It is also related to the fundamental concept that individuals are motivated when they are provided with the means to achieve their goals.

The characteristics required in jobs if they are to be intrinsically motivating are that first, individuals must receive meaningful feedback about their performance, preferably by evaluating their own performance and defining the feedback they require; second, the job must be perceived by individuals as requiring them to use abilities they value in order to perform the job effectively; and third, individuals must feel that they have a high degree of self-control over setting their own goals and defining the paths to these goals.

Influence

People can be motivated by the drive to exert influence or to exercise power. David McClelland's (35) research established that alongside the need for achievement, the need for power was a prime motivating force for managers, although the need for 'affiliation', ie warm, friendly relationships with others was always present. The organization, through its policies for involvement, can provide motivation by putting people into situations where their views can be expressed, listened to and acted upon. This is another aspect of empowerment.

Personal growth

In Maslow's (34) hierarchy of needs, self-fulfilment or self-actualization is the highest need of all and is therefore the ultimate motivator. He defines self-fulfilment as 'the need to develop potentialities and skills, to become what one believes one is capable of becoming'.

Ambitious and determined people will seek and find these opportunities for themselves, although the organization needs to clarify the scope for growth and development it can provide (if it does not, they will go away and grow elsewhere).

Increasingly, however, individuals at all levels in organizations, whether or not they are eaten up by ambition, recognize the importance of continually upgrading their skills and of progressively developing their careers. Many people now regard access to training as a key element in the overall reward package. The availability of learning opportunities, the selection of individuals for high-prestige training courses and programmes, and the emphasis placed by the organization on the acquisition of new skills as well as the enhancement of existing ones, can all act as powerful motivators.

Achieving high levels of motivation

The following steps need to be taken if you wish to achieve higher levels of motivation:

1. Set and agree demanding goals.
2. Provide feedback on performance.
3. Create expectations that certain behaviours and outputs will produce worthwhile rewards when people succeed but will result in penalties if they fail.
4. Design jobs which enable people to feel a sense of accomplishment, to express and use their abilities and to exercise their own decision-making powers.
5. Provide appropriate financial incentives and rewards for achievement (pay-for-performance).
6. Provide appropriate non-financial rewards such as recognition and praise for work well done.
7. Communicate to individuals and publicize generally the link between performance and reward – thus enhancing expectations.
8. Select and train team leaders who will exercise effective leadership and have the required motivating skills.
9. Give people guidance and training which will develop the knowledge, skills and competences they need to improve their performance.
10. Show individuals what they have to do to develop their careers.

Chapter 31
Negotiating

Negotiation is the process of coming to terms and, in so doing, getting the best deal possible for your firm, your union or yourself.

Negotiations involve a conflict of interest. Sellers prefer a high price to a low one and buyers prefer a low price to a high one. Unions want the highest settlement they can get, management wants the lowest. What one side gains the other loses. No one likes to lose, so there is conflict, which has to be managed if an amicable agreement is to be achieved. And negotiators do, or should, try to end up on friendly terms, whatever differences of opinion have occurred on the way. After all, they may well meet again.

Another important feature of negotiations is that they take place in an atmosphere of uncertainty. Neither side necessarily knows what the other wants or will give.

There are two main types of negotiation – commercial and trade union.

Commercial negotiations

Commercial negotiations are mainly about the price and the terms for supplying goods or services.

In their simplest form they are no more than a haggle between buyer and seller, much the same as what happens when you trade in your car for a new one. At their more complex they concern a package in which a number of extras are on offer along with the basic product. Sellers can usually offer a range of prices to suit the needs of the buyer: an 'ex-works' price, a delivered price, an installed price and a price which includes service. Various methods of staging payments or providing credit may also be offered.

Negotiations of this type usually start with the buyer producing a specification. The seller then produces a proposal and negotiation starts.

The seller will have included a negotiating margin in the proposal and will be prepared to vary the price according to the package required.

Commercial negotiations are usually conducted in a friendly manner, and that's your major problem. You can too easily be seduced into accepting a less than satisfactory deal by the blandishments of the negotiator.

Trade union negotiations

Trade union negotiations can be much tougher. They may involve a simple pay settlement, but usually they involve a package. Extra benefits will be at issue, which can be traded for concessions if need be.

In this type of negotiation, both parties are probably quite clear as to the maximum they will give or the minimum they will accept. They will have predetermined their opening demands and offers and their shopping list of extras will have been analysed to determine which points can be conceded in return for some benefit.

There are a number of bargaining conventions used in union negotiations, of which the following are the most generally accepted:

- Whatever happens during the bargaining, both parties hope to come to a settlement.
- Attacks, hard words, threats and (controlled) losses of temper are treated by both sides as legitimate tactics and should not be allowed to shake either party's belief in the other's integrity, or their desire to settle without taking drastic action.
- Off-the-record discussions (beneficial as a means of probing attitudes and intentions) should not be referred to specifically in formal bargaining sessions, unless both sides agree in advance.
- Each side should be prepared to move from its original position.
- It is normal, although not inevitable, for the negotiation to proceed by a series of offers and counter-offers which lead steadily towards a settlement.
- Concessions, once made, cannot be withdrawn.
- Firm offers must not be withdrawn, although it is legitimate to make and withdraw conditional offers.
- A third party should not be brought in until both parties are agreed that no further progress would be made without one.
- The final agreement should mean exactly what it says. There should be no trickery and the terms agreed should be implemented without amendment.

- If possible, the final settlement should be framed so that both sides can save face and credibility.

The process of negotiation

In both cases the process is much the same. Here each stage is illustrated by a summary of what took place in an actual trade union negotiation.

Stage 1: Preparation – Setting objectives (or drawing up specifications), assembling data, and deciding on negotiating strategy
The union's aim was to achieve a settlement at, or above, the current rate of inflation (8 per cent). Its strategy was to force management on to the defensive by asking them to make an offer without divulging what the union wanted. In addition, the union asked for a reduction of one hour in the working week, an extra three days' holiday and a Christmas bonus of one week's pay.

The management's objective was to settle at no more than the rate of inflation, and to concede nothing that would raise the total cost of the package above 8 per cent. There was some debate within the management team about strategy. One hawk wanted to pre-empt the union claim by starting with the final offer, allowing no room for bargaining. He was overruled on the grounds that this would cause a confrontation and hence long-term damage to relations with the union. The next question was how much room for manoeuvre should be allowed between the opening and closing offer. Some wanted to start as low as possible, say 3 per cent, so as to close well below the 15 per cent claim expected from the union. The prevailing view, however, was that too low an offer would prolong the negotiations unnecessarily. It was thought better to start at 5 per cent, so that, if it had to, the firm could take two steps of $1\frac{1}{2}$ per cent before reaching its maximum of 8 per cent.

Stage 2: Opening – Negotiators reveal their initial bargaining positions to their opposite numbers
The union started by stating its case. It wanted a substantial increase to protect its members from inflation and to restore the differentials lost over the previous three years. The extras (reduced working week, etc) were thrown in almost as make-weights, giving management the clue that there might be scope for some trading later on.

Management stated that no 'substantial offer' could be expected. It emphasized the poor trading results of the firm and the fact that, overall, the pay of the union's members compared favourably with other workers. The point was also made (it was to be repeated many times in ensuing meetings) that the firm could not guarantee that pay increases would match inflation. Having set out their opening positions and their main arguments the two parties agreed to adjourn the meeting.

Stage 3: Bargaining – At this stage both parties have the same aims. As a negotiator you will be trying: (a) to probe the weaknesses in the other side's case, and (b) to convince the other side that they must abandon their position and move closer to your own. You will also be checking to see if your own position holds good in the light of information received from your opponents and their reactions to your case. Your original judgement may be confirmed or you may have to adjust it now. You may also decide to apply pressure or give concessions now in order to move towards a satisfactory conclusion.

In the bargaining stage three meetings were held. At each of them the arguments of both management and union teams were the same as in the opening phase.

Each party aimed to discover how strongly the other believed in their arguments and to what extent they were prepared to shift position. Every phrase was analysed to discover just what was behind it, both sides seeking hints as to how much support the other was getting – from the shop floor and top management respectively.

Management opened with a 5 per cent offer and got the usual reaction: it was 'derisory', 'insulting', and so on. The union refused to state exactly what it wanted, hoping to mystify and wrong-foot the management.

Between the second and third meetings the management team were agreed in the belief that the union was hoping to get 10 per cent but, if pushed, might settle for 8. It was decided that an offer to reduce the working week by 30 minutes might be made, but only as a last-minute trade-off if a reasonable settlement seemed unlikely.

At the third meeting, management increased its offer to 7 per cent, saying that this was as far as it could go. When pressed to state whether this was, or was not, their final offer, the management team refused to elucidate. The union rightly interpreted this to mean that there was more in the kitty and that top management would release it if pressed hard enough. The union demanded 10 per cent *and* the other concessions.

Stage 4: Closing – Each party judges whether the other side is determined to stick to its position or will settle for a compromise. The final moves are made. It is during this stage that final 'trade-offs' may lead to a settlement.

The final meeting lasted all day and into the night. Management stuck to its 7 per cent offer and made no other concessions. The union tried several tactics. Pleading, controlled loss of temper and threats of industrial action were all used. The management team finally judged that the only way to get a settlement was to attempt a trade-off. They offered 7 per cent plus one hour off the working week, in return for an agreement to abolish the customary five minutes' 'wash-up' time (a practice that had been consistently abused).

Management reiterated that this was the final offer and was as much as the firm could afford and managed to convince the union by sheer force of argument that it meant what it said. The union accepted the offer after balloting its members.

Negotiating tactics

(a) Preparation

1. Define your bargaining objectives as follows:

   * *Ideal* – the best you can hope to achieve.
   * *Minimum* – the least you would be prepared to settle for.
   * *Target* – what you are going to try for and believe, realistically, you have a good chance of achieving.

2. Consider how you might build up a package which would allow concessions to be exchanged. For example, could you accept a higher price for a concession on payment terms, or increase a pay offer if the union agrees to remove a restrictive practice?

3. Assess what the other party wants or is prepared to offer. For example, if you are a manufacturer negotiating terms with a store it pays to know, say, that the buyer is constrained by company policy which insists on a three times mark-up. Knowing the retail price that the store will want to charge you will have a good idea of the maximum the buyer will pay. You can then judge whether you should press for a larger order to justify a lower selling price than you would normally accept.

   In a typical wage negotiation the union or representative body making the claim will come to the table with a predetermined target, minimum and opening claims. Similarly, you, as the employer, will have your own target, maximum and opening offer.

   The difference between their claim and your offer is the negotiating range. If your maximum exceeds their minimum this will indicate the settlement zone. This is demonstrated in Figure 31.1. In this example the chance of settlement without too much trouble is fairly high. It is when your maximum is less than their minimum, as in Figure 31.2, that the trouble starts.

4. Decide on your strategy and tactics – your opening offer, the steps

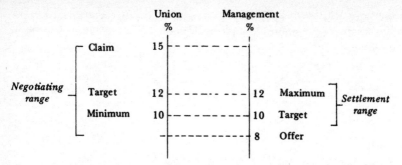

Figure 31.1: *Negotiating range with a settlement zone*

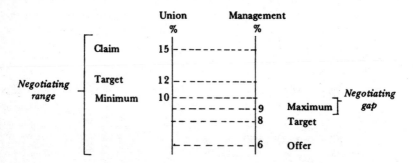

Figure 31.2: *Negotiating range without a settlement zone*

you are going to take, the concessions you are prepared to offer and the arguments you are going to use.

5. Collect the facts needed to support your case.
6. Assemble any documents you need, such as standard contract terms.
7. In a trade union negotiation:

   • Select the negotiating team. This should never have fewer than two members, and for major negotiations should have three or more: one to take the lead, one to take notes and feed the negotiator with any supporting information needed, and the others to observe their opposite numbers and play a specific part in negotiations in accordance with their brief.

   • Brief the members of the negotiating team on their roles and the negotiating strategy and tactics that are to be adopted. If appropriate, prepared statements or arguments should be issued at this stage to be used as required by the strategic plan.

   • Rehearse the members of the team in their roles. They can be asked to repeat their points to other members and deal with responses from them; or someone can act as devil's advocate and force the leader or other members of the team to handle awkward points or negotiating ploys.

At this stage it may be possible to meet your opponents informally to sound out their position, while they sound out yours. You can use such a session as an 'early warning' system to get your opponents to modify their initial demands by convincing them of the strength of your own position or your determination to resist.

In a recent trade union negotiation these 'corridor tactics' met with success. The union concerned had asked management to introduce a new technology agreement with the usual clauses about consultation, job protection and health precautions.

During the first two meetings management stuck firmly to its view that all these requirements were catered for by existing agreements and published policies. But the union insisted that this was not so. The negotiation seemed to have reached an impasse. Whatever the union leader felt, he could not weaken too obviously during the actual meetings. Neither could the general manager who was heading the management team.

To break the impasse the general manager asked his industrial relations manager to hold an off-the-record meeting with the trade union leader. At this meeting it was made clear that the company would not agree to a separate new technology agreement in any circumstances. But the industrial relations manager suggested that the company would be prepared to add a stronger prior consultation clause to the existing agreement.

From previous experience, the union leader knew this man meant what he said. He saw no point in having a major confrontation on this issue and knew he would get little support from his members, who did not see new technology as a real issue. But he felt that if he had to give a concession he should get something back. In other words, he wanted a trade-off.

He therefore agreed to go along with the idea, so long as the company let the union monitor the introduction of any major new technology schemes over the next six months. This was accepted by the industrial relations manager. Both parties understood the convention that there was no commitment and that no reference would be made to their discussion in future formal meetings. They then cleared the informal understanding with their respective committees and, at the subsequent formal meeting, the terms were agreed without any difficulty. What looked like being a major problem had been solved by corridor negotiations.

(b) Opening

Your tactics when opening the negotiation should be to:

- Open realistically and move moderately
- Challenge your opponents' position as it stands, but on no account limit their ability to move
- Explore attitudes, ask questions, observe behaviour and, above all, listen; assess your opponents' strengths and weaknesses, their tactics and the extent to which they may be bluffing
- Make no concessions of any kind at this stage
- Be non-committal about proposals and explanations (do not talk too much).

(c) Bargaining

Your aim is to narrow the gap between the two initial positions and to persuade your opponents that your case is so strong that they must accept less than they had planned. You should:

- Always make conditional proposals: 'If you will do this I will consider doing that'
- Never make one-sided concessions: always trade-off against a concession from the other party: 'If I concede x then I expect you to concede y'
- Negotiate on the whole package: never allow your opponents to pick you off item by item; keep all the issues open so as to extract the maximum benefit from potential trade-offs.

Reading the signals

During the bargaining stage you must be sensitive to any signals made by the other party. Every time they make a conditional statement it shows that they are prepared to move. Explore the possibilities with questions. Try to get behind what people *say* and understand what they really *mean*. For example:

What they say	What they mean
That's as far as I can go.	I might be able to persuade my boss to go further.
We don't usually give more than 5 per cent discount.	We're prepared to give more if you give us something in return.
Let's think about that point.	I'm prepared to negotiate.
I need notice of that question.	It's difficult, but not impossible. Try again.
It will be very difficult for us to meet that requirement.	It's not impossible but we'll want a trade-off.

What they say	*What they mean*
I shall certainly consider your offer.	I am going to accept it but I don't want to appear to be too easy a touch.
This is our standard contract.	We're prepared to negotiate on the terms.
We're prepared to offer you £x per 1000 units.	The price is negotiable.
That's my final offer.	My boss *might* go further if pushed (or if it is made worth his while).
We couldn't meet your delivery requirements at that price.	I will negotiate on delivery or price.

Arguing

During the bargaining stage much of your time will be spent in arguing. Clear thinking (see Chapter 7) will help you to present your case and expose the fallacies in your opponent's arguments.

You should also consider the *manner* in which you argue. You are not there to beat your opponent into the ground. In fact, in the interests of future good relationships (which will benefit *you* as well as your opponent) it is wise to leave an escape route. As Victor Feather said: 'Always leave the other fellow the price of his bus ticket home.'

Avoid brow-beating your opponent. Disagree firmly, but don't shoot him down. Don't try to make your opponent look small. Score points, if you must, to discredit arguments or expose fallacious reasoning but never in order to discredit him as a person. If you indulge in personal attacks or abuse, your opponents will close ranks.

To argue effectively you must be prepared to listen both to the stated, and to the implied, points made by your opponent. Don't talk too much yourself; it will prevent you reading signals, and you may give too much away. Wherever you can, challenge your opponent to justify the case on an item-by-item basis. Put the onus on him by questioning for clarification. Answer a question with another question if you want time to consider.

Argue calmly and without emotion, but emphasize the points you really want to ram home either by raising your voice slightly and slowing down to highlight your argument, or by repetition.

Control your anger. Express yourself strongly, by all means, but you will lose everything if you lose your temper.

Always remember that you are *not* trying to win at all costs. If your opponent wants something which you cannot give, don't just say no. Offer an alternative package. If your opponent is asking for a higher specification than you normally provide for the price and wants a delivery date which you cannot meet without incurring extra overtime costs, say that you can meet the specifications and the delivery deadline as long as he is prepared to cover the costs.

Gambits

There are a number of standard bargaining gambits. Here are a few of the more common ones:

- *Uttering threats* – 'Agree to what I want or I'll call out the lads'; or '. . . I'll take my custom elsewhere'. Never react to such threats and never utter empty ones.

- *No negotiation under duress* – 'We refuse to discuss your claim unless and until you cancel your overtime ban.' An excellent approach, if you can get away with it.

- *It will reflect badly on you* – 'Do you really want to get the reputation of being a heartless employer?' This is an emotional appeal and, as such, should be discounted.

- *The bluff direct* – 'I have two or three quotations lower than yours.' The answer to this gambit is to call your opponent's bluff – 'What are they offering for the price?' 'OK, why not accept them, why bother talking to me?'

- *The leading question* – 'Do you think it is a good idea to reward people according to merit?' 'Yes.' 'Then why do you insist on retaining this fixed incremental scheme which benefits everybody irrespective of how well they've done?' Never fall for a leading question.

- *The piecemeal or 'salami' technique* – In this your opponent will try to pick off the items one by one. 'That's the price agreed, now we can deliver in three months, OK?' 'Right, we've agreed the delivery terms, now this is how we charge for maintenance.' Always negotiate the whole package. Don't allow yourself to be railroaded into a piecemeal approach.

- *The yes, but . . . approach* – 'Yes, we agree to accept an increase of 8 per cent but before we can agree to everything there is this other problem of compensation for redundancy we must tackle.' To avoid being caught in a yes/but trap, always make offers on one part of a package conditional on accepting another part: 'We are prepared to consider an 8 per cent offer but only if you agree to drop your claim for enhanced redundancy pay.'

(d) Closing

When and how you close depends on your assessment of the strength of your opponent's case and his or her determination to see it through. You may close by:

1. Making a concession, preferably a minor one, and trading it off against an agreement to settle. The concession can be offered more positively than at the bargaining stage: 'If you will agree to settle at x, I will concede y.'
2. Doing a deal: You might split the difference, or bring in something new – such as extending the settlement time-scale, agreeing to back payments, phasing increases, making a joint declaration of intent to do something in the future (for example to introduce a productivity plan), or offering an incentive discount.
3. Summarizing what has happened to date, emphasizing the concessions that have been made and the extent to which you have moved, and stating that you have reached your final position.
4. Applying pressure through a threat of the consequences which will follow if your offer is not accepted.
5. Giving your opponent a choice between two courses of action.

Do not make a final offer unless you mean it. If it is not really your final offer and your opponent calls your bluff, you will have to make further concessions and your credibility will be undermined. He or she will, of course, attempt to force you into revealing how close you are to your final position. Do not allow yourself to be hurried into this. If you want to avoid committing yourself and thus devaluing the word 'final', state as positively as you can that this is as far as *you* are prepared to go.

Chapter 32
Objective setting

One of your most important tasks as a manager is to make sure that the members of your team understand what is expected of them. Each individual and the team as a whole must know what they have to do and achieve. This is the management of expectations aspect of your role.

Your task is to ensure that performance requirements expressed as objectives are defined and agreed. You will then be in a position to review achievements in relation to agreed objectives. This is done through agreed performance measures and indicators.

What are objectives?

An objective describes something which has to be accomplished – a point to be aimed at. Objectives or goals (the terms are interchangeable) define what organizations, functions, departments, teams and individuals are expected to achieve.

There are two main types of objective: work and personal.

Work objectives

Work or operational objectives refer to the results to be achieved or the contribution to be made to the accomplishment of team, departmental and corporate objectives. At *corporate level* they are related to the organization's mission, core values and strategic plans.

At *departmental or functional level* they are related to corporate objectives, spelling out the specific mission, targets and purposes to be achieved by a function or department.

At *team level* they will again be related specifically to the purpose of the team and the contribution it is expected to make to achieving departmental and corporate goals.

At *individual level* they are job-related, referring to the principal accountabilities, main activity areas or key tasks which constitute the individual's job. They focus on the results individuals are expected to achieve and how they contribute to the attainment of team, departmental and corporate goals and to upholding the organization's core values.

Personal objectives

Personal or learning objectives are concerned with what individuals should do and learn to improve their performance (performance improvement plans) and/or their knowledge, skills and overall level of competence (training and personal development plans).

How are individual work objectives expressed?

Individual objectives define the results to be achieved and the basis upon which performance in attaining these results can be measured. They can take the form of target- or project-related objectives or standing objectives.

Target- or project-related objectives

Individual objectives can be expressed as quantified output or improvement targets (open 24 new accounts by 31 December, reduce cost per unit of output by 2.5 per cent by 30 June) or in terms of projects to be completed (open distribution depot in Northampton by 31 October). Targets may be reset regularly, say once a year or every six months, or be subject to frequent amendments to meet new requirements or changed circumstances.

Standing objectives

Objectives for some aspects of a job (or for all aspects of some jobs) can be what might be described as 'standing objectives'. These are concerned with the permanent or continuing features of a job. They incorporate or lead to defined standards of performance which may be expressed in quantified terms such as the requirement to ensure that all deliveries are made within three days of receiving an order. Alternatively, they may have to be defined as qualitative standards such as:

> Performance will be up to standard if requests for information are dealt with promptly and helpfully on a can do/will do basis and are delivered in the form required by the user.

Qualitative standing objectives may also be defined for behaviour which will contribute to upholding the core values of the organization. For example, if one of the core values relates to the development of the skills and competences of employees, a performance standard for employee development could be one of the objectives agreed for all managers and team leaders.

What is a good work objective?

Good work or operational objectives are:

- *Consistent* with the values of the organization and departmental and organizational objectives
- *Precise:* clear and well-defined, using positive words
- *Challenging:* to stimulate high standards of performance and to encourage progress
- *Measurable:* they can be related to quantified or qualitative performance measures
- *Achievable:* within the capabilities of the individual. Account should be taken of any constraints which might affect the individual's capacity to achieve the objectives; these could include lack of resources (money, time, equipment, support from other people), lack of experience or training, external factors beyond the individual's control, etc
- *Agreed* by the manager and the individual concerned. The aim is to provide for the ownership, not the imposition, of objectives, although there may be situations where individuals have to be persuaded to accept a higher standard than they believe themselves capable of attaining
- *Time-related* – achievable within a defined time-scale (this would not be applicable to a standing objective)
- *Teamwork orientated* – emphasize teamwork as well as individual achievement.

Some organizations use the acronym SMART to define a good objective:

S = stretching
M = measurable
A = agreed
R = realistic
T = time-related.

Defining work objectives

The process of agreeing objectives need not be unduly complicated. It must start from an agreed list of the principal accountabilities or main tasks of the job. It is then simply a matter of jointly examining each area and agreeing targets and standards of performance as appropriate. Agreement can also be reached on any projects to be undertaken which might be linked to a specific accountability, or maybe more general projects which fall broadly within the remit of the jobholder.

Define targets

The first step is to identify the key result areas of the job from the list of accountabilities or main tasks to which targets can be attached.

Targets are quantified and time based – they always define specific and measurable outputs and when they have to be reached. The target may be to achieve a specified level of output or to improve performance in some way. Targets may be expressed in financial terms such as profits to be made, income to be generated, costs to be reduced or budgets to be worked within. Or they may be expressed in numerical terms as a specified number of units to be processed, responses to be obtained or clients or customers to be contacted over a period of time.

Output targets are expressed in financial or unitary terms, for example:

- Achieve sales of £1.6 million by 30 June.
- Maintain inventory levels at no more than £12 million.
- Maintain throughput at the rate of 800 units a day.

Performance improvement targets may be expressed in terms such as:

- Increase sales turnover for the year by 8 per cent in real terms.
- Reduce the overhead to sales ratio from 22.6 to 20 per cent over the next 12 months.
- Increase the ratio of successful conversions (enquiry to sales) from 40 to 50 per cent.

Define performance standards

The next stage is to define performance standards for any area (accountability or main task) to which specific, time-based targets cannot be attached. These are sometimes described as standing or continuing objectives because, as explained earlier in this chapter, their essential nature may not change significantly from one review period to the next if the key task remains unaltered, although they may be modified if new circumstances arise.

Performance standards should have been broadly defined in outcome terms in the why part of the accountability/task definition. But the broad definition should be expanded and, as far as possible, particularized. They should preferably be quantified in terms, for example, of level of service or speed of response. Where the standard cannot be quantified, a more qualitative approach may have to be adopted, in which case the standard of performance definition would in effect state: 'this job or task will have been well done if . . . (the following things happen)'. Junior or more routine jobs are likely to have a higher proportion of standing objectives to which performance standards are attached than senior and more flexible or output-orientated jobs.

The following are some examples of performance standards which spell out the end results required in quantitative terms:

- Prepare and distribute management accounts to managers within three working days of the end of the accounting period.
- Deal with 90 per cent of customer complaints within 24 hours – the remainder to be acknowledged the same day and answered within five working days.
- Hear job evaluation appeals within five working days.

It may not always be possible to quantify performance standards as in the examples given above. The end results required may have to be defined in qualitative terms.

It is often assumed that qualitative performance standards are difficult to define. But all managers make judgements about the standards of performance they expect and obtain from their staff, and most people have some idea of whether or not they are doing a good job. The problem is that these views are often subjective and are seldom articulated. Even if, as often happens, the final definition of a performance standard is somewhat bland and unspecific, the discipline of working through the requirements in itself will lead to greater mutual understanding of performance expectations.

A performance standard definition should take the form of a statement that performance will be up to standard if a desirable, specified and observable result happens.

The following are some examples of qualitative performance standards:

- Performance will be up to standard if line managers receive guidance on the interpretation and implementation of inventory policies which is acted upon and makes a significant contribution to the achievement of inventory targets.
- Performance will be up to standard when callers are dealt with courteously at all times, even when they are being difficult.

- Performance will be up to standard if proposals for new product development are fully supported by data provided from properly conducted product research, market research and product testing programmes, and are justified by meeting return on investment criteria policies.

Define projects

Projects may already have been defined as part of a team, departmental or functional plan, and when setting individual objectives it is simply necessary to agree on the part that the individual will play and the contribution he or she is expected to make. Alternatively, projects may be linked to one or more specific accountabilities or they may be related generally to the overall purpose of the job.

Objective setting for projects will specify the required outcome of the project (results to be achieved), its budget and its time-scale.

When a number of projects have to be undertaken by the jobholder, agreement should be reached on priorities.

Project or task achievement objectives may be expressed in terms such as:

- Introduce new stock control system by 30 November.
- All employees to have received training on the implementation of equal opportunities policies by 1 June.
- New distribution centre to be operational by 1 March.
- Reorganization of finance department to be completed by 1 October.

For each project or task it would also be necessary to set out the success criteria, for example:

Introduce a new stock control system by 30 November to provide more accurate, comprehensive and immediate information on stock and thus enable inventory targets to be achieved without prejudicing production flows or customer service levels.

Performance measures

Measurement is a key aspect of managing performance on the grounds that 'if you can't measure it you can't improve it'. It is pointless to define objectives or performance standards unless there is agreement and understanding on how performance in achieving these objectives or standards will be measured.

Performance measures should provide evidence of whether or not the intended result has been achieved and the extent to which the jobholder has produced that result. This will be the basis for generating feedback information for use not only by you but also by individuals to monitor their own performance.

Types of measure

Performance measures may refer to such matters as income generation, sales, output, units processed, productivity, costs, delivery-to-time, 'take up' of a service, speed of reaction or turnround, achievement of quality standards or customer/client reactions.

Sun Life, for example, uses the three criteria of work quality, output and 'timeliness' (eg how many cases are dealt with over a given period of time). These are measured by a management information system. Cambridgeshire County Council has identified four distinct types of measurement: money, time, effect and reaction.

- *Money measures* include maximizing income, minimizing expenditure and improving rates of return.
- *Time measures* express performance against work timetables, the amount of backlog and speed of activity or response.
- *Measures of effect* include attainment of a standard, changes in behaviour (of colleagues, staff, clients or customers), physical completion of the work and the level of take-up of a service.
- *Reaction* indicates how others judge the jobholder and is therefore a less objective measure. Reaction can be measured by peer assessments, performance ratings by internal or external clients or customers, or the analysis of comments and complaints.

Defining performance measures

It is important to agree performance measures at the same time as objectives are defined. This is the only way in which a fair assessment of progress and achievements can be made, and the successful definition of performance measures will provide the best basis for feedback.

The following are guidelines for defining performance measures:

- Measures should relate to results not efforts.
- The results must be within the jobholder's control.
- Measures should be objective and observable.
- Data must be available for measurement.
- Existing measures should be used or adapted wherever possible.

Chapter 33
Organizing

An effective enterprise ensures that collective effort is organized to achieve specific ends. Organizing involves dividing the overall management task into a variety of processes and activities and then establishing means of ensuring that these processes are carried out effectively and that the activities are coordinated. It is about differentiating activities in times of uncertainty and change, integrating them – grouping them together to achieve the organization's overall purpose – and ensuring that effective information flows and channels of communication are maintained.

Organization design

Organization design is based on the analysis of activities, processes, decisions, information flows and roles. It produces a structure which consists of positions and units between which there are relationships involving cooperation, the exercise of authority and the exchange of information.

Within the structure there will be line managers who are responsible for achieving results in the organization's key areas of activity by managing teams and individuals, and specialists who provide support, guidance and advice to the line.

The structure must be appropriate to the organization's purpose, technology and the environment in which it exists. It must be flexible enough to adapt itself easily to new circumstances – organization design is a continuous process of modification and change, it is never a one-off event. It must also be recognized that, although the formal organization structure may define who is responsible for what and the ostensible lines of communication and control, the way in which it actually operates will depend on informal networks and other relationships which have not been defined in the design process and arise from people's daily interaction.

The approach to organization design

Organization design aims to clarify roles and relationships so far as this is possible in fluid conditions. It is also concerned with giving people the scope and opportunity to use their skills and abilities to better effect – this is the process of empowerment which is examined in Chapter 21. Jobs should be designed to satisfy the requirements of the organization for productivity, operational efficiency and quality of product or service. But they must also meet the needs of individuals for interest, challenge and accomplishment. These aims are interrelated and an important aim of organization and job design is to integrate the needs of the individual with those of the organization.

When it comes to designing or modifying the structure a pragmatic approach is necessary. It is first necessary to understand the environment, the technology and the existing systems of social relationships. An organization can then be designed which is *contingent* upon the circumstances. There is always some choice, but designers should try to achieve the best fit they can. And in making their choice, they should be aware of the structural, human, process and systems factors which will influence the design, and of the context within which the organization operates.

Organization design is ultimately a matter of ensuring that the structure, processes and methods of operation fit the strategic requirements of the business and its technology within its environment. Disruption occurs if internal and external coherence and consistency is not achieved. And, as Mintzberg (38) suggests: 'Organizations, like individuals, can avoid identity crises by deciding what they wish to be and then pursuing it with a healthy obsession.'

Organization design is always an empirical and evolutionary process for which absolute principles cannot be laid down. But there are a number of broad guidelines which should be taken into account even if they are not followed slavishly.

Organization guidelines

Allocation of work

Related activities should be grouped logically together into functions and departments. Unnecessary overlap and duplication of work, either horizontally or vertically within a hierarchy, should be avoided.

A matrix organization may be developed in which multi-disciplinary project teams are created specially to accomplish a specified task but the members of those teams are responsible on a continuing basis to a functional leader who allocates them to projects, assesses their performance, provides rewards and deals with training and career development needs.

Close attention should be given to the processes within the business. These are the interconnected sequence of activities which convert inputs into outputs. Thus, 'order fulfilment' is a process which starts with an order as its input and results in an 'output', ie the delivery of the ordered goods. The organization design should ensure that the flow of such processes can proceed smoothly, efficiently and effectively.

Business process re-engineering, as described in Chapter 43, can help to achieve this by subjecting the processes that link key organizational functions together from initiation to completion to critical examination and, as necessary, redesign. It is sometimes better to organize these processes properly before becoming over-involved in the design of rigid structures which can inhibit the flow of work.

The work that needs to be done and accountabilities for results should be defined and agreed with teams and individual jobholders.

Matters requiring a decision should be dealt with as near to the point of action as possible by individuals or self-managing teams (see Chapter 47). Managers should not try to do too much themselves, nor should they supervise too closely.

Levels in the structure

Too many levels of management and supervision inhibit communication and teamwork and create extra work (and unnecessary jobs). The aim should be to reduce the number of levels to a minimum. However, the elimination of middle managers and wider spans of control mean that more attention has to be paid to improving teamwork, delegation and methods of integrating activities.

Span of control

There are limits to the number of people anyone can manage or supervise well, but these vary considerably between different jobs. Most people can work with a far greater span of control than they imagine, as long as they are prepared to delegate more effectively, to avoid becoming involved in too much detail, and to develop good teamwork among the individuals reporting to them. In fact, wide spans of control are beneficial in that they can enforce delegation and better teamwork and free the higher-level manager to spend more time on policy-making and planning.

Limited spans of control encourage managers to interfere too much with the work going on beneath them and therefore constrain the scope that should be given to their subordinates to grow with their jobs.

One person, one boss

Generally speaking, individuals should be accountable only to one boss for the results they achieve, to avoid confusion on operational matters. But in a project-based or matrix organization individuals might be responsible to their project leader for contributing to the outcome of the project while also being responsible to their departmental manager or the head of their discipline for the continuing requirements of their role and for achieving agreed standards of overall performance.

Individuals in functional roles such as finance or personnel may be directly responsible to a line manager but may also have a 'dotted line' relationship of responsibility to the head of their function on matters of corporate policy.

Decentralization

Authority to make decisions should be delegated as close to the action as possible.

Optimize the structure

Develop an ideal organization by all means, but also remember that it may have to be modified to fit in the particular skills and abilities of key individuals.

Relevance to organizational needs

The organization has to be developed to meet the needs of its situation. In today's conditions of turbulence and change this inevitably means a tendency towards more decentralized and flexible structures, with greater responsibility given to individuals and an extension of the use of task forces and project teams to deal with opportunities or threats. This implies an informal, non-bureaucratic, organic approach to organization design – the form of the organization will follow its function, not the other way around.

The organization may be largely based on multi-disciplinary project teams, as in a matrix organization, or greater emphasis will be placed on ensuring that flows of work involved in the key business processes are properly catered for rather than the creation of a traditionally formal and hierarchical structure.

The basic approach to organization design

The basic approach to organization design is to:

- Define what the organization exists to do – its purpose and objectives
- Analyse and identify the processes, activities or tasks required to do it and, as appropriate, the flow of decision-making and work throughout the organization
- Allocate related activities to teams and individual jobholders as appropriate
- Group related activities carried out by teams and individual jobholders logically into organizational units while ensuring that the flow of work across organizational boundaries is not inhibited
- Provide for the management and coordination of the processes and activities at each level of responsibility
- Ensure that attention is given to developing the processes of teamwork and communication
- Establish reporting and communicating relationships
- Recognize the importance of informal networks as means of communicating information and joint decision-making
- Provide, as far as possible, for organizational processes to adapt to change.

Defining structures

Structures are usually defined by means of organization charts. Such charts have their uses in planning and reviewing organizations. They can indicate how work is allocated and how activities are grouped together. They show who is responsible to whom, and they illustrate lines of authority. Drawing up a chart can be a good way of clarifying what is currently happening: the mere process of putting the organization down on paper will highlight any problems. And when it comes to considering changes, charts are the best way of illustrating alternatives.

The danger with organization charts is that they can be mistaken for the organization itself. They are no more than a snapshot of what is supposed to be happening at a given moment. They are out of date as soon as they are drawn, and they leave out the informal organization and its networks. If you use little boxes to represent people, they may behave as if they were indeed little boxes, sticking too closely to the rule book.

Charts can make people very conscious of their superiority or inferiority in relation to others. They can make it harder to change things, they can freeze relationships, and they can show relationships as they are supposed to be, not as they are. Robert Townsend (56) said of organization charts: 'Never formalize, print and circulate them. Good organizations are living bodies that grow new muscles to meet challenges.'

Defining roles

Role definitions describe the part to be played by individuals in fulfilling their job requirements. Roles therefore indicate the behaviour required to carry out a particular task or the group of tasks contained in a job – they will set out the context within which individuals work as part of a team as well as the tasks they are expected to carry out.

The traditional form for defining roles is the job description but, like organization charts, job descriptions can be too rigid and stifle initiative. It is better to use a role definition format along the following lines:

- Job title
- Reporting relationships
- Main purpose of the role – a brief description of why the role exists
- Main areas of responsibility – these are defined in terms of the results expected; no attempt should be made to go into any detail of how the work is done
- Context – how the job fits in with others, flexibility requirements, decision-making authority, any particular requirements or pressures.

A role definition emphasizes the dynamic aspects of a job in terms of output, relationships and flexibility. It should focus on performance and delivery, not on tasks and duties.

Implementing structures

At the implementation stage it is necessary to ensure that everyone concerned:

- Knows how they will be affected by the change
- Understands how their relationships with other people will change
- Accepts the reasons for the change and will not be reluctant to participate in its implementation.

It is easy to tell people what they are expected to do; it is much harder to get them to understand and accept how and why they should do it. The implementation plan should therefore cover not only the information to be given but also how it should be presented. The presentation will be easier if, in the analysis and design stage, full consultation has taken place with the individuals and groups who will be affected by the change. Too many organizational changes have failed because they have been imposed from above or from outside without proper consideration for the views and feelings of those most intimately concerned.

Implementation is often attempted by purely formal means – issuing edicts, distributing organization manuals or handing out job descriptions. These may be useful as far as they go, but while they provide information, they do not necessarily promote understanding and ownership. This can only be achieved on an informal but direct basis. Individuals must be given the opportunity to talk about what the proposed changes in their responsibilities will involve – they should already have been given the chance to contribute to the thinking behind the change, so discussions on the implications of the proposals should follow quite naturally. There is no guarantee that individuals who feel threatened by change will accept it, however much they have been consulted. But the attempt should be made. Departmental, team and interfunctional meetings can help to increase understanding. Change management is discussed in more detail in Chapter 6.

The implementation plan may have to cater for the likelihood that all the organizational changes cannot be implemented at once. Implementation may have to be phased to allow changes to be introduced progressively, to enable people to absorb what they will be expected to do and to allow for any necessary training. Changes may in any case be delayed until suitable people for new positions are available.

Chapter 34
Performance management

Performance management is a means of obtaining better results from the organization, teams and individuals by understanding and managing performance within an agreed framework of planned goals, objectives and standards of achievement and competence.

It can be defined as a process or set of processes for establishing shared understanding about what *is* to be achieved, and of managing and developing people in a way which increases the probability that it *will* be achieved in the short and longer term.

Perhaps the most important point to remember about performance management is that it is a *continuous* process shared between managers and the people for whom they are responsible. It is about improving both results and the quality of working relationships. Good performance management means that people are clear about what their priorities are, what they should be doing currently, what they should be aiming for, the level of competence they should achieve and how well this contributes to both team and company performance. It grows from open, positive and constructive discussion between managers, individuals and teams to produce agreement on how to focus on doing the job better.

The process of performance management

Initiation

Performance management starts at the top level in an organization with definitions of mission, strategy and objectives. These lead to more detailed definitions of functional or departmental missions, plans and objectives.

Performance agreements

Performance agreements are then made between individuals and their managers which set out:

- The key result areas of the job
- The objectives and standards of performance associated with these key result areas
- Work and personal development plans
- The skills and competences required to fulfil job requirements.

Continuous review

The performance of individuals and their development is reviewed continuously as part of the normal process of management. It is not deferred until a formal performance review takes place at the end of the year when it will have lost its immediacy and where the relative formality of the proceedings may prevent a constructive discussion.

Effective performance is reinforced with praise, recognition and the opportunity to take on more responsible work. Less effective performance is dealt with as it happens by reiterating the standards and competences required, indicating areas for improvement, and agreeing the actions necessary to effect improvements. Coaching and counselling is provided as necessary.

Formal performance review

There is a periodic formal review which, in effect, is a stocktaking exercise but its emphasis is on looking forward to the next period and redefining the performance agreement rather than raking over past events.

The review leads to a revised performance agreement. It also provides individuals with the opportunity to raise any concerns about their work and future.

Performance management skills

The effective management of performance requires you to deploy a number of demanding skills. These comprise:

- Giving feedback as described below (page 226)
- Conducting review meetings, also described later in this chapter (pages 226 to 228)
- Setting objectives (see Chapter 32)
- Coaching (see Chapter 8)
- Counselling (see Chapter 16).

Giving feedback

An essential element of performance management is the process of feedback – ensuring that people know how well, or badly, they are doing. The following approaches should be used:

1. *Build feedback into the job.* To be effective feedback should be built into the job or provided within 48 hours of the activity taking place.
2. *Provide feedback on actual events.* Feedback should be provided on actual results or observed behaviour. It should not be based on supposition about the reason for the behaviour. You should, for example, say: 'We have received a complaint from a customer that you have been rude, would you like to comment on this?', rather than: 'You tend to be aggressive.'
3. *Describe, don't judge.* The feedback should be presented as a description of what has happened, it should not be accompanied by a judgement. If you start by saying: 'I have been informed that you have been rude to one of our customers; we can't tolerate that sort of behaviour' you will instantly create resistance and prejudice an opportunity to encourage improvement.
4. *Refer to specific behaviour.* Relate all your feedback to specific items of behaviour. Don't indulge in transmitting general feelings or impressions.
5. *Ask questions.* Ask questions rather than make statements: 'Why do you think this happened?'; 'On reflection, is there any other way in which you think you could have handled the situation?'; 'How do you think you should tackle this sort of problem in the future?'
6. *Select key issues.* Select key issues and restrict yourself to them. There is a limit to how much criticism anyone can take. If you overdo it, the doors will be shut and you will get nowhere.
7. *Focus.* Focus on aspects of performance which can be improved. It is a waste of time to concentrate on areas which the individual can do little or nothing about.
8. *Provide positive feedback.* Provide feedback on the activities that the individual did well in addition to areas for improvement.

Conducting performance reviews

There are ten golden rules for conducting performance review meetings:

1. *Be prepared.* You should prepare by referring to a list of agreed objectives and any notes you have made on performance throughout the year (it is a good idea to make notes about particular

successes – or failures). Form views about the reasons for success or failure and decide where to give praise, which performance problems should be mentioned and what steps might be undertaken to overcome them. Thought should also be given to any changes that have taken place or are contemplated in the individual's role and to work and personal objectives for the next period.

Individuals should also prepare in order to identify achievements and problems, and to be ready to assess their own performance at the meeting. They should also note any points they wish to raise about their work and prospects.

2. *Create the right atmosphere.* A successful meeting depends on creating an informal environment in which a full, frank but friendly exchange of views can take place. It is best to start with a fairly general discussion before getting into any detail.

3. *Work to a clear structure.* The meeting should be planned to cover all the points identified during preparation. But time should be allowed for the individual to express his or her views fully.

4. *Use praise.* If possible, you should begin with praise for some specific achievement, but this should be sincere and deserved. Praise helps people to relax – everyone needs encouragement and appreciation.

5. *Let individuals do most of the talking.* This enables them to get things off their chest and helps them to feel that they are being given a fair hearing. Use open-ended questions (ie questions that invite the individual to think about what to reply rather than indicating the expected answer). This is to encourage people to expand.

6. *Invite self-appraisal.* This is to see the situation from the individual's point of view and to provide a basis for discussion – many people underestimate themselves. Ask questions such as:

- How do you feel you have done?
- What do you feel are your strengths?
- What do you like most/least about your job?
- Why do you think that project went well?
- Why do you think you didn't meet that target?

7. *Discuss performance not personality.* Discussions on performance should be based on fact not opinion. Always refer to actual events or behaviour and to results compared with agreed performance measures. Individuals should be given plenty of scope to explain why something did or did not happen.

8. *Encourage analysis of performance.* Don't just hand out praise or

blame. Analyse jointly and objectively why things went well or badly and what can be done to maintain a high standard or to avoid problems in the future.

9. *Don't deliver unexpected criticisms.* There should be no surprises. The discussion should be concerned only with events or behaviours which have been noted at the time they took place. Feedback on performance should be immediate. It should not wait until the end of the year. The purpose of the formal review is to reflect briefly on experiences during the review period and on this basis to look ahead.

10. *Agree measurable objectives and a plan of action.* The aim should be to end the review meeting on a positive note.

Managing under-performers

Performance management is a positive process, building on strengths and taking steps to overcome weaknesses. It may be necessary, however, to take specific action to deal with under-performers and the steps required to manage them are set out below:

1. Identify and agree the problem

Analyse the feedback and, as far as possible, obtain agreement from the individual on what the shortfall has been.

2. Establish the reason(s) for the shortfall

When seeking the reasons for any shortfalls you should not crudely be trying to attach blame. The aim should be for you and the individual jointly to identify the facts that have contributed to the problem. It is on the basis of this factual analysis that decisions can be made on what to do about it by the individual, yourself or the two of you working together.

It is necessary first to identify any causes which are external to the job and outside the control of either you or the individual. Any factors which are within the control of the latter and/or yourself can then be considered. What needs to be determined is the extent to which the reason for the problem is because the individual:

- Could not do it – ability
- Did not know how to do it – skill
- Would not do it – attitude
- Did not receive adequate support or guidance from you
- Did not fully understand what he or she was expected to do.

3. Decide and agree on the action required

Action may be taken by the individual, yourself or both parties. This could include:

- Taking steps to improve skills or change behaviour – the individual
- Changing attitudes – this is up to individuals as long as they accept that their attitudes need to be changed. The challenge for managers is that people will not change their attitudes simply because they are told to do so. They can only be helped to understand that certain changes to their behaviour could be beneficial not only to the organization but also to themselves. A counselling approach is desirable, as described in Chapter 16
- Providing more support or guidance – yourself
- Clarifying expectations – joint
- Developing abilities and skills – joint, in the sense that individuals may be expected to take steps to develop themselves but you can provide help in the form of coaching, additional experience or training.

Whatever action is agreed, both parties must understand how they will know that it has succeeded. Feedback arrangements can be made but individuals should be encouraged to monitor their own performance and take further action as required.

4. Resource the action

Provide the coaching, training, guidance, experience or facilities required to enable agreed actions to happen.

5. Monitor and provide feedback

Both you and the individual monitor performance, ensuring that feedback is provided or obtained and analysed, and agreeing on any further actions that may be necessary.

Case study – The National Australia Bank Group

The National Australia Bank Group operates the following banks in the UK and the Republic of Ireland:

- The Clydesdale Bank
- The National Irish Bank
- The Northern Bank
- The Yorkshire Bank.

The Group operates a total of about 800 branches and has 17,000 employees.

Reason for introducing performance management

The two overriding reasons for introducing performance management were: first, to achieve a closer link throughout the Group to its strategic objectives; and second, to achieve a greater focus on performance. This was decided against the background of a changing business environment and the need to develop further a sales and service culture common to all parts of the group.

The development programme

It was decided that for the purpose of developing a market performance-focused culture throughout the Group, a single system of performance management should be introduced, although some of the banks already had their own performance management or appraisal systems.

The scheme was designed by a team of human resources representatives from the banks, with the help of an outside consultant, Dr Trevor Bentley, and in consultation with focus groups set up in each bank. The system took about six months to devise and is described below.

Definition of performance management

Performance management in the National Australia Bank Group is based on the simple idea that when people know and understand what is expected of them, and have been able to take part in forming these expectations, they can and will perform to meet them.

Why it was needed

After discussions with staff, the following suggestions were made on why performance management was needed:

- We need to be offered encouragement and support to perform well.
- When our performance is assessed it needs to be as objective as possible.
- We should all be part of the same process of performance assessment.
- We need to believe and have confidence in a system which is fair to everyone.
- We need everybody to be trained so that the approach is fully understood and can be applied consistently.
- We all need to be involved in the process with advance information, time for preparation, and an opportunity to assess ourselves.

How it works

Performance management works in stages that represent a cycle from the initial planning of the individual's performance and development to the final appraisal at the end of the period.

In the introduction to performance management across the Group it was stated that:

It is difficult to say exactly how you will benefit because so much of what you get out of performance management depends on what you put in. However, here are a few suggestions:

- You will be clear about what is expected of you.
- You will be able to participate in agreeing your performance plan.
- You and your manager will plan your ongoing performance development.
- You will learn about the benefits of coaching.
- You will be encouraged to assess your own performance based on objective criteria.
- You will participate in a fair and consistent approach applied equally to everyone.
- You will receive the same comprehensive learning materials as your colleagues.
- You will learn from these materials at your own pace and have the opportunity to discuss your learning with your colleagues.

How the organization will benefit

The statement in the introductory notes reads:

The organization depends for its success on the combined performance of all its people, including you. So if your performance improves, your organization's performance improves because:

- It will have your input as a well-trained, committed member of staff
- It will benefit from your improved development
- The quality of your performance will improve the service it offers its customers
- It will benefit from improved management systems in support of the quality, professionalism and productivity of its people, which includes you.

Chapter 35
Persuading

A manager's job is 60 per cent getting it right and 40 per cent putting it across. Managers spend a lot of time persuading other people to accept their ideas and suggestions.

Persuasion is just another word for selling. You may feel that good ideas should sell themselves, but life is not like that. Everyone resists change and anything new is certain to be treated with suspicion. So it's worth learning a few simple rules that will help you to sell your ideas more effectively.

Six rules for effective persuasion

1. *Define your objective and get the facts.* Decide what you want to achieve and why. Assemble all the facts you need to support your case. Eliminate emotional arguments so that you and others can judge the proposition on the facts alone.

2. *Find out what 'they' want.* Never underestimate people's natural resistance to change. But bear in mind that such resistance is proportional, not to the total extent of the change, but to the extent to which it affects them personally. When asked to accept a proposition, the first questions people ask themselves are: 'How does this affect me?' 'What do I stand to lose?' 'What do I stand to gain?' These questions must be answered before persuasion can start.

   The key to all persuasion and selling is to see your proposition from the other person's point of view. If you can really put yourself into the other person's shoes you will be able to foresee objections and present your ideas in the way most attractive to him or her.

   You must find out how people look at things – what they want. Listen to what they have to say. Don't talk too much. Ask questions. If they ask you a question reply with another question. Find out what they are after. Then present your case in a way that highlights its benefits to them, or at least reduces any objections or fears.

3. *Prepare a simple and attractive presentation.* Your presentation should be as simple and straightforward as possible. Emphasize the benefits. Don't bury the selling points. Lead them in gently so there are no surprises. Anticipate objections.

4. *Make them a party to your ideas.* Get them to contribute, if at all possible. Find some common ground in order to start off with agreement. Don't antagonize them. Avoid defeating them in arguments. Help them to preserve their self-esteem. Always leave a way out.

5. *Positively sell the benefits.* Show conviction. You are not going to sell anything if you don't believe in it and communicate that belief. To persuade effectively you have to sell yourself. You must spell out the benefits. *What* you are proposing is of less interest to the individuals concerned than the effects of that proposal on them.

6. *Clinch and take action.* Choose the right moment to clinch the proposal and get out. Make sure that you are not pushing too hard, but when you reach your objective don't stay and risk losing it. Take prompt follow-up action. There is no point in going to all the trouble of getting agreement if you let matters slide afterwards.

Chapter 36
Planning

As a manager you will normally plan ahead over a relatively short period of time – up to one or, at most, two years. And your objectives, targets and budgets will probably have been fixed by the corporate plan or company budget.

You plan to complete tasks on time without using more resources than you were allowed. Your aim should be to avoid crises and the high costs that they cause; to have fewer 'drop everything and rush this' problems. Planning warns you about possible crises and gives you a chance to avoid them. Contingency or fall-back plans should be prepared if you have any reason to believe that your initial plan may fail for reasons beyond your control.

When you plan, you choose certain courses of action and rule out others; that is to say, you lose flexibility. This will be a disadvantage if the future turns out differently from what you expected – which is only too likely. Try to make plans that you can change at reasonable cost if you have to. It is a bad plan that admits no change.

Planning activities

As a manager, there are eight planning activities you need to carry out:

- *Forecasting*
  - What sort of work has to be done, how much and by when
  - How the workload might change
  - The likelihood of the department being called on to undertake specialized or rush jobs
  - Possible changes within or outside the department which might affect priorities, the activities carried out, or the workload.

- *Programming* – deciding the sequence and time-scale of operations and events required to produce results on time.

- *Staffing* – deciding how many and what type of staff are needed and considering the feasibility of absorbing peak loads by means of overtime or temporary staff.

- *Setting standards and targets* – for output, sales, times, quality, costs or for any other aspect of the work where performance should be planned, measured and controlled.

- *Procedure planning* – deciding how the work should be done and planning the actual operations by defining the systems and procedures required.

- *Materials planning* – deciding what materials, bought-in parts or subcontracted work are required and ensuring that they are made available in the right quantity at the right time.

- *Facilities planning* – deciding on the plant, equipment, tools and space required.

- *Budgeting*.

Planning techniques

Most of the planning you do as a manager is simply a matter of thinking systematically and using your common sense. Every plan contains three key ingredients:

- Objective – the innovation or improvement to be achieved.
- Action programme – the specific steps required to achieve the right objective.
- Financial impact – the effect of the action on sales, turnover, costs and, ultimately, profit.

Figure 36.1, overleaf, is an example of how a manufacturing plan could be set out.

Bar charts should be used to express plans more graphically wherever there is more than one activity and care has to be taken to sequence them correctly. The manufacturing plan illustrated overleaf could be expressed as a Gantt chart (see Figure 36.2, page 237).

A more refined method of planning activities in a complex programme, where many interdependent events have to take place, is network planning. This requires the recording of the component parts and their representation in a diagram as a network of interrelated activities. Events are represented

Objective

To reduce the frequency and cost of faulty castings received from the XYZ Company.

Action Programme

Steps	Responsibility	Completion by
1. Ensure recognition by supplier of problem with 'hard spots' in castings.	Purchasing Manager Production Manager	15 January
2. Negotiate price concession on all castings received during weeks when we return more than ten bad castings.	Purchasing Manager	31 January
3. Set up storage area to accumulate ruined castings.	Facilities Manager	15 February
4. Establish procedures to record machine downtime and cutter breakage with individual castings.	Production Controller	1 March
5. Ensure XYZ Company agrees new arrangements.	Purchasing Manager	15 March

Profit Impact

		£ 19.. Profit Increase (Decrease)
Price concessions		7,000
Effect of improved quality	Scrap	8,500
	Overtime	3,500
	Expense tools	9,000
	Lost production	20,000
	Other	12,000
Modifications in storage area		(2,000)
Recording procedures		(1,000)
Other costs		(3,000)
	Total profit impact	£54,000

Figure 36.1: *Example of a manufacturing plan*

Step (detailed in action programme)	Responsibility	January	February	March
1. Get XYZ Company to recognize problem.	Purchasing Manager	▭		
2. Negotiate price concession.	Purchasing Manager		▭	
3. Set up storage area.	Facilities Manager		▭	
4. Establish downtime recording procedures.	Production Controller		▭	
5. Get XYZ Company to agree new arrangements.	Purchasing Manager			▭

Figure 36.2: *A Gantt chart*

by circles, activities by arrows, and the time taken by activities by the length of the arrows. There can also be dotted arrows for dummy activities between events that have a time rather than an activity relationship. A critical path can be derived which highlights those operations or activities which are essential for the completion of the project within the allocated time-scale. An illustration of part of a basic network is given in Figure 36.3.

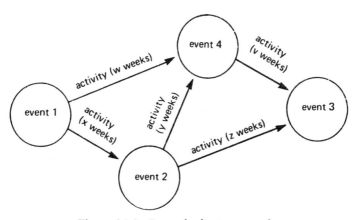

Figure 36.3: *Part of a basic network*

There may be occasions when even more sophisticated planning techniques, using computer models, can be made available to help the manager, especially when large quantities of information have to be processed against a number of fixed assumptions or parameters, or where alternative assumptions have to be assessed. In Book Club Associates, for example, the loading required in the warehouse in terms of machine time and work hours can be projected two years ahead by feeding parameters for projected activity levels into the programme. Plans can then be made to ensure that workers and machine capacity are available to deal with forecast work levels.

Chapter 37
Policies

What are policies?

Anything which indicates what you can or cannot do in certain situations is a policy. It does not have to be written. It may not even have been stated explicitly. But if there is an understanding 'that this is the way we do things round here' then there is a policy.

For example, one business may lay down that 'company salary levels should be at the upper quartile of the range of salaries paid for comparable jobs elsewhere'. This is quite clear, although salary administrators can get bogged down in defining what is comparable and what is not.

Another business may have a salary structure which has developed in a more haphazard way. There may have been a general understanding that the company is prepared to pay above the going rate to get and to keep good quality staff, but nothing so precise as the upper quartile has been defined and nothing has been written down.

Both these companies have salary policies. Which of them has the best policy? There is only one answer to this question. The one that works. A clearly defined, almost rigid policy, quoting the upper quartile is fine if people find out what the upper quartile is and try their best to match it. Otherwise it is useless. A policy of paying above the going rate is great if that is what happens, and as long as the application of the policy is consistent between different jobs and different parts of the company.

Inconsistency is, of course, the danger of ill-defined policies, just as undue restraint of judgement and initiative is the danger of a policy which is too rigid.

Why have policies?

When faced with a crisis or difficult decision it is helpful to have a guide.

When running a business or a department it is essential to let people know what they can and cannot do.

A direct selling business will tell its agents in the field what they can do – they are to sell direct to housewives who are broadly in the middle income group. It will also tell them what they must not do – it is not the firm's policy to go in for high-pressure selling.

A retail store will tell its buyers what it wants them to do – to achieve a three times mark-up on the cost of the goods they purchase. It will also tell them what it does not want them to do – to sacrifice the firm's reputation for quality in the pursuit of low-cost merchandise.

What makes a good policy?

A good policy is one that works. But what makes it work? In general, policies will work if they are appropriate – if they clearly take you in the direction you want to go. They need to be understood, which does not mean that they *have* to be written down. Oral tradition can be a more powerful force than an unused and dusty policy manual.

Policies need to be clear, which is easier said than done. If you try to be completely unambiguous you may only achieve a flood of words which defeat your purpose. Or, worse, your policy may become a prison rather than a pathway. There is a limit to how much you can or should spell out. Take this example:

> Divisional general managers may fix prices for the products under their control so long as:
>
> (a) those prices produce gross profit margins in line with agreed budgets
> (b) price reductions do not adversely affect prices in other divisions.

It looks clear enough, but is it? What does 'in line with' really mean? At what point are prices 'adversely affected'? There is scope for different interpretations in this definition. But is it clear enough? Yes. It gives the divisional managers concerned a general guideline sufficient to keep them from going off the rails. Some room for discretion is, however, allowed. And at this level, this is what policies must do. They should not act as strait-jackets.

Policies must have a degree of permanence or they are not really policies at all. If you constantly change them, no one, in or out of the organization, knows what to count on. But they should not become so hard and fast that they stop a company looking ahead.

How to formulate policies

You cannot just sit down and say 'let's formulate a policy'. Policies should either emerge as a result of a series of decisions forced upon you by events or be part of a deliberate planning process which includes setting objectives and the broad strategies required to achieve them.

Policies should be formulated in response to needs: people require guidance on what or what not to do; plans can only be realized if the line to take is defined; points of reference are required in unfamiliar areas of decision-making.

There is a lot to be said for defining policies in writing. But not in a vast policy manual which no one will read. Make your policy statement as clear and succinct as you can. Ensure that it gets to those who have to implement the policy and check that they understand the policy and are taking steps to put it into practice.

How to implement policies

If your policies are inappropriate or ambiguous the implementation will be hard. If not, all you need to do is to ensure that your staff are clearly briefed on what they are to do and how they are expected to do it. If there are areas left to their discretion, point this out. Less experienced staff may need more explicit guidance at this stage on how they should exercise their discretion. Give them an idea of the circumstances in which you would expect them to come to you for further guidance.

For example, a company introducing a 'promotion from within' policy might express it like this:

> Wherever possible, vacancies should be filled by the most effective people available from within the company subject to the right of the company to recruit from outside if there are no suitable internal candidates.

Experienced personnel officers would know what to do if, say, a departmental manager refused to release a member of staff who had successfully applied for an internal vacancy. They would quote the policy without browbeating the manager with it, and use their powers of persuasion, based on past experience, to convince the manager to release the member of staff. Inexperienced personnel officers, on the other hand, should be warned in advance that this problem might arise. They should be told not to rely too much on the rigid application of the policy and to use their discretion to decide whether they can gently persuade the manager and, if not, must be prepared to go to the personnel manager for advice on how to handle the situation.

Once you have briefed staff, all you need to do is to follow up and make sure that the policy is being applied properly and is appropriate. This gives you an opportunity for training your staff, or, if the policy is not working, for recommending amendments to it. You can only find out if a policy works by checking on how it works, and this means talking to the people who have to implement it.

Chapter 38
Power and politics

Power and politics in an organization go together. You may feel, like Nietzsche, that 'power has crooked legs'. But things don't get done without the exercise of authority, and authority requires the use of power. Furthermore, one way of getting authority and power is to indulge in company politics. You may deplore it, and many chief executives deny that it happens in their organizations. It does take place, however, because people seek power and often use political means to attain it.

Power – good or bad?

In his analysis of power in British industry, Antony Jay (27) commented: 'Power lies in the acceptance of your authority by others, their knowledge that if they try to resist you they will fail and you will succeed. Real power does not lie in documents etc – it lies in what you can achieve.'

And Mary Parker Follett (19) wrote: 'Our task is not to learn where to plan power; it is how to develop power. Genuine power can only be grown, it will slip from every arbitrary hand.'

Power is legitimate if it is used to pursue legitimate ends and is wielded in a responsible way by responsible people. But it can be employed in a harsh way.

David McClelland's (35) studies of power in action involving over 500 managers from 25 different US corporations led him to conclude:

[Managers] must possess a high need for power, that is, a concern for influencing people. However, this need must be disciplined and controlled so that it is directed towards the benefit of the institution as a whole and not towards the manager's personal aggrandizement ... [Managers motivated by a need for power] are able to create a greater sense of responsibility in their divisions and, above all, a greater team spirit.

Here are two cases of power being used effectively:

Case 1: One of the best managers we have in the company has lots of power based on one thing or another over most people. But he seldom if ever just tells or asks someone to do something. He almost always takes a few minutes to try to persuade them. The power he has over people generally induces them to listen carefully and certainly disposes them to be influenced. That, of course, makes the persuasion process go quickly and easily. And he never risks getting the other person upset by making what that person thinks is an unfair request or command.

Case 2: Product manager Stein needed plant manager Billings to 'sign off' on a new product idea (Product X) which Billings thought was terrible. Stein decided there was no way he could logically persuade Billings because Billings just would not listen to him. With time, Stein felt, he could have broken through that barrier. But he did not have that time. Stein also realized that Billings would never, just because of some deal or favour, sign off on a product he did not believe in. Stein also felt it not worth the risk of trying to force Billings to sign off, so here is what he did:

On Monday, Stein got Reynolds, a person Billings respected, to send Billings two market research studies that were very favourable to Product X, with a note attached saying, 'Have you seen this? I found them rather surprising. I am not sure if I entirely believe them, but still . . .'

On Tuesday, Stein got a representative of one of the company's biggest customers to mention casually to Billings on the phone that he had heard a rumour about Product X being introduced soon and was 'glad to see you guys are on your toes as usual'.

On Wednesday, Stein had two industrial engineers stand about three feet away from Billings as they were waiting for a meeting to begin and talk about the favourable test results on Product X.

On Thursday, Stein set up a meeting to talk about Product X with Billings and invited only people whom Billings liked or respected and who also felt favourably about Product X.

On Friday, Stein went to see Billings and asked him if he was willing to sign off on Product X. He was.

Sources of power

Power is clearly linked to position and rank. But to a certain degree it has to be earned. You can give orders to your subordinates but you are going to get more out of them if you obtain their willing cooperation rather than their grudging submission. Power is bestowed upon you as a manager but you have to justify your use of it.

There are, however, other sources of power, namely:

- *Access to other people with power*. Proximity or a direct line obviously gives you more scope to exert influence, actual or perceived. That is why secretaries are important.

- *Control over information.* 'Knowledge is power' or, alternatively, 'authority goes to the one who knows'. If you are in the know, you are in a better position to control events or, if you want to play politics, to put spokes in other people's wheels.
- *Control over resources.* If you have control over resources such as money, workforce, equipment or services that you or anyone else needs, you have power.
- *Control over rewards and punishments.* You also have power if you can give rewards or punishments or influence others who control them.
- *Expertise.* You gain and keep power if you can convince others that you are the expert.
- *Identification.* You can achieve power over others if you persuade them to identify with what you are doing or with you personally. This is what charismatic leaders do by enthusiasm, dedication, involving people and by sheer force of personality.
- *Sense of obligation.* If you develop a sense of obligation by doing favours for people you can reasonably expect that they will feel an obligation to return those favours.

Using power

John Kotter (33) interviewed over 250 managers who were in a position to use power. He found that the successful ones had the following characteristics:

- They use their power openly and legitimately. They are seen as genuine experts in their field and consistently live up to the leadership image they build for themselves.
- They are sensitive to what types of power are most effective with different types of people. For example, experts respect expertise.
- They develop all their sources of power and do not rely too much on any particular technique.
- They seek jobs and tasks which will give them the opportunity to acquire and use power. They constantly seek ways to invest the power they already have to secure an even higher positive return.
- They use their power in a mature and self-controlled way. They seldom if ever use power impulsively or for their own aggrandizement.
- They get satisfaction from influencing others.

Politics – good or bad?

To be politic, according to the *Oxford English Dictionary*, you can be sagacious, prudent, judicious, expedient, scheming or crafty. So political behaviour in an organization could be desirable or undesirable.

Organizations consist of individuals who, while they are ostensibly there to achieve a common purpose, will, at the same time, be driven by their own needs to achieve their own goals. Effective management is the process of harmonizing individual endeavour and ambition to the common good. Some individuals will genuinely believe that using political means to achieve their goals will benefit the organization as well as themselves. Others will rationalize this belief. Yet others will unashamedly pursue their own ends. They may use all their powers of persuasion to legitimize these ends to their colleagues, but self-interest remains the primary drive. These are the corporate politicians whom the *Oxford English Dictionary* describes as 'shrewd schemers, crafty plotters or intriguers'. Politicians within organizations can be like this. They manoeuvre behind people's backs, blocking proposals they do not like. They advance their own reputation and career at the expense of other people's. They can be envious and jealous and act accordingly. They are bad news.

But it can also be argued that a political approach to management is inevitable and even desirable in any organization where the clarity of goals is not absolute, where the decision-making process is not clear-cut and where the authority to make decisions is not evenly or appropriately distributed. And there can be few organizations where one or more of these conditions do not apply.

Andrew Kakabadse (28) recognizes this point when he says in *The Politics of Management*: 'Politics is a process, that of influencing individuals and groups of people to your point of view, where you cannot rely on authority.' In this sense, a political approach can be legitimate as long as the ends are justifiable from the viewpoint of the organization.

Political approaches

Kakabadse identifies seven approaches that organizational politicians adopt:

1. Identify the stakeholders, those who have a commitment to act in a particular way.
2. Keep the stakeholders comfortable, concentrating on behaviour,

values, attitudes, fears and drives that the individuals will accept, tolerate and manage (comfort zones).

3. Fit the image – work on the comfort zones and align their image to that of the people with power.
4. Use the network – identify the interest groups and people of influence.
5. Enter the network – identify the gatekeepers, adhere to the norms.
6. Make deals – agree to support other people where this is of mutual benefit.
7. Withhold and withdraw – withhold information as appropriate and withdraw judiciously when the going gets rough.

Some of these precepts are more legitimate than others. Organizational life requires managers to identify the key decision-makers when they are involved in developing new approaches and getting things done. Before coming to a final conclusion and launching a fully fledged proposal at a committee or in a memorandum, it makes good sense to test opinion and find out how other people may react. This testing process enables managers to anticipate counter-arguments and modify their proposals either to meet legitimate objections or, when there is no alternative, to accommodate other people's requirements.

Making deals may not appear to be particularly desirable, but it does happen, and managers can always rationalize this type of behaviour by reference to the end result. Withholding information is not legitimate behaviour, but people do indulge in it in recognition of the fact that knowledge is power. Judicious withdrawal may also seem to be questionable, but most managers prefer to live to fight another day rather than launch a doomed crusade.

Dangers

The danger of politics, however, is that they can be carried to excess, and they can then seriously harm the effectiveness of an organization. The signs of excessive indulgence in political behaviour include:

- Back-biting
- Buck-passing
- Secret meetings and hidden decisions
- Feuds between people and departments
- Paper wars between armed camps – arguing by memoranda, always a sign of distrust
- A multiplicity of snide comments and criticisms
- Excessive and counter-productive lobbying

- The formation of cabals – cliques which spend their time intriguing.

Dealing with organizational politicians

One way to deal with this sort of behaviour is to find out who is going in for it and openly confront them with the damage they are doing. They will, of course, deny that they are behaving politically (they wouldn't be politicians if they didn't) but the fact that they have been identified might lead them to modify their approach. It could, of course, only serve to drive them further underground, in which case their behaviour will have to be observed even more closely and corrective action taken as necessary.

A more positive approach to keeping politics operating at an acceptable level is for the organization to manage its operations as openly as possible. The aims should be to ensure that issues are debated fully, that differences of opinion are dealt with frankly and that disagreements are de-personalized, so far as this is possible. Political processes can then be seen as a way of maintaining the momentum of the organization as a complex decision-making and problem-solving entity.

Use of politics

There are occasions when a subtle appeal rather than a direct attack will pay dividends; and sometimes you have to exercise your powers of persuasion indirectly on those whose support you need. The following case study illustrates the legitimate use of politics:

James Hale was the personnel director of a large divisionalized group in the food industry. The rate of growth by expansion and acquisitions had been very rapid. There was a shortage of really good managers and a lack of coordination between the divisions in the group and between those divisions and head office. Hale believed that setting up a group management training centre would be a good way of helping to overcome these problems. He knew, however, that he would have to get agreement to this plan not only from the managing director, who would be broadly sympathetic, but also from his co-directors. The MD would not act without the support of a majority on his board.

In any case Hale genuinely felt that there was no point in developing a facility of this sort for people who were not interested in it. He therefore sat back and deliberately worked out a strategy for getting agreement to his proposal. He knew that a frontal attack might fail. Management development was perceived by his colleagues as a somewhat airy-fairy idea which had little relevance to their real concerns as directors. He therefore had to adopt a more subtle approach. He did not call it a political campaign, but that is what it was. He was setting out to influence people indirectly.

The basis of his plan was an individual approach to each of his colleagues, adjusted to their particular interests and concerns. In the case of the marketing director, he got the general sales manager to advocate the need for training in sales management for divisional sales staff. He ran several pilot courses in hotels and invited the marketing director to the winding-up session. He made sure that the marketing director was impressed, not only by what the divisional sales staff had learned from the course, but also by the new spirit of identification with group aims and policies engendered by the training. Casually, the personnel director let slip the thought that if the group had its own training centre this feeling of commitment could be developed even more strongly.

The same basic technique was used with the production director. In addition he was helped to come to the view that a centre owned by the group could speed up the introduction of new ideas and provide a facility for communicating directly with key staff which was not available at present.

The finance director was a more difficult person to convince. He could easily assess the costs but found it difficult to accept largely subjective views of the potential benefits. In this case James Hale did not try too hard to persuade him against his will. He knew that the majority of the board was now in favour of the plan, including the managing director. Hale felt safe in leaving his financial colleague in an isolated and ultimately untenable position. The qualitative arguments, as absorbed by the other members of the board, including the managing director, had the ring of truth about them which no purely quantitative arguments could overcome.

Hale was content that he had enough support. To clinch the argument he played his last political card by warning the marketing and production directors that there might be some financial opposition. He then got them to agree with the thesis that they wouldn't allow 'Mr Money Bags' to adopt a narrow financial view and thus dictate the destiny of the firm.

James Hale had no difficulty in getting his proposal accepted at the next board meeting.

The non-legitimate use of politics

The following is an example of non-legitimate use of politics. Unfortunately, it is a fairly common one. In most organizations there are people who want to get on, and do not have too many scruples about how they do it. If it involves treading on other people's faces, then so be it.

Two directors of a company both aspired to be the next managing director. Mr Black, the finance director, had the ear of the MD. Mr White, the technical director, was more remote.

Mr White had a number of ideas for introducing new technology and had proved, to his own satisfaction at least, that the pay-off was considerable. Unfortunately, he jumped the gun in order to anticipate comments from Black, and presented a paper to the managing director which was not as well argued as it might be. Black carefully lobbied the MD and convinced him that the proposal was full of holes – he also hinted that this was yet another example of White's inability to understand the wider commercial issues.

The MD accepted this view more or less completely and agreed with Black's suggestion that the whole proposal should be off-loaded on to a board sub-committee – a well-known device to delay if not to stifle new ideas. This was done, and the introduction of new technology was unnecessarily delayed by 18 months. But Black had made his point as the practical man of affairs who would not allow the company to get involved in expensive and unrewarding projects.

Chapter 39
Presentations and effective speaking

A manager's job usually includes giving formal or informal presentations at meetings, and addressing groups of people at conferences or training sessions. To be able to speak well in public is therefore a necessary management skill which you should acquire and develop.

The three keys to effective speaking are:

- Overcoming nervousness
- Thorough preparation
- Good delivery.

Overcoming nervousness

Some nervousness is a good thing. It makes you prepare, makes you think and makes the adrenalin flow, thus raising performance. But excessive nervousness ruins your effectiveness and must be controlled.

The common reasons for excessive nervousness are: fear of failure, fear of looking foolish, fear of breakdown, a sense of inferiority and dread of the isolation of the speaker. To overcome it there are three things to remember and six things to do.

Three things to remember about nervousness

- Everyone is nervous. It is natural and, for the reasons mentioned earlier, a good thing.
- Speaking standards are generally low. You can do better than the other person.
- You have something to contribute. Otherwise why should you have been asked to speak?

Six things to do about nervousness

- *Practise.* Take every opportunity you can get to speak in public. The more you do it, the more confident you will become. Solicit constructive criticism and act on it.
- *Know your subject.* Get the facts, examples and illustrations which you need to put across.
- *Know your audience.* Who is going to be there? What are they expecting to hear? What will they want to get out of listening to you?
- *Know your objective.* Make sure that you know what you want to achieve. Visualize, if you can, each member of your audience going away having learned something new which he or she is going to put into practical use.
- *Prepare.*
- *Rehearse.*

Preparation

Allow yourself ample time for preparation in two ways. First, leave yourself plenty of low-pressure time; start thinking early – in your bath, on the way to work, mowing your lawn, any place where you can freely develop new ideas on the subject. Second, you should leave yourself lots of time actually to prepare the talk. There are eight stages of preparation.

1. Agreeing to talk

Do not agree to talk unless you know you have something to contribute to *this audience* on *this subject*.

2. Getting informed

Collect facts and arguments for your talk by: brainstorming and writing down all the points as they occur; reading up the subject; talking to colleagues and friends and keeping cuttings and files on subjects you may have to speak on.

3. Deciding what to say

Start by defining your objective. Is it to persuade, inform, interest or inspire? Then decide the main message you want to put across. Adopt the 'rule of three'. Few people can absorb more than three new ideas at a time. Simplify your presentation to ensure that the three main points you want to convey come over loud and clear. Finally, select the facts and arguments which best support your message.

Never try to do too much. The most fatal mistake speakers can make is to tell everything they know. Select and simplify using the rule of three.

4. Structuring your talk

Good structure is vital. It provides for continuity, makes your thoughts easy to follow, gives the talk perspective and balance and, above all, enables you to ram your message home.

The classic method of structuring a talk is to 'tell them what you are going to say – say it – tell them what you have said'. This is the rule of three in action again, as applied to attention span. Your audience will probably only listen to one-third of what you say. If you say it three times in three different ways they will at least hear you once.

You were no doubt told at school that an essay should have a beginning, a middle and an end. Exactly the same principle applies to a talk.

Tackle the middle of your talk first and:

- Write the main messages on separate postcards
- List the points you want to make against each main message
- Illustrate the points with facts, evidence, examples and introduce local colour
- Arrange the cards in different sequences to help you to decide on the best way to achieve impact and a logical flow of ideas.

Then turn to the opening of your talk. Your objectives should be to create attention, arouse interest and inspire confidence. Give your audience a trailer to what you are going to say. Underline the objective of your presentation – what *they* will get out of it.

Finally, think about how you are going to close your talk. First and last impressions are very important. End on a high note.

Think carefully about length, reinforcement and continuity. Never talk for more than 40 minutes at a time. Twenty or thirty minutes is better. Very few speakers can keep people's attention for long. An audience is usually very interested to begin with (unless you make a mess of your opening) but interest declines steadily until people realize that you are approaching the end. Then they perk up. Hence the importance of your conclusion.

To keep their attention throughout, give interim summaries which reinforce what you are saying and, above all, hammer home your key points at intervals throughout your talk.

Continuity is equally important. You should build your argument progressively until you come to a positive and overwhelming conclusion.

Provide signposts, interim summaries and bridging sections which lead your audience naturally from one point to the next.

5. Prepare your notes

The best sort of notes are the postcards used in preparing the talk. Each card should cover one section and include the main headings. Avoid using too many words on each; they will only confuse you.

Cards of this type can easily be referred to during your talk and should not distract your audience. It is quite a good idea, however, to write out your opening and closing remarks, in full, on separate cards. You can then learn these by heart, ensuring a confident start and a positive end to your presentation.

6. Prepare visual aids

As your audience will only absorb one-third of what you say, if that, reinforce your message with visual aids. Appeal to more than one sense at a time. Flip charts, slides and so on all provide good back-up, but don't overdo them and keep them simple. Too many visuals can be distracting, and too many words, or an over-elaborate presentation, will distract, bore and confuse your audience.

7. Rehearse

Rehearsal is vital. It instils confidence, helps you to get your timing right, enables you to polish your opening and closing remarks and to coordinate your talk and visual aids.

Rehearse the talk to yourself several times and note how long each section takes. Get used to expanding your notes without waffling. Never write down your talk in full and read it during rehearsal. This will guarantee a stilted and lifeless presentation.

Practise giving your talk out loud – standing up, if that is the way you are going to present it. Some people like to tape record themselves but that can be off-putting. It is better to get someone to hear you and provide constructive criticism. It may be hard to take but it could do you a world of good.

Finally, try to rehearse in the actual room in which you are going to speak, using your visual aids and with someone listening at the back to make sure you are audible.

8. Check and prepare arrangements on site

Check the visibility of your visual aids. Make sure that you know how to use them. Test and focus the overhead or slide projector. Brief your film projector operator and get him or her to run through the film to ensure that there are no snags.

If you are using slides in a carousel go through the lot to check that the sequence is right and none is upside down.

Be prepared for something to go wrong with your equipment. You may have to do without it at short notice. That is why you should not rely too much on visual aids.

Before you start your talk, check that your notes and visual aids are in the right order and to hand. There is nothing worse than a speaker who mixes up his or her speech and fumbles helplessly for the next slide.

Delivery

With thorough preparation you will not fail. You will not break down. But the way you deliver the talk will affect the impact you make. Good delivery depends on technique and manner.

Technique

Your *voice* should reach the people at the back. If you don't know that you can be heard, ask. It is distracting if someone shouts 'speak up'. Vary the pace, pitch and emphasis of your delivery. Pause before making a key point, to highlight it, and again afterwards to allow it to sink in. Try to be conversational. Avoid a stilted delivery. This is one reason why you should *never* read your talk. If you are your natural self the audience is more likely to be on your side.

Light relief is a good thing if it comes naturally. People are easily bored if they feel they are being lectured, but you should never tell jokes unless you are good at telling jokes. Don't drag them in because you feel you must. Many effective and enjoyable speakers never use them.

Your *words* and *sentences* should be simple and short.

Your *eyes* are an important link with your audience. Look at them, measure their reaction and adjust to it. Don't fret if people look at their watches; it's when they start shaking them to see if they've stopped that you should start to worry.

Use *hands* for gesture and emphasis only. Avoid fidgeting. Don't put your hands in your pockets.

Stand naturally and upright. Do not stand casually. Be and look like someone in command. If you pace up and down like a caged tiger you will distract your audience. They will be waiting for you to trip over some equipment or fall off the edge of the platform.

Manner

Relax and show that you are relaxed. Convey an air of quiet confidence. Relaxation and confidence will come with thorough preparation and practice.

Don't preach or pontificate to your audience. They will resent it and turn against you.

Show sincerity and conviction. Obvious sincerity, belief in your message, positive conviction and enthusiasm in putting your message across count more than any technique.

Conclusion

- You can learn to become an effective speaker with practice. Seize every opportunity to develop your skills.
- Nervousness can be controlled by preparation and knowledge of technique.
- Good preparation is more than half the battle.
- Technique is there to help you to exploit your personality and style to the full, not to obliterate them.

Chapter 40
Problem-solving and decision-making

Problems and opportunities

It is often said that 'there are no problems, only opportunities'. This is not universally true, of course, but it does emphasize the point that a problem should lead to positive thinking about what is to be done now, rather than to recriminations. If a mistake has been made, the reasons for it should be analysed, to ensure that it does not happen again. But it is then water under the bridge.

Faced with a continuous flow of problems and decisions you may occasionally feel utterly confused. We all feel like that sometimes.

Improving your skills

How can you improve your ability to solve problems and make decisions? There are a few basic approaches you should use:

Improve your analytical ability

A complicated situation can often be resolved by separating the whole into its component parts. Such an analysis should relate to facts, although, as Peter Drucker points out, when trying to understand the root causes of a problem you may have to start with an opinion. Even if you ask people to search for the facts first, they will probably look for those facts that fit the conclusion they have already reached.

Opinions are a perfectly good starting point as long as they are brought out into the open at once and then tested against reality. Analyse each hypothesis and pick out the parts which need to be studied and tested.

Mary Parker Follett's (19) 'law of the situation' – the logic of facts and events – should rule in the end. And although you may start out with a hypothesis, when testing it, use Rudyard Kipling's six honest serving men:

> I keep six honest serving men
> (They taught me all I knew)
> Their names are What and Why and When
> and How and Where and Who.

Adopt a systematic approach

Use the methods discussed in Chapter 7: analysing the situation, identifying possible courses of action, weighing them up and deciding what to do.

But do not expect the system to produce a black and white solution. Remember that Drucker (15) says in *The Effective Executive*:

> A decision is a judgement. It is a choice between alternatives. It is rarely a choice between right and wrong. It is at best a choice between almost right and probably wrong – but much more often a choice between two courses of action neither of which is probably more nearly right than the other.

You should not expect, or even welcome, a bland consensus view. The best decisions emerge from a clash of conflicting points of view. This is Drucker's first law of decision-making – 'one does not make a decision without disagreements'. You need a clash of opinion to prevent people falling into the trap of starting with the conclusion and then looking for the facts that support it.

Alfred P Sloan of General Motors knew this. At a meeting of one of his top committees he said: 'Gentlemen, I take it we are all in complete agreement on the decision here.' Everyone round the table nodded assent. 'Then,' continued Mr Sloan, 'I propose we postpone further discussion of this matter until our next meeting to give ourselves time to develop disagreement and perhaps gain some understanding of what the decision is all about.'

Use your imagination

A strictly logical answer to the problem may not be the best one. Use lateral thinking, analogies and brainstorming, as described in Chapter 17, to get off your tramlines and dream up an entirely new approach.

Keep it simple

One of the first principles of logic is known as Occam's razor. It states that 'entities are not to be multiplied without necessity'. That is, always believe the simplest of several explanations.

Implementation

A problem has not been solved until the decision has been implemented. Think carefully not only about how a thing is to be done (by whom, with what resources and by when) but also about its impact on the people concerned and the extent to which they will cooperate. You will get less cooperation if you impose a solution. The best method is to arrange things so that everyone arrives jointly at a solution freely agreed to be the one best suited to the situation (the law of the situation again).

Problem-solving and decision-making techniques

Effective problem-solving and decision-making require the following steps:

1. *Define the situation.* Establish what has gone wrong or is about to go wrong.
2. *Specify objectives.* Define what you are setting out to achieve now or in the future as you deal with an actual or potential problem or a change in circumstances.
3. *Develop hypotheses.* If you have a problem, develop hypotheses about the cause.
4. *Get the facts.* In order to provide a basis for testing hypotheses and developing possible courses of action, find out what is happening now and/or what is likely to happen in the future. If different people are involved, get both sides of the story and, where possible, check with a third party. Obtain written evidence wherever relevant. Do not rely on hearsay.

   Define what is supposed to be happening in terms of policies, procedures or results and contrast this with what is actually happening. Try to understand the attitudes and motivation of those concerned. Remember that people will see what has happened or is happening, in terms of their own position. Obtain information about internal or external constraints that affect the situation.
5. *Analyse the facts.* Determine what is relevant and what is irrelevant. Establish the cause or causes of the problem. Do not be tempted to concentrate on symptoms rather than causes. Dig into what lies behind the problem. When analysing future events, try to make a realistic assessment in terms of existing trends both within and outside the organization. But be careful not to indulge in crude extrapolations. Consider the various internal and external organizational and environmental factors which may affect future developments.

6. *Consider possible courses of action.* List the possible courses of action in the light of the factual analysis. Where appropriate, use brainstorming and creative-thinking techniques to identify courses of action which may not be immediately evident.

7. *Evaluate possible courses of action.* Consider the possibilities, listing pros and cons and comparing anticipated results with your specified objectives. Evaluate the immediate and future consequences both inside and outside the organization. Compare costs with benefits. Assess how far the needs of those involved will be met and the extent to which your decisions will be acceptable. Consider the risk of creating dangerous precedents. Consider also the implications of any internal or external constraints that might exist. Ensure that all concerned participate in the evaluating and decision-making process. Note, however, that the degree of participation will depend on the nature of the problem and the participation procedures and management style of the organization.

8. *Decide and implement.* Decide which, on balance, is the preferred course of action, and discuss it with those concerned. Consider carefully how the decision is likely to affect them. Decide on the method of presentation, giving the reasons for the decision and, so far as possible, allaying any fears. Before implementing the decision ensure that everyone who needs it gets the relevant information.

9. *Monitor implementation.* Check on how effectively the decision is being implemented. Obtain the reactions of those affected. Take corrective action where necessary.

Chapter 41
Productivity improvement

The benefits of improved productivity

Work measurement programmes usually show that staff not on an incentive scheme perform at about 50 to 60 per cent of the standard that can reasonably be expected from an average worker.

It has been established that productivity audits of manufacturing and distribution activities consistently pinpoint opportunities of improving output by from 25 to 40 per cent with much the same plant and human resources. Similarly, clerical work measurement programmes can almost always save more than 15 per cent of staff without affecting output or quality. The scope for improvement is tremendous and so is the pay-off, as the following analysis shows.

Payroll as a percentage of sales	Percentage increase in profit before tax* from improvement in productivity of:			
	5%	10%	20%	40%
20	20	40	80	160
30	30	60	120	240
40	40	80	160	320
50	50	100	200	500
* Assumes a return on sales of 5 per cent.				

The pay-off from improving productivity is high, but how can you achieve it?

The first thing to do is to overcome apathy. Both managers and workforce must be persuaded somehow that they have a common interest in increasing output per head. This is a difficult exercise. It requires considerable powers of leadership from the top and this means positive programmes for motivating and involving all concerned to obtain their commitment to improvement.

A continuous drive for productivity is required and a productivity improvement programme based on a productivity audit should be the instrument.

Productivity improvement programme

The objective of a productivity improvement programme should be to achieve a significant change for the better in the relationship between outputs and inputs or, to put it another way, an improvement in the following ratio:

$$\frac{\text{Performance achieved}}{\text{Resources consumed}}$$

What are the factors for success?

A successful productivity improvement campaign depends on:

- A well-planned programme based on a productivity audit, with positive objectives and a clearly defined timetable
- A commitment on the part of management and supervisors to the programme
- The involvement of employees in the programme so that they are prepared, with suitable safeguards concerning their future, to participate in implementing it
- A recognition that the benefits resulting from the programme should be shared among everyone concerned: the organization, management and all other employees.

These are demanding criteria and they are not easily achieved. Things can go wrong. Managers, supervisors and other employees will all be suspicious of the programme. They will see it either as a device for exposing their inadequacies, an instrument for producing unacceptable change or a threat to their livelihood. These are emotional reactions and, once emotion comes in at the door, reason goes out of the window. So communication, education, involvement and persuasion are essential aspects of the programme.

Even if your powers of persuasion are great and you manage to involve employees in the programme sufficiently to overcome their natural resistance to change, there are a number of mistakes to be avoided in implementing productivity improvements. These include:

- Making recommendations based on inaccurate information or conclusions
- Making recommendations on new equipment, methods or procedures without properly evaluating the cost-effectiveness of the proposals
- Making recommendations without properly evaluating the impact of changes on other departments
- Proposing changes without giving sufficient consideration to the reactions of those involved.

These are common, but avoidable, errors. Those responsible for productivity improvement programmes will be much less likely to commit them if they are made aware of the dangers in advance. This is why it is important to be quite clear about who runs the programme and how it should be conducted.

Who runs the programme?

The programme for improving productivity must be run by top management. They should set the objectives, define terms of reference, appoint the executive responsible for the programme, provide him or her with the necessary resources and monitor the results achieved.

A senior manager responsible directly to the chief executive should be in charge of the programme. Never use a committee. It will spend its time talking, not doing. The productivity executive will need help – from organization and methods, work study, personnel and accounts departments – and he or she should get aides involved directly, rather than sitting them round a table to talk to one another. It may be necessary to set up small project teams comprising members of different departments to carry out tasks, but they should be given specific things to do.

The employment of outside consultants will have to be considered. You should normally only use them as an 'extra pair of hands' providing expertise and resources not necessarily available within the organization. But they should be kept under control. They are there to work under the direction of the productivity executive, not to pursue their own line.

Consultants are often used as hatchet men to put forward the unpleasant recommendations that no one else wants to make. This is a pity. If you believe in productivity, you should realize that its achievement may not always be a comfortable process. You ought to be prepared to take justified action yourself and not rely on others to do it for you.

When you have decided who runs the programme, make sure that they know what you want them to achieve and that they adopt a systematic approach along the lines of the following productivity audit checklist.

Productivity audit checklist

What to look for

When you conduct a productivity audit you should look first at performance:

1. Actual compared with company standards and trends
2. Actual compared with other organizations
3. Reasons for unsatisfactory performance, which should be listed under the following headings:

   - Poor planning, budgeting and control procedures
   - Inefficient methods or systems of work
   - Inadequate use of work measurement
   - Insufficient mechanization or inadequate plant and machinery
   - Poor management
   - Poorly motivated employees
   - Badly paid employees
   - Too many restrictive practices
   - Inadequate training
   - Excessive waste.

The audit should then examine the following areas. Each one should be checked to discover what *should* be done; to what extent it *is* being done; and comment on any remedial action required.

1. Planning, budgeting and control – check that:

(a) Productivity performance tasks and standards are clearly defined, attainable, accurate and measurable
(b) Individuals are fully aware of the targets and standards they are expected to achieve
(c) Staffing plans and budgets are specifically concerned with setting and achieving realistic productivity targets
(d) Control reports clearly identify variances and deviations from the plan
(e) Individuals are fully accountable for failures to achieve targets or standards
(f) Prompt corrective action is taken by management to deal with adverse variances or results.

2. **Work methods** – check that:

  (a) A continuous programme of reviewing and improving work methods in all parts of the organization is in existence

  (b) The method improvement programme has the support of management, trade unions and employees

  (c) The programme is producing real improvements in productivity.

3. **Work measurement** – check that:

  (a) Work measurement is used, wherever feasible, to develop standards, give better controlled information and improve methods and procedures

  (b) Work measurement is used to provide the basis for effective incentive schemes.

4. **Technology** – check that:

  (a) There is a constant search by management for ways of improving productivity by the use of new technology – mechanization, computerization and automation

  (b) Investment in equipment or machinery is justified on a cost-benefit basis

  (c) Use of existing equipment is managed to achieve maximum productivity.

5. **Management** – check that:

  (a) Management is fully conscious of the need for productivity

  (b) Management and supervisors take active and successful steps to improve the productivity consciousness of their staff

  (c) Productivity performance is treated as a key criterion in assessing the capabilities and rewards of management and supervisors

  (d) The organization of work ensures that decisions on key aspects of productivity are taken at the point where work is carried out and the impact is greatest

  (e) Research into methods of improving productivity is an important function in the organization.

6. **Motivation and involvement** – check that:

  (a) Employees are motivated by management and supervisors to achieve greater productivity

  (b) A continuous review is carried out by management into ways of improving motivation for productivity

(c) Employees are involved in seeking ways of improving productivity

(d) Employees appreciate that improvements in productivity benefit themselves as well as the company.

7. Pay – check that:

(a) Payment-by-results schemes are used wherever possible to boost productivity

(b) Payment-by-results schemes are kept under close review to ensure that they are cost effective

(c) Rewards to those not on payment-by-results schemes are related to achievement

(d) Schemes for sharing the rewards from increased productivity among employees are used to promote further gains in productivity.

8. Restrictive practices – check that:

(a) Productivity agreements are negotiated with trade unions to buy out restrictive practices

(b) The agreements are cost effective; that is, that the value of improvements in productivity resulting from the elimination of restrictive practices outweighs the cost of buying them out.

9. Training – check that:

(a) Analyses of training needs concentrate on ways of improving productivity

(b) Training programmes are derived from such analyses

(c) All those who can benefit from training to improve their productivity, especially new employees, are given such training

(d) The impact of training is followed up to ensure that it is cost effective; that is, that gains on productivity resulting from training outweigh the cost of training.

10. Elimination of waste – check that:

(a) There is a continuous attack led by top management on all forms of excessive staffing costs and wasteful use of staff

(b) Work and method study is used to improve the use of the workforce by introducing more efficient techniques, systems and procedures

(c) Increases of staff, enlargement of support departments and the engagement of indirect workers is rigidly controlled

(d) Managers and supervisors are held strictly accountable for wasteful practices.

Implementing improvements

It will be much easier to implement improvements in productivity if the objectives of your programme are understood and accepted by all concerned. Clear direction from the top and a systematic approach to conducting investigations are also important. But you will fail to achieve the results you want if you cannot get your workforce involved in the programme.

If you can get your staff involved they will identify themselves with the results. This will reduce their natural resistance to change and ensure their cooperation. It will become *their* programme rather than something imposed upon them.

Chapter 42
Profit improvement

Robert Heller (25) wrote that 'businesses and managers don't earn profits, they earn money. Profit is an abstraction from the true, underlying movement of cash in and cash out.' It can be argued that profit is the result, not the objective, of efficient management.

On its own, profit, as shown on the balance sheet, is not necessarily an accurate measure of success in business. Profit figures can be 'influenced' by factors quite distinct from the trading performance of the company. These include how research and development is treated in the accounts, how stocks and work in progress are valued and how the flow of funds resulting from investments and realization of investments is dealt with. Rolls Royce is the classic example of a company whose profit figures proved to be misleading because of the way research and development expenditure was treated.

The president of International Harvester once said: 'All you have to do in business is to make some stuff and sell it to someone else for more than you paid for it.' And the controller of Bethlehem Steel stated: 'We're not in business to make steel, we're not in business to build ships, we're not in business to erect buildings. We're in business to make money.'

Both these statements are, of course, gross over-simplifications, but at least they emphasize the importance of the flow of money. Profit improvement is about increasing the flow of money into the business and reducing the flow of money out. It is not about maximizing an abstraction called 'profit' which is subject to so many extraneous influences. Perhaps we should think of it as performance improvement measured in financial terms rather than profit improvement. But profit improvement is what most people call it, and this is the term used here, with the reservations expressed above.

Factors affecting profit improvement

The three key factors are sales, costs and effectiveness.

Sales

The maximization of sales revenue depends first on good marketing. There are two approaches to marketing.

One is to assess the market in terms of what existing and potential customers will buy. This means an analysis of existing wants and buying patterns along with possible future needs. The other is to assess the scope for creating wants which do not exist at the moment, by developing and offering new products or services.

A company can maximize its market penetration by moving into market development (new markets for existing products), product development (improved or new products for existing markets) and diversification (new products for new markets).

Good marketing ensures that the company and its products are presented to customers by advertising, merchandizing and public relations in a way which will best promote sales.

Finally, good marketing ensures that prices match what customers can be persuaded to pay, with the objective of maximizing contribution to profits and direct overheads. Maximizing profit means getting the right balance between high margins and high sales volume.

Sales depend on good marketing but do not necessarily follow from it. A well-trained, well-motivated and well-controlled sales force is an essential ingredient.

The final, but often neglected, ingredient is distribution. Effective marketing and selling will go for nought if order processing is inefficient, if the turnround of customer orders takes too long, if the wrong distribution channels are used from the point of view of speed, reliability and cost, or if customer queries and complaints are not dealt with properly.

Costs

One of the many wise things Peter Drucker has said (15) is that: 'Cost, after all, does not exist by itself. It is always incurred – in intent at least – for the sake of a result. What matters therefore is not the absolute cost level but the rates between efforts and their results.'

The approach to cost reduction should therefore be to distinguish between those costs which are producing results and those which are not. Indiscriminate attacks on all costs – the 10 per cent slash approach – are counter-productive. On a selective basis, it may be better to cut something out altogether than to try and make a series of marginal cost reductions. As Drucker says: 'There is little point in trying to do cheaply what should not be done at all.'

Effectiveness

The objective should be effectiveness rather than just efficiency: to do the right things rather than merely to do things right.

Effectiveness should be aimed for in the areas of:

- *Productivity* – getting more for less, whether it is workforce (output per head), capital (return on investment) or equipment (output per unit)
- *Finance* – tightening credit policies, cracking down on bad debts, controlling quantity and settlement discounts, optimizing cash holdings while gaining maximum interest on surplus cash and reducing interest payments on bank overdrafts to a minimum
- *Inventory* – keeping the amount tied up in working capital to the minimum consistent with the need to satisfy customer demand
- *Buying* – using supplier's warehouse space by 'calling off' at specified intervals, ensuring that competitive bids are obtained for all new or renewed contracts, specifying to buyers how they should use 'clout' to get good terms, resisting the temptation to over-order, having clearly laid down policies on mark-ups.

Approach to profit improvement

Profit improvement should be a continuous exercise. It should not be left until a crisis forces you to think about it. Use benchmarking as described in Chapter 3 to find out what other businesses are doing, what lessons can be learnt from their experience and successes and decide on how they might be applied profitably in your company. Avoid the mistake of trying to transfer someone else's idea or practice into your business without ensuring that it will fit your circumstances – your technology, market position, culture and management style.

Pick up further ideas from writers – books, magazines, articles on the business pages of newspapers. But beware of falling for the latest fad without thinking through very carefully how it might work in your business.

Your route to profit improvement may be through a form of business process re-engineering as described in Chapter 43. This can be the basis for radical and fundamental change and a quantum leap on performance, founded on the questioning of all existing assumptions about how your business is run and concentrating on process – why the organization is doing things the way it does and whether it should be doing them at all.

As part of your business process re-engineering exercise (or instead of it, if you do not want to go quite so far) start with an analysis of your current situation, using the checklist at the end of this chapter. Look at the whole product range for each market and assess the relative profitability and potential of all products and markets. Try to spot those which are fading and the up-and-coming ones. For fading products or markets, consider whether remedial or surgical treatment is appropriate. For up-and-coming products or markets, work out how their progress can be assured and, possibly, accelerated.

Use the 80/20 rule (Pareto's Law) to suggest the 20 per cent of your products/markets which generate 80 per cent of your profits. Concentrate on maximizing the effectiveness of the 20 per cent of areas where the impact will be greatest.

Identify those factors within the business which are restraining its potential and, in Drucker's (15) words, 'convert into opportunity what everybody else considers dangers'. Build on strengths rather than weaknesses.

Then look ahead. Project trends, anticipate problems and, where appropriate, innovate so that you can challenge the future rather than being overwhelmed by it.

Above all, bear in mind the results of the following highly pertinent research carried out by William Hall (21). Hall looked at 64 companies in depth to determine which had the best hopes of surviving in a hostile environment. Writing in the *Harvard Business Review* he identified two key factors. The best business survivors are, first, those which can deliver their products at the lowest cost, and/or second, those which have the 'highest differentiated position'. This means having the product which the customers perceive most clearly as being different and, in important respects, rather better than the competition.

How to stay in business

You may possibly be faced with the situation, not just of seeking to improve your profitability, but of having to take steps to stay in business, such as one or more of the following:

- Improve your terms of trade by extending the terms of credit you receive and reducing the credit you give.
- Rent, lease or hire fixed assets instead of buying them. This avoids

increasing commercial lending and allows greater financial flexibility.

- Refuse tough orders: ration production by raising prices.
- Consider factoring your debt to improve cashflow. You receive most of the money and pay a factoring agent's commission of 1 to 3 per cent.
- Consider a new partner who can inject fresh capital.
- Speed up the financial money-go-round by reducing stocks and debtors.
- Renegotiate bank overdrafts for term loans and equity investments. These are more appropriate for financing capital investment as repayment can be scheduled to suit revenues.

Profit improvement checklist

Corporate analysis

1. Analyse result areas (divisions, markets, products) according to the revenue contribution they make and the costs they generate.
2. Assess for each product line or product in each market:

   (a) The extent to which it is thriving, static or retracting
   (b) Its potential for the future on the basis of different assumptions about the level of investment or cost necessary for development or survival.

3. Analyse corporate sales performance against plan and explain variances.
4. Analyse direct and overhead costs against plan and explain variances.
5. Assess development achievements (product and market) against plan and explain deviations.
6. Analyse key financial ratios (currents and trends) and establish reasons for variations from the norm.
7. Conduct a zero- or priority-based budgeting exercise to assess the justification for all major expenditure.
8. Find the answers to three key questions:

   (a) What business are we in?
   (b) What business should we be in?
   (c) What are we good at doing?

9. Assess corporate strengths and weaknesses in the fields of organization, management ability, calibre of staff, industrial

relations, planning, development, marketing, selling, distribution, buying, inventory, financial base, productivity, production methods and facilities, use of new technology, including computers, management information and financial control.

10. Assess threats and opportunities:

(a) External, eg competition, government policies and interventions, market and product developments, inflation, exchange rates

(b) Internal, eg staff, innovation, systems, financial resources (including cash flow).

Strategic plans

11. Prepare strategic plans which:

(a) Exploit opportunities and strengths revealed by the corporate analysis

(b) Are based on realistic assumptions and projections of future trends

(c) Take into account the cash required to finance expansion and product or market development.

Marketing

12. Find out everything possible about existing customers: buying habits, likes and dislikes, desire for changes or improvements to products or services.

13. Identify potential for getting new customers: what the company can do to meet existing needs or to create new wants.

14. Segment the market where this will reach different customers and can be profitable.

15. Penetrate new markets if this can be done profitably.

16. Check on cost-effectiveness of advertising and promotional expenditure. Rejig and expand advertising campaigns where it is confidently believed that this will improve results.

17. Pay more attention to merchandizing, eg advising retailers/agents on selling, holding special promotions, providing better point-of-sale material.

Product mix and development

18. Redistribute resources (finance, people, production and distribution) between products, as required, to optimize returns on investment.

19. Maximize product profitability by:

    (a) Cutting high-risk, high-capital projects
    (b) Developing low-cost, low-risk products
    (c) Cutting costs – advertising, promotion, packaging material, servicing or selling
    (d) Reducing stockholding
    (e) Reducing discounts
    (f) Increasing prices.

20. Develop new products or services to meet defined market needs or to create new wants.
21. Eliminate unprofitable products or markets.

Sales

22. Improve the order-to-call ratio of sales representatives by better field supervision and training and more effective incentives.
23. Concentrate upon key accounts.
24. Eliminate unprofitable accounts.
25. Develop more high-volume accounts.
26. Improve discount structure.
27. Provide incentives for customers to place larger orders or to remain loyal to the company's products.
28. Provide better support to sales representatives in the form of advertising, sales literature, merchandizing and direct mail shots.
29. Speed response to customer enquiries.

Distribution

30. Analyse transport costs and switch to more economic methods.
31. Rationalize depot structure to speed deliveries and cut distribution and storage costs.
32. Use fewer, larger capacity vehicles and lengthen their life.
33. Introduce automatic handling methods wherever justified by the return on investment.
34. Make better use of storage space.

Production

35. Use quick sharp doses of method study to identify areas where output can be improved, eg eliminating bottlenecks, illogical work flows, inefficient work scheduling.

36. Use value analysis techniques to reduce material costs.
37. Use group technology techniques to group associated processes into self-contained and easily controlled work units.
38. Rationalize product design so that more parts are interchangeable.
39. Ensure that procedures exist to relate customer orders and priorities to shop-floor capacity.
40. Improve shop loading and production control techniques in order to smooth work flow, rationalize distribution of work, and eliminate delays because of shortages in materials, parts or tools.
41. Revise design standards and tolerances to match production facilities.
42. Reduce waste and scrap rates.
43. Increase machine utilization.
44. Introduce automation (mechanization) where justified by return on investment.

Buying

45. Use 'clout' to get better terms (but beware of placing orders which are too large).
46. Find alternative, cheaper or more reliable sources of supply.
47. Reserve capacity if there is a genuine and predictable need.
48. Place guaranteed orders in exchange for bulk prices.
49. Analyse for over-specification and reduce specifications to the minimum safe level.
50. Use 'call-off' system for regular supplies to cut storage costs.
51. Alter product design to allow for standard parts purchasing.

Inventory

52. Use economic order-quantity techniques to establish order points, taking into account inventory carrying charges, order preparation costs and demand for the item.
53. Use material requirements planning (MRP) techniques to ensure that the exact quantity of material wanted is on hand or is delivered not too long before it is required in accordance with sales demands.
54. Use computer modelling techniques to determine optimum stock levels, balancing the need to reduce working capital with the need to avoid being out of stock.
55. Improve information on inventory so that action can be taken in good time to reduce stock to optimum levels.

Cost reduction

56. Look at the scope for cutting costs in all the major areas where expenses are incurred:

    (a) Labour costs – look for overstaffing, especially in indirect, service and staff departments.
    (b) Manufacturing costs – streamline production methods, reduce material costs.
    (c) Selling costs – advertising, promotions, public relations, packaging and display material.
    (d) Inventory – stock levels too high.
    (e) Operating – space, computers, services, plant and equipment.

57. Use zero- or priority-based budgeting and organization and methods techniques to analyse every activity not directly concerned with production. Establish the extent to which each is essential and the degree to which costs could be cut without making a significant impact on the productivity and efficiency of the business.

58. Reduce waste created by the company by eliminating:

    (a) Unnecessary forms
    (b) Over-complicated paperwork procedures
    (c) Too many levels of management
    (d) Delays in decision-making because authority is not delegated down the line
    (e) Bottlenecks and inefficient work flows.

59. Reduce waste created by staff, eg time wasting, absenteeism, extravagant use of the company's facilities and equipment.

Productivity

60. Extend or introduce a comprehensive method improvement programme.
61. Use work measurement to develop standards, give better control information and improve methods and procedures.
62. Introduce new technology, when justified, on a cost/benefit basis.
63. Set productivity performance targets.
64. Buy out restrictive practices by productivity bargaining.

People

65. Identify effective managers and promote them.
66. Identify ineffective managers and remove them.

67. Introduce payment schemes which have a significant effect on motivation.
68. Encourage and train managers and supervisors to motivate their staff better.
69. Achieve better motivation by improving organization (more direct and immediate management) and the quality of working life. Get employees involved in productivity and quality improvement programmes.

Finance

70. Tighten credit policies.
71. Set priorities for capital expenditures.
72. Take steps to reduce bad debts.
73. Delay payments for as long as creditors will stand.
74. Analyse key ratios (eg profits as a percentage of sales and cash flow to current liabilities) and ensure that steps are taken to remedy adverse trends.
75. Ensure that management information, which allows proper control to be maintained over all aspects of the business, is available promptly.

Chapter 43
Re-engineering the business

Even when a business is functioning well there is much to be said for conducting a thorough analysis and review of the key business processes to ensure that they will be capable of sustaining growth and the creation of added value. Business process re-engineering is a method of conducting such a review.

Business process re-engineering (BPR) is essentially about business *process* which can be defined as:

> The collection of activities that takes one or more kinds of input and creates an output that is of value to the customer.

This 'order fulfilment' is a process which starts with an order as its input and results in the delivery of the ordered goods. This delivery is the value that the process creates. It is much wider than simply a selling or distribution activity. Business process re-engineering does not look at related functions as separate entities. Instead, it examines the process that contains and links those functions together from initiation to completion.

Approaches to business process re-engineering

The chief tool of business process re-engineering is a clean sheet of paper. Re-engineers start from the future and work backwards. They are unconstrained by existing methods, people or departments. In effect they ask, 'If we were a new company, how would we run the place?' Then they take what are usually drastic steps to make the company conform to that vision.

Conventional process structures are fragmented and piecemeal. Work tends to be organized as a sequence of narrowly defined tasks. The people carrying out these tasks are then aggregated into departments and managers are installed to administer them. Control systems funnel information up the hierarchy to the few who are presumed to know what to do with it.

Re-engineering takes a much broader and radical view. It looks at the fundamental processes of a business from a cross-functional perspective. Its aim is to achieve integration. It breaks away from conventional wisdom and the constraints of organizational boundaries. It uses information technology not to automate an existing process but to facilitate a new one. Expert systems, for example, are used to enable people to use accumulated and systematized knowledge to make decisions on the spot without having to refer to higher authority or bring in specialists.

Re-engineers ask two fundamental questions: 'Why?' and 'What if?' In that respect they are following in the footsteps of good methods engineers who use critical examination techniques to challenge assumptions, indeed to question the very existence of an activity, and only when they receive a satisfactory answer, to explore better (ie quicker, less costly, more efficient) ways of doing it. The critical examination questions they ask are:

- What is done? Why do it?
- How is it done? Why do it that way?
- Where is it done? Why do it there?
- When is it done? Why do it then?
- Who does it? Why that person?

The difference between this traditional and often very effective approach and business process re-engineering is that the latter carries out an even more fundamental look at business processes across the organization. This examination is driven by top management as a means of achieving radical change affecting the whole business or a major part of it. Method study tended to be more piecemeal and not integrated with a business strategy for comprehensive change and improvement.

Another significant difference is that business process re-engineering is much more concerned with exploiting the power of information technology. Again, however, systems design in BPR cuts across functional boundaries and, in contrast to the traditional approach to systems analysis, is focused on producing new and fully integrated solutions.

The considerations which should be taken into account in a BPR exercise are described below.

Get the strategy straight first

One of the mottoes of BPR is: 'Don't fix stuff you shouldn't be doing in the first place.' Re-engineering is about processes and operations; only strategy can tell you which ones matter. It is necessary to start with a long hard look at what business the organization is in and how it intends to

279

make money out of it. It is equally important to identify the core competences of the organization and ensure that the business is built round them.

Lead from the top

The one crucial factor for success in re-engineering is executive leadership with real vision. Moreover, because re-engineering is cross-functional, it must be driven by people with the authority to oversee a process from end to end and top to bottom. There should be a core team of functional heads led by the chief executive.

Create a sense of urgency

Re-engineering will break apart under political pressure or peter out after a few easy gains unless the case for doing it is compelling, urgent and constantly refreshed.

Methodology

Business process re-engineering cannot be planned meticulously and accomplished in small and cautious steps. It tends to be an all-or-nothing proposition, often with an uncertain result. It is therefore a high-risk undertaking and not worth attempting unless there is a pressing need to rethink what the organization is doing overall or in a major area.

Process re-engineering should not spend too much time studying existing work flows. But the review process should aim to identify points of leverage where new thinking will provide the greatest benefit.

Applications

Business process re-engineering can be used to carry out a complete and fundamental review of the organization's strategy, structure and business processes as in the case of Barr and Stroud, a Glasgow engineering firm that had to introduce radical changes in response to new business conditions and demands. The changes included focusing on the core competences, reducing management layers from nine to four and the establishment of multi-disciplinary teams with the remit to strip time and waste out of the system.

BPR is not a relevant approach in discrete functions. In the United States, for example, Ford established that there was no point in re-engineering a single function such as accounts payable. It was only a viable proposition if fundamental processes of the business were looked at from a cross-functional perspective. Ford therefore re-engineered the whole accounts payable process, covering the separate functions of purchasing, material control and accounts, with the result that they introduced a system of invoiceless processing which achieved a 75 per cent reduction in headcount.

If re-engineering is done well it can deliver impressive gains in speed, productivity and profitability. For example, in the United States, Union Carbide eliminated $400 million of fixed costs in just three years, GTE expects to double revenues and halve costs in its telephone operations; Mutual Benefit Life reduced its turnaround of customer applications from 5 to 25 days to an average of 2 to 5 days and eliminated 100 field office positions; IBM Credit cut its time for preparing quotes from 7 days to 1; and Bell Atlantic cut its delivery times from 15 days to just 1.

It is claimed that BPR can deliver tenfold improvements in performance but only when it works well, and that is not easy. A large proportion of companies do not achieve good results because they fail to think the process through first (functions must be simplified before information technology is brought in), do not engage hearts and minds sufficiently, or simply act on bad advice.

Requirements for success

A re-engineering project, like any major change programme, can produce lasting results only if senior executives invest considerable time and energy in it. Without strong leadership from the top, the disruption that accompanies such radical change can sabotage the project.

To be successful, the project should be based on an analysis which identifies those processes which are critical for value creation in the overall business. BPR is not just concerned with single activities or isolated processes, its aim is to cover wider groups of related processes or interrelated activities so that improvements extend throughout the business. But it is unwise to adopt too wide or indiscriminate an approach. To enhance a company's ability to deliver value to its customers it is essential to focus on the two or three key elements which create such value and tackle these with vigour and a determination to achieve continuous improvement over the longer term.

Chapter 44
Report writing

The ability to express oneself clearly on paper and to write effective reports is one of a manager's most important skills. As often as not, it is through the medium of reports that you will convey your ideas and recommendations to your superiors and colleagues and inform them of the progress you are making.

What makes a good report?

The purpose of a report is to analyse and explain a situation, to propose and gain agreement to a plan. It should be logical, practical, persuasive and succinct.

To be an effective report writer you start by having something worthwhile to say. Clear thinking (Chapter 7), creative thinking (Chapter 17), problem-solving (Chapter 40) and trouble-shooting (Chapter 50) techniques will all help. Your analysis of opinions and facts and your evaluation of options should provide a base for positive conclusions and recommendations.

There are three fundamental rules for report writing:

- Give your report a logical structure.
- Use plain words to convey your meaning.
- Remember the importance of good, clear presentation of material.

Structure

A report should have a beginning, a middle and an end. If the report is lengthy or complex it will also need a summary of conclusions and recommendations. There may also be appendices containing detailed data and statistics.

Beginning

Your introduction should explain: why the report has been written, its aims, its terms of reference, and why it should be read. It should then state the sources of information upon which the report was based. Finally, if the report is divided into various sections, the arrangement and labelling of these sections should be explained.

Middle

The middle of the report should contain the facts you have assembled and your analysis of those facts. The analysis should lead logically to the conclusions and recommendations included in the final section. One of the most common weaknesses in reports is for the facts not to lead on naturally to the conclusions; the other is for the conclusions not to be supported by the facts.

Summarize the facts and your observations. If you have identified alternative courses of action, set out the pros and cons of each one, but make it quite clear which one you favour. Don't leave your readers in mid-air.

A typical trouble-shooting report would start by describing the present situation; it would then list any problems or weaknesses in that situation, and proceed to explain why these have occurred.

End

The final section of the report should set out your recommendations, stating how each of them will help to achieve the stated aims of the report or overcome any weaknesses revealed by the analytical studies.

The benefits and costs of implementing the recommendations should then be explained. The next stage is to propose a method of proceeding – the programme of work, complete with deadlines and the names of people who would carry it out. Finally, tell the recipient(s) of the report what action, such as approval of plans or authorization of expenditure, you would like them to take.

Summary

In a long or complex report it is very helpful to provide a summary of conclusions and recommendations. It concentrates the reader's mind and can be used as an agenda in presenting and discussing the report. It is useful to cross-reference the items to the relevant paragraphs or sections of the report.

Plain words

'If language is not correct, then what is said is not what is meant; if what is said is not what is meant, then what ought to be done remains undone.' (Confucius)

The heading of this section is taken from Sir Ernest Gowers' *The Complete Plain Words* (20). This book is required reading for anyone interested in report writing. Gowers' recommendations on how best to convey meaning without ambiguity, and without giving unnecessary trouble to the reader, are:

1. Use no more words than are necessary to express your meaning, for if you use more you are likely to obscure it and to tire your reader. In particular do not use superfluous adjectives and adverbs, and do not use roundabout phrases where single words would serve.
2. Use familiar words rather than the far-fetched if they express your meaning equally well; for the familiar are more likely to be understood.
3. Use words with a precise meaning rather than those that are vague, for they will obviously serve better to make your meaning clear; and in particular, prefer concrete words to abstract for they are more likely to have a precise meaning.

You will not go far wrong if you follow these precepts.

Presentation

The way in which you present your report affects its impact and value. The reader should be able to follow your argument easily and not get bogged down in too much detail.

Paragraphs should be short and each one should be restricted to a single topic. If you want to list or highlight a series of points, tabulate them or use bullet points. For example:

Pay reviews
Control should be maintained over increments by issuing guidelines to managers on:

- The maximum percentage increase to their pay roll allowable for increments to individual salaries

- The maximum percentage increase that should be paid to a member of staff.

Paragraphs may be numbered for ease of reference. Some people prefer the system which numbers main sections 1, 2, etc, sub-sections 1.1, 1.2, etc, and sub-sub-sections 1.1.1, 1.1.2, etc. However, this can be clumsy and distracting. A simpler system, which eases cross-referencing, is to number each paragraph, *not* the headings, 1, 2, 3, etc; sub-paragraphs or tabulations are identified as 1(a), 1(b), 1(c), etc and sub-sub-paragraphs if required as 1(a)(i), (ii), (iii), etc (or use bullet points).

Use headings to guide people on what they are about to read and to help them to find their way about the report. Main headings should be in capitals and sub-headings in lower case.

A long report could have an index listing the main and sub-headings and their paragraph numbers like this:

	Paragraphs
PAY ADMINISTRATION	83–92
Pay structure	84–88
Job evaluation	89–90
Pay reviews	91–92

Your report will make most impact if it is brief and to the point. Read and re-read your draft to cut out any superfluous material or flabby writing. Use bullet points to simplify the presentation and to put your messages across clearly and succinctly.

Do not clutter up the main pages of the report with masses of indigestible figures or other data. Summarize key statistics in compact, easy-to-follow tables with clear headings. Relegate supporting material to an appendix.

Chapter 45
Strategic management

To provide for a successful, long-term future organizations must have a clearly defined purpose, a sense of direction and an idea of the resources they will need. They do this by managing strategically. This requires managers to understand the nature of strategy, to use strategic management processes and to prepare strategic plans, while recognizing that strategy is constantly evolving and adapting to changing circumstances.

Strategy – aim and purpose

The overall aim of strategy at corporate level will be to match or fit the organization to its environment in the most advantageous way possible.

Strategy defines where the organization wants to go to fulfil its purpose and achieve its mission. It provides the framework for guiding choices which determine the organization's nature and direction. These choices relate to the organization's products or services, markets, key capabilities, growth, return on capital and allocation of resources. A strategy is therefore a declaration of intent; it defines what the organization wants to become in the longer term.

Strategies form the basis for strategic management and the formulation of strategic plans.

Strategic management

Strategic management is the process of formulating strategies and managing the organization to achieve them.

Organizations and managers who think and act strategically are looking ahead and defining the direction in which they want to go in the middle and longer term. Although they are aware of the fact that businesses, like managers, must perform well in the present to succeed in the future, they are concerned with the broader issues they face, and the general direction in which they must go to deal with these issues.

Strategic management takes place within the context of the mission of the organization, and a fundamental task of strategic management will be to ensure that the mission is defined and relevant to the basic purpose of the organization within its changing environment. Strategic management is concerned with both ends and means. As an end, it describes a vision of what the organization will look like in a few years' time; as means, it shows how it is expected that the vision will be realized. Strategic management is therefore visionary management, concerned with creating and conceptualizing ideas of where the organization is going. But it must be translatable into empirical management, which decides how, in practice, it is going to get there.

Strategic management creates a perspective which people can share and which guides their decisions and actions. The focus will be on identifying the organization's mission and goals, but attention is also concentrated on the resource base required to make it succeed. It is always necessary to remember that strategy is the means to create value.

Managers who think strategically will have a broad and long-term view of where they are going. But they will also be aware that they are responsible first for planning how to allocate resources to opportunities which contribute to the implementation of strategy and, second, for managing these opportunities in ways which will significantly add value to the results achieved by the organization.

Key concepts in strategic management

The key concepts used in strategic management are:

- *Distinctive competence* – working out what the organization is best at, and what its special or unique capabilities are.
- *Focus* – identifying and concentrating on the key strategic issues.
- *Sustainable competitive advantage* – as formulated by Michael Porter (49), this concept states that to achieve competitive advantage, firms should create value for their customers, select markets where they can excel and present a moving target to their competitors by continually improving their position. Three of the most important factors are innovation, quality and cost reduction.
- *Synergy* – developing a product-market posture with a combined performance which is greater than the sum of its parts.
- *Environmental scanning* – scanning the internal and external environment of the firm to ensure that its management is fully aware

of its strengths and weaknesses and the threats and opportunities it faces (SWOT analysis).

- *Resource allocation* – understanding the human, financial and material resource requirements of the strategy, and ensuring that the resources are made available and their use is optimized.

Formulating strategies

As Henry Mintzberg (39) has pointed out, strategy formulation is not necessarily a rational and continuous process. He believes that while most of the time management pursues a given strategic orientation, changes in strategies, when they do occur, happen in brief quantum loops. In practice, 'a realized strategy can emerge in response to an evolving situation'.

Lester Dignam (12) also believes that strategy-making is not always a rational step-by-step process. He suggests that most strategic decisions are event driven, not programmed. They are expressed as preferences rather than as exercises in applied logic. Strategy formulation, according to Dignam, is about correct decision-making, not about the formulation of detailed plans. The most effective strategists are usually creative, intuitive people, employing an adaptive and flexible process.

There is a lot of truth in what Dignam says but there are still strong arguments for adopting a systematic approach to the formulation of strategic plans, as described below.

Strategic planning

Strategic planning is a systematic, analytical approach which reviews the business as a whole in relation to its environment with the object of:

- Developing an integrated, coordinated and consistent view of the route the organization wishes to follow
- Facilitating the adaptation of the organization to environmental change.

The aim of strategic planning is to create a viable link between the organization's objectives and resources and its environmental opportunities.

Formulating strategic plans

A systematic approach to formalizing strategic plans consists of the following steps:

1. *Define the organization's mission* – its overall purpose.
2. *Set objectives* – definitions of what the organization must achieve to fulfil its mission.
3. *Conduct environmental scans* – internal appraisals of the strengths and weaknesses of the organization and external appraisals of the opportunities and threats which face it (a SWOT analysis).
4. *Analyse existing strategies* – determining their relevance in the light of the environmental scan. This may include gap analysis to establish the extent to which environmental factors might lead to gaps between what is being achieved and what could be achieved if changes in existing strategies were made. In a corporation with a number of distinct businesses, an analysis of the viability of each strategic business unit (portfolio analysis) can take place to establish strategies for the future of each unit.
5. *Define strategic issues* in the light of the environmental scan, the gap analysis and, where appropriate, the portfolio analysis.
6. *Develop new or revised strategies* and amend objectives in the light of the analysis of strategic issues.
7. *Decide on the critical success factors* related to the achievement of objectives and the implementation of strategy.
8. *Prepare operational, resource and project plans* designed to achieve the strategies and meet the critical success factor criteria.
9. *Implement* the plans.
10. *Monitor results* against the plans and feed back information which can be used to modify strategies and plans.

However carefully you plan, remember that strategy is often no more (and no less) than 'just keeping that herd heading broadly west,' as the cowboys used to say.

Chapter 46
Stress management

The activities of most managers are characterized by brevity, variety and fragmentation. They are constantly exposed to change – indeed chaos. They are frequently working under pressure which within reason is normal, perhaps desirable, as a motivating force. It can make the adrenalin flow and concentrates the mind wonderfully. It is only when the pressure becomes excessive that it can turn into stress, which will then have a demotivating effect. Because some degree of stress is almost inevitable in these turbulent times, it is desirable to understand something about the varieties of stress, its causes and how to cope with it.

Varieties of stress

Emotionally induced stress can be classified into four general categories:

1. *Time stress.* This is an anxiety reaction, either to the feeling that something, or a number of things, must be done before a deadline, or to the general feeling that time is running out and something terrible will happen when it does.
2. *Anticipatory stress.* This is commonly known as 'worry'. This is a feeling of anxiety about an impending event. It is often a generalized anxiety, with little or no specific basis.
3. *Situational stress.* This is anxiety as a result of finding oneself excessively pressurized by events or people. It occurs in situations which are threatening and wholly or partially beyond one's control. It can also happen when there is conflict or distrust between people.
4. *Encounter stress.* This is anxiety about dealing with individuals or groups of people who are perceived as potentially unpleasant or unpredictable.

Causes of stress

The main causes of stress are:

- *Working conditions* – unpleasant working conditions, such as the need to work fast or expend a lot of physical effort or excessive or inconvenient hours, can affect both physical and mental health.
- *Work overload* – either having too much work to do, or carrying out work that is beyond one's capacity.
- *Role ambiguity* – when individuals are unclear about the scope and responsibilities of their jobs or the authority they have to make decisions.
- *Role conflict* – where individuals have conflicting job demands, are doing things they do not want to do, or are having to do things which are outside the specification of their jobs.
- *Responsibility* – increased responsibility for people means being involved more in interacting with others, attending meetings and meeting deadline pressures and schedules. Such people may also worry about 'carrying the can' for the mistakes or inadequacies of their staff.
- *Accountability* – accountability for results can increase stress because of the pressure on meeting targets and improving standards of performance, especially in conditions where the future is uncertain.
- *Change* – coping with rapid technological change, the acquisition of new skills, different responsibilities in the job and the variety of tasks to be undertaken in turbulent conditions.
- *Relationships with subordinates* – inability to delegate, critical or uncooperative staff, difficulties in exercising authority.
- *Relationships with colleagues* – office politics, rivalry, competitiveness, lack of support, difficulties in achieving cooperation on joint projects.
- *Job security* – fears of redundancy, obsolescence or early retirement.
- *Lack of status* – actual or perceived.
- *Feelings about job or career* – frustration at reaching career ceiling, lack of prospects, under- or over-promotion.
- *Impact of the organization* – pressurized or tense climate, autocratic management style, restrictions on behaviour, lack of information and involvement.
- *External pressures* – clash between demands made by the organization and those made by the family or other external interests; problems at home created by excessive hours at work; priority being given to work rather than partner and family; travelling away from home, company transfers.

These causes can combine in many ways. They are probably most acute for middle managers who are pressurized from above and from below, are busy making their mark and advancing their career, are having to travel and move with the company, yet who may be married with growing responsibilities at home. But older managers may also be subject to stress either because of the extra weight of responsibility or because their career has 'plateaued' and their ambitions are not being realized.

Coping with stress

How people deal with stress will depend on their personality, tolerance for ambiguity and ability to live with change. Motivation also comes into it. Motivation is a form of pressure. People can be too highly motivated and pressure becomes stress when they cannot achieve what they set out, or are expected, to do.

Stress can be managed by adaptive behaviour. An overworked manager may adapt successfully by delegating more work and spending more time in managing time (see Chapter 48). But someone else may accept the overload, with the result that pressure and stress increase and performance deteriorates.

The following are various ways in which you can manage stress:

1. Build rewarding, pleasant, supportive relationships with your boss, colleagues and subordinates.
2. If in any doubt about your role, seek clarification from your boss.
3. If there are problems between you and other managers, bring the issues out into the open and discuss them in a frank but friendly way.
4. Take steps to clarify your objectives and have them agreed by your boss.
5. However much you may wish to present yourself as the willing horse, don't take on extra work and make promises you will have great difficulty in keeping. Don't refuse outright or you will get the reputation of being uncooperative. Don't plead overwork or you may be regarded as a shirker. Simply say that you have a set of priorities which you have to keep to and that, while you will be glad to help, you will have to give this job a lower priority, unless your other priorities can be changed. If the task is completely beyond your capabilities, say so, but offer to help in finding someone who has the required skills and knowledge.
6. Appraise your own strengths and weaknesses. If your problems are

because of an identifiable weakness, do something about it or seek help.

7. Determine a goal in your career which is realistic in relation to your own self-appraisal. Check on the competences and qualifications required to move to where you want to be. If you are confident that you have them, pursue your ambition vigorously. If you do not have the qualities required, decide whether or not you can build them. If so, go ahead. If not, think of an alternative goal and career path which is within your capabilities.

8. If you are under pressure to meet deadlines or have too many balls in the air at once, plan your priorities to fit the time available, and delegate as much work as possible.

9. If you are facing a crisis, take time to decide how to tackle it. Don't run in all directions at once like a headless chicken.

10. If under extreme pressure, deliberately allow yourself time to relax for a few minutes.

11. Use time management techniques as described in Chapter 48 to plan your working day, always allowing some time – even if only ten minutes – for complete privacy and freedom from pressure.

12. Try to make sure that you are placed in a job suitable to your characteristics and talents.

13. Face up realistically to what you can do and achieve.

14. Do whatever you can to achieve an acceptable balance between yourself, your work and your family.

15. Foster relationships which help you to cope with work pressure, and enable you to admit, and take steps to remedy, work-related stress.

Chapter 47
Team management

One of your most important tasks as a manager is to make the best use of the capacity of your team so that all its members will work well together to deliver superior levels of performance.

This key process of team management means that you have to clarify the team's purpose and goals, ensure that its members work well together, build commitment and self-confidence, strengthen the team's collective skills and approach, remove externally imposed obstacles, and create opportunities for team members to develop their skills and competences.

To carry out this task effectively you need to understand:

- The significance of teams
- The use of self-managing teams
- The factors which contribute to team effectiveness
- What to do to achieve good teamwork
- How to conduct team performance reviews
- How to analyse team performance.

The significance of teams

As defined by Katzenbach and Smith (31):

A team is a small number of people with complementary skills who are committed to a common purpose, performance goals and approach for which they hold themselves mutually accountable.

They suggested that some of the main characteristics of teams are as follows:

- Teams are the basic units of performance for most organizations. They meld together the skills, experiences and insights of several people.

- Team work applies to the whole organization as well as specific teams. It represents 'a set of values that encourage behaviours such as listening and responding cooperatively to points of view expressed by others, giving others the benefit of the doubt, providing support to those who need it and recognizing the interests and achievements of others'.
- Teams are created and energized by significant and demanding performance challenges.
- Teams outperform individuals acting alone or in large organizational groupings, especially when performance requires multiple skills, judgements and experiences.
- Teams are flexible and responsive to changing events and demands. They can adjust their approach to new information and challenges with greater speed, accuracy and effectiveness than can individuals caught in the web of larger organizational connections.
- High-performance teams invest much time and effort exploring, shaping and agreeing on a purpose that belongs to them, both collectively and individually. They are characterized by a deep sense of commitment to their growth and success.

Richard Walton (57) has commented that in the new commitment-based organization it will often be teams rather than individuals who will be the organizational units accountable for performance.

However, teamwork, as Peter Wickens (61) has said, 'is not dependent on people working in groups but upon everyone working towards the same objectives'. The Nissan concept of teamwork, as quoted by Wickens, is expressed in its General Principles and emphasizes the need to:

- Promote mutual trust and cooperation between the company, its employees and the union
- Recognize that all employees, at whatever level, have a valued part to play in the success of the company
- Seek actively the contributions of all employees in furthering these goals.

Waterman (59) has noted that teamwork 'is a tricky business; it requires people to pull together towards a set of shared goals or values. It does not mean that they always agree on the best way to get there. When they don't agree they should discuss, even argue, these differences.'

Richard Pascale (42) underlined this point when he wrote that successful companies can use conflict to stay ahead: 'We are almost always better served when conflict is surfaced and channelled, not suppressed.' The pursuit of teamwork should not lead to a 'bland' climate in the organization in which nothing new or challenging ever happens. It is all very well to be 'one big happy family' but this could be disastrous if it breeds complacency and a cosy feeling that the family spirit comes first, whatever is happening in the outside world.

Self-managing teams

Tom Peters (46) strongly advocates the use of self-managing teams. He calls it 'the small within big principle' and states that if the organization is built around teams the result will be 'enhanced focus, task orientation, innovativeness and individual commitment'.

A self-managed team typically has the following characteristics:

- The team might be quite large – 12 to 15 members or even more, depending on the work involved, with one team leader.
- Team leaders are accountable for the achievement of schedule, quality, cost and people development goals, as well as being responsible for 'boundary management' for their groups, ie relating to more senior management and support staff and external contacts and working with other groups.
- However, the role of team leaders is primarily to act as coordinators and facilitators; their style is expected to be more supportive and participative than directive.
- The team is highly autonomous, responsible to a considerable degree for planning and scheduling work, problem-solving, developing its own performance indicators and setting and monitoring team performance and quality standards.
- Job specialization is minimized, team members operate flexibly within the group, tasks are rotated among them and they are multi-skilled.
- The team meets at least once a week as a group.
- Effectiveness as a team member is a major performance criterion in appraisals.
- Some form of team pay, related to group performance, may be provided.
- The team is encouraged to develop new ideas for improving performance – awards for suggestions are team based.

Team effectiveness

An effective team is likely to be one in which the structure, leadership and methods of operation are relevant to the requirements of the task. There will be commitment to the whole group task and people will have been grouped together in a way which ensures that they are related to each other by way of the requirements of task performance and task interdependence.

In an effective team its purpose is clear and its members feel the task is important, both to them and to the organization. According to Douglas McGregor (36) the main features of a well-functioning, creative team are as follows:

1. The atmosphere tends to be informal, comfortable and relaxed.
2. There is a lot of discussion in which initially everyone participates, but it remains pertinent to the task of the group.
3. The task or objective of the team is well understood and accepted by the members. There will have been free discussion of the objective at some point until it was formulated in such a way that the members of the team could commit themselves to it.
4. The members listen to each other. Every idea is given a hearing. People do not appear to be afraid of being considered foolish by putting forth a creative thought even if it seems fairly extreme.
5. There is disagreement. Disagreements are not suppressed or overridden by premature team action. The reasons are carefully examined, and the team seeks to resolve them rather than to dominate the dissenter.
6. Most decisions are reached by consensus in which it is clear that everybody is in general agreement and willing to go along. Formal voting is at a minimum; the team does not accept a simple majority as a proper basis for action.
7. Criticism is frequent, frank and relatively comfortable. There is little evidence of personal attack, either openly or in a hidden fashion.
8. People are free in expressing their feelings as well as their ideas both on the problem and on the group's operation.
9. When action is taken, clear assignments are made and accepted.
10. The leader of the team does not dominate it, nor does the team defer unduly to him or her. There is little evidence of a struggle for power as the team operates. The issue is not who controls, but how to get the job done.

What to do to achieve good teamwork

1. Establish urgency and direction.
2. Select members based on skills and skill potential who are good at

working with others but still capable of taking their own line when necessary.

3. Pay particular attention to first meetings and actions.

4. Set immediate performance-orientated tasks and goals.

5. Set overlapping or interlocking objectives for people who have to work together. These will take the form of targets to be achieved or projects to be completed by joint action.

6. Assess people's performance not only on the results they achieve but also on the degree to which they are good team members. Recognize and reward people who have worked well in teams (using team bonus schemes where appropriate) bearing in mind that being part of a high performance team can be a reward in itself.

7. Encourage people to build networks – results are achieved in organizations, as in the outside world, on the basis of who you know as well as what you know.

8. Set up interdepartmental project teams with a brief to get on with it.

9. Describe and think of the organization as a system of interlocking teams united by a common purpose. Don't emphasize hierarchies. Abolish departmental boundaries if they are getting in the way, but do not be alarmed if there is disagreement – remember the value of *constructive* conflict.

10. Hold special 'off-the-job' meetings for work teams so they can get together and explore issues without the pressures of their day-to-day jobs.

11. Use training programmes to build relationships. This can often be a far more beneficial result of a course than the increase in skills or knowledge which was its ostensible purpose.

12. Use teambuilding and interactive skills training to supplement the other approaches. But do not rely upon them to have any effect unless the messages they convey are in line with the organization's culture and values.

Team performance reviews

Team performance review meetings analyse and assess feedback and control information on their joint achievements against objectives and work plans.

The agenda for such a meeting could be as follows:

1. General feedback – review of:

- Progress of the team as a whole
- General problems encountered by the team which have caused difficulties or delayed progress
- Overall help and hindrance to the effective operation of the team.

2. Work reviews

- How well the team has functioned (a checklist for analysing team performance is given below)
- Review of the individual contribution made by each team member
- Discussion of any new problems encountered by team members.

3. Group problem-solving

- Analysis of reasons for any major problems
- Agreement of steps to be taken to solve them or to avoid their recurrence in the future.

4. Update objectives and work plans

- Review of new requirements, opportunities or threats
- Amendment and updating of objectives and work plans.

Checklist for analysing team performance

- How well do we work together?
- Does everyone contribute?
- How effectively is the team led?
- How good are we at analysing problems?
- How decisive are we?
- How good are we at initiating action?
- Do we concentrate sufficiently on the priority issues?
- Do we waste time on irrelevancies?
- To what extent can people speak their minds without being squashed by other team members?
- If there is any conflict, is it openly expressed and is it about issues rather than personalities?

Team management at Boots the Chemists (a Kinsley Lord Ltd case study)

As far back as the mid-1970s, Boots the Chemists estimated that very similar stores could have turnover levels varying by 15 per cent or more, with the differences entirely attributable to the respective abilities of the managers to motivate their staff. The company's heavy, long-term investment in training reflects its belief that people make the difference. Its customer charter helps to focus staff on the highest standards of customer service. Now the company is moving further into involving the sales assistants at the front line in defining their own roles and developing their skills and contributions. For example, teams of staff in stores now meet regularly to plan and implement better ways of further improving their store performance.

Chapter 48
Time management

I wasted time, now doth time waste me (*Richard II*).

If you were told by your chairman that you were needed for a special assignment which would mean working directly under him, give you the opportunity to deal with strategic issues, broaden your experience and provide you with excellent promotion prospects, would you take it? The answer would, of course, be yes. If, however, you were told that you would spend one day a week on this assignment and carry out your present duties in the remaining four days, would you still accept the job? Of course you would. But you would be admitting that you could, if you organized yourself better, do your existing work in four-fifths of the time you spend at the moment.

To recover that one-fifth or more, you need to think systematically about how you use your time. You can then take steps to organize yourself better and to get other people to help or at least not to hinder you.

Analysis

The first thing to do is to find out where there is scope for improving your use of time.

Your job

Start with your job – the tasks you have to carry out and the objectives you are there to achieve. Try to establish an order of priority between your tasks and among your objectives.

It is more difficult to do this if you have a number of potentially conflicting areas of responsibility. A good example of this was a director of administration who had a ragbag of responsibilities including property, office services and staff. He had perpetual problems with conflicting priorities and, all too frequently, at the end of the day he would say to himself: 'I have wasted my time, I have achieved next to nothing.'

He took a day off to think things through and realized that he had to take a broad view before getting into detail. He felt that if he could sort out the relative importance of his objectives he would be in a better position to attach priorities to his tasks. He quickly realized that, as an administrator, his first objective was to set up and maintain systems which would run smoothly. Having done this, he could rely on preventive maintenance to reduce problems. But when a crisis did occur – which was inevitable in his area – he could concentrate on fire-fighting in one place without having to worry about what was going on elsewhere.

His second objective, therefore, was to give himself sufficient free time to concentrate on major problems so that he could react swiftly to them. He then classified the sort of issues that could arise and decided which could safely be delegated to others and which he should deal with himself. He was thus prepared to allocate priorities as the problems landed on his desk and to select the serious ones to deal with himself, knowing that the administrative system would go on without interruption.

How you spend your time

Having sorted out your main priorities you should analyse in more detail how you spend your time. This will identify time-consuming activities and indicate where there are problems as well as possible solutions to them.

The best way to analyse time is to keep a diary. Do this for a week, or preferably two or three, as one week may not provide a typical picture. Divide the day into 15-minute sections and note down what you did in each period. Against each space, summarize how effectively you spent your time by writing V for valuable, D for doubtful and U for useless. If you want to make more refined judgements give your ratings pluses or minuses. For example:

Time	Task	Rating
9.00– 9.15	Dealt with incoming mail	V
9.15– 9.30	Dealt with incoming mail	V
9.30– 9.45	Discussed admin problem	D
9.45–10.00	Discussed admin problem	D
10.00–10.15	Deputized at meeting	U
10.15–10.30	Deputized at meeting	U
10.30–10.45	Deputized at meeting	U
10.45–11.00	Deputized at meeting	U

At the end of the week analyse your time under the following headings:

- Reading

- Writing
- Dictating
- Telephoning
- Dealing with people (individuals or groups)
- Attending meetings
- Travelling
- Other (specify).

Analyse also the VDU ratings of the worth of each activity under each heading.

This analysis will provide you with the information you need to spot any weaknesses in the way in which you manage time. Use the time-consumer's checklist at the end of this chapter to identify problems and possible remedies.

Organizing yourself

Such an analysis will usually throw up weaknesses in the way you plan your work and establish your priorities. You have to fit the tasks you must complete into the time available to complete them, and get them done in order of importance.

Some people find it difficult, if not impossible, to plan their work ahead. They find that they work best if they have to achieve almost impossible deadlines. Working under pressure concentrates the mind wonderfully, they say. Journalists are a case in point.

But ordinary mortals, who work under a variety of conflicting pressures, cannot rely upon crisis action to get them out of log-jams of work. For most of us it is better to try to minimize the need for working under exceptional pressure by a little attention to the organization of our week or day. At the very least you should use your diary for long-range planning, organize your weekly activities in broad outline and plan each day in some detail.

Use the diary

Attempt to leave at least one day a week free of meetings and avoid filling any day with appointments. In other words leave blocks of unallocated time for planning, thinking, reading, writing and dealing with the unexpected.

Weekly organizer

Sit down at the beginning of each week with your diary and plan how you are going to spend your time. Assess each of your projects or tasks and work out priorities. Leave blocks of time for dealing with correspondence and seeing people. Try to preserve one free day, or at least half a day, if it is at all possible.

If it helps you to put everything down on paper, draw up a simple weekly organizer form and record what you intend to do each morning, afternoon and, if it's work, evening.

Daily organizer

At the beginning of each day, consult your diary to check on your plans and commitments. Refer to the previous day's organizer to find out what is outstanding. Inspect your pending tray and in-tray to check on what remains and what has just arrived.

Then write down the things to do:

1. Meetings or interviews
2. Telephone calls
3. Tasks in order of priority:

    A – must be done today
    B – ideally should be done today but could be left till tomorrow
    C – can be dealt with later.

Plan broadly when you are going to fit your A and B priority tasks into the day. Tick off your tasks as they have been completed. Retain the list to consult next day.

You do not need an elaborate form for this purpose. Many successful time managers use a blank sheet of paper, but a simple form which you can use is shown below.

DAILY ORGANIZER Date ....

Meetings and appointments

Committee/person	Where	When

To telephone

Person	About what	When

To do

Tasks *(in order of priority)*	Priority rating* A, B or C	Approximate timing

* A = must be done today. B = ideally done today. C = later.

Organizing other people

Your first task is to organize yourself, but other people can help, if you can guide and encourage them. They include your secretary, boss, colleagues, subordinates and outside contacts.

Your secretary

A secretary can be a great help: sorting incoming mail into what needs immediate attention and what can be looked at later; managing appointments within your guidelines; keeping unwanted callers at bay; intercepting telephone calls; dealing with routine or even semi-routine correspondence; sorting and arranging your papers and the filing system for easy accessibility; getting people on the telephone for you, and so on. The list is almost endless. Every efficient boss will recognize that he or she depends a lot on an efficient secretary.

Your boss

Your boss can waste your time with over-long meetings, needless interruptions, trivial requests and general nitpicking. Maybe there is nothing you can do about this. But you can learn how to avoid doing the same to your own staff.

On your own behalf you can cultivate the polite art of cutting short tedious discussions. Such formulas as 'I hope you feel we have cleared up this problem – I'll get out of your hair now and get things moving' are useful. And you might be able, subtly, to indicate that your boss is going to get better performance from you if he or she leaves you alone. It's difficult but it's worth trying.

Your colleagues

Try to educate them to avoid unnecessary interruptions. Don't anger them by shutting them out when they have something urgent to discuss. But if it can wait, get them to agree to meet you later at a fixed time. Try to avoid indulging in too many pleasantries over the telephone. Be brisk but not brusque.

Your subordinates

You will save a lot of time with your subordinates if you systematically decide what work you can delegate to them. You save even more time if you delegate clearly and spell out how and when you want them to report back.

An 'open door' policy is fine in theory but time wasting in practice. Learn to say no to subordinates who want to see you when you are engaged on more important business. But always give them a time when they can see you and stick to it.

Talking generally to your staff about their job and outside interests can be time well spent if it helps to increase mutual understanding and respect. Allow for this in your schedule and be prepared to extend business discussions into broader matters when the opportunity arises. But don't overdo it.

Outside contacts

The same rules apply to outside contacts. Prevent them from seeing you without an appointment. Ask your secretary to block unwanted telephone calls. Brief your contacts on what you expect from them and when meetings should be arranged.

Time-consumer's checklist

Problem	Possible remedies
TASKS	
1. Work piling up	• Set priorities
	• Set deadlines
	• Make realistic time estimates – most people underestimate – add 20 per cent to your first guess.
2. Trying to do too much at once	• Set priorities
	• Do one thing at a time
	• Learn to say no to yourself as well as other people.
3. Getting involved in too much detail	• Delegate more.

Problem	*Possible remedies*
4. Postponing unpleasant tasks	• Set a timetable and stick to it • Get unpleasant tasks over with quickly – you will feel better afterwards.
5. Insufficient time to think	• Reserve blocks of time – part of a day or week – for thinking. No paperwork, no interruptions.

PEOPLE

6. Constant interruptions from people calling into your office	• Use secretary to keep unwanted visitors out • Make appointments and see that people stick to them • Reserve block times when you are not to be interrupted.
7. Constant telephone interruptions	• Get your secretary to intercept and, where appropriate, divert calls • State firmly that you will call back when convenient.
8. Too much time spent in conversation	• Decide in advance what you want to achieve when you meet someone, and keep pleasantries to a minimum at the beginning and end • Concentrate on keeping yourself and the other person to the point – it is too easy to divert or be diverted • Learn how to end meetings quickly but not too brusquely.

PAPERWORK

9. Flooded with incoming paper	• Get your secretary to sort it into three folders: action now, action later, information • Take yourself off the circulation list of useless information • Only ask for written memos and reports when you really need them • Encourage people to present information and reports clearly and succinctly • Ask for summaries rather than the whole report • Take a course in rapid reading.

Problem	*Possible remedies*
10. Too many letters/memos to write or dictate	• Use the telephone more • Avoid individually typed acknowledgements • Practise writing a succinct 'yes/no/ let's talk' on the memos you receive and return them to the sender.
11. Paperwork piling up	• Do it now • Set aside the first half hour or so in the day to deal with urgent correspondence • Leave a period at the end of the day for less urgent reading • Aim to clear at least 90 per cent of the paper on your desk every day.
12. Lost or mislaid papers	• Arrange, or get your secretary to organize, papers on current projects in separate, easily accessible folders • Don't hang on to papers in your pending tray – clear it daily • Set up a filing and retrieval system which will enable you to get at papers easily • Ensure that your secretary keeps a day book of correspondence as a last resort method of turning up papers • Keep a tidy desk.

MEETINGS

13. Too much time spent in meetings	• If you set up the meeting: avoid regular meetings when there is nothing that needs saying regularly, review all the meetings you hold and eliminate as many as you can • Get yourself taken off committees if your presence is not essential or if someone else is more appropriate • As chairman: set limits for the duration of meetings and keep to them, cut out waffle and repetition, allow discussion but insist on making progress, have a logical agenda and stick to it

Problem	*Possible remedies*
	• As a member: don't waffle, don't talk for the sake of talking, don't waste time scoring points or boosting your ego.
TRAVELLING	
14. Too much time spent on travelling	• Use the phone or post
	• Send someone else
	• Ask yourself, every time you plan to go anywhere, 'is my journey really necessary?'
	• Plan the quickest way – air, rail or car.

Chapter 49
Total quality management

Total quality management (TQM) is a systematic way of guaranteeing that all activities within an organization happen the way they have been planned in order to meet the defined needs of customers and clients. The emphasis is on involving everyone in the organization in activities which provide for continuous improvement and for achieving sustained high levels of quality performance.

The TQM approach

The TQM approach is about gaining commitment to quality. Everyone at every level in the organization has genuinely to believe in quality and to act on that belief. Total quality can be described as an attitude of mind which leads to appropriate behaviour and actions.

Basic concepts of TQM

1. Customer satisfaction

The only real measure of the quality of a product or service is the extent to which it delivers customer satisfaction. The word 'satisfaction' can be defined as when all customers' wants, needs and expectations are met, whether or not they have been expressed.

2. The significance of internal customers

Another key concept in total quality is the significance of the internal customer. This refers to the fact that everyone who receives goods or services from a colleague within an organization is a customer of that colleague. These goods or services can include materials, tools, parts, subassemblies, completed goods for despatch, designs, drawings, information, advice, help, guidance, administrative assistance, etc.

Suppliers of these goods and services have to be just as aware of the need to achieve high levels of quality for their colleagues as for their ultimate customers. In the last analysis, of course, the quality of the services provided to internal customers will affect the quality delivered to the external customer. But the final result can only be guaranteed if attention is paid to quality in all aspects of the transactions and processes which take place within the organization.

3. Total quality

The concept of total quality indicates the requirement for *all* employees in the organization to be *involved* all the time in meeting *all* customer requirements.

The development of TQM

TQM must, by definition, extend to all aspects of a company's operation and its relationships with internal and external customers. It is essentially a *process*, a way of doing things, which makes use of a number of techniques but ultimately depends on the attitudes and behaviour of all those involved; and that means everyone in the organization and its suppliers.

The steps required to develop TQM are described below:

Formulate a TQM policy

A TQM policy might cover the following points:

- The goal of the organization is to achieve customer satisfaction by meeting the requirements of both external and internal customers.
- The need is to establish customer requirements and respond quickly and effectively to them.
- It is essential to concentrate on prevention rather than cure.
- Everyone is involved – all work done by company employees, suppliers and product outlets is part of a process which creates a product or service for a customer.
- Each employee is a customer for work done by other employees and has the right to expect good work from them and the obligation to contribute work of high calibre to them.
- The standard of quality is 'zero defect' or 'no failures' – everyone has

311

to understand the standards required and the need to do it right first time.

- Sustained quality excellence requires continuous improvement.
- Quality performance and costs should be measured systematically.
- Continuous attention must be paid to satisfying educational and training needs.
- High quality performance will be recognized and rewarded.
- Quality improvement is best achieved by the joint efforts of management and employees.

Determine quality standards

Quality standards in manufacturing organizations may simply be expressed as a zero defect policy but it is still necessary to define what a zero defect situation is for each key operation and service. This means the clarification of what constitutes a defect or failure to achieve a standard, how that will be measured or recognized and what steps may be required to prevent the occurrence of the defect.

Measure quality

The measurement of quality may involve process control or similar techniques in a manufacturing company which include the analysis of the system, the collection of information on variations from the norm or attributes (data on whether a process is meeting or not meeting specification) and the use of techniques for establishing process capability and performance.

Plan for quality

Planning for quality involves:

- Recording the series of events and activities constituting the total process (where applicable) by the use of flowcharting and other means of activity analysis
- Analysing the existing processes and system flows to establish inconsistencies and potential sources of variations and defects
- Specifying for each activity the necessary quality-related activities, including material and packaging specifications, quality control procedures, process control systems, and sampling and inspection procedures
- Developing, as appropriate, just-in-time (JIT) systems which provide for the right quantities to be produced or delivered at the right time and ensure that there is no waste
- Determining how to achieve quality in the purchasing system, with

particular reference to the development of long-term relationships with suppliers so that dependable product quality and delivery standards can be defined and maintained

- Developing planned maintenance systems in manufacturing or distribution organizations to reduce the incidence of emergency maintenance
- Designing quality into the product or service, making sure that the standards and specifications meet customer or client needs and can be achieved by existing processes (or, if not, by improving these processes in particular ways)
- Conducting process capability studies to ensure that it will be possible to achieve quality standards through existing processes or, if not, what changes are required.

Organize for quality

Organizing for quality means looking at the accountabilities of each member of the organization and ensuring that the responsibility for quality performance is clearly specified.

The organization for quality should aim to take account of the development of joint responsibility for quality in production or distribution teams. The focus should be on teamwork for quality.

Finally, consideration should be given to placing responsibility with individuals and/or task forces to oversee the development and implementation of TQM.

Train for quality

The achievement of improved standards of quality will require additional and higher levels of skills and knowledge. Training needs therefore have to be identified and continuous training programmes developed – quality training is not a one-off process. The employee development system has to operate within a learning, self-development, continuous improvement culture.

Gain commitment to quality

Procedures and systems for laying down standards and measuring quality performance are all very well, but significant results from TQM will not be obtained unless total commitment to quality is achieved at all levels of the organization. The emphasis should be on self-responsibility for quality. This can be a long-term process – it will not be achieved by running a few short courses. Commitment is achieved by example from the top and, more importantly, by involving people in quality improvement programmes.

Quality circles or improvement groups are one approach to achieving commitment, but they will not succeed by themselves. Total quality has to be seen as a permanent and fundamental part of everyday working. The Japanese approach, as translated to Nissan Motor (UK), involves seeing quality as a team affair to be discussed by all members at five-minute meetings at the start of every day.

Motivate for quality

Motivating for quality means reviewing the reward system so that it supports the strategic objectives of the total quality programme. If the system is essentially production driven and based on individual rewards, it is likely to conflict with a quality-driven teamwork approach. The reward system should not only include financial rewards. There are other ways of rewarding people by non-financial means such as recognizing achievements and providing additional learning and promotion opportunities.

Chapter 50
Trouble shooting

No matter what you do, things will sometimes go wrong. As a manager, you will often be called upon to put them right, or to employ other people to do it for you.

Trouble shooting requires diagnostic ability, to size up the difficulties; know-how, to select the required solution and decide how to implement it; and managerial skill, to put the solution into effect. It can be divided into three main parts:

- Planning the campaign.
- Diagnosis.
- Cure.

Planning the campaign

Even if you decide to do it yourself without using management consultants, you can still take a leaf out of the consultant's book. A good management consultant will go through the following stages:

- Analysis of the present situation – what has happened and why.
- Development of alternative solutions to the problem.
- Decision as to the preferred solution, stating the costs and benefits of implementing it.
- Defining a method of proceeding – how and over what time-scale should the solution be implemented, who does it and with what resources. If a staged implementation is preferred, the stages will be defined and a programme worked out.

The most important task at the planning stage is to define the problem, clarify objectives and terms of reference. A problem defined is a problem half solved. And it is the difficult half. The rest should follow quite naturally if an analytical approach is adopted.

Once you know what the problem is you can define what you want done and prepare terms of reference for those who are conducting the investigation, including yourself. These should set out the problem, how and by whom it is to be tackled, what is to be achieved and by when. All those concerned in the exercise should know what these terms of reference are.

The next step is to programme the trouble-shooting assignment. Four points need to be decided: the information you need, where you get it from, how you obtain it and who receives it. Draw up lists of facts required and the people who can supply them. Remember you will have to deal with opinion as well as fact; all data are subject to interpretation. List those who are likely to understand what has happened and why; those who might have good ideas about what to do next.

Then draw up your programme. Give notice that you require information. Warn people in plenty of time that you want to discuss particular points with them and that you expect them to have thought about the subject *and* have supporting evidence to hand.

Diagnosis

Diagnosis means finding out *what* is happening – the symptom – and then digging to establish *why* it is happening – the cause. There may be a mass of evidence. The skilled diagnostician dissects the facts, sorts out what is relevant to the problem and refines it all down until he or she reveals the crucial pieces of information which show the cause of the problem and point to its solution.

Analytical ability – being able to sort the wheat from the chaff – is a key element in diagnosis. It is a matter of getting the facts and then submitting each one to a critical examination, in order to determine which is significant.

During the process of diagnosis you must remain open-minded. You should not allow yourself to have preconceptions or to be over-influenced by anyone's opinion. Listen and observe, but suspend judgement until you can arrange all the facts against all the opinions.

At the same time, do whatever you can to enlist the interest and support of those involved. If you can minimize their natural fears and suspicions, those close to the problem will reveal ideas and facts which might otherwise be concealed from you.

Trouble-shooting checklist

Base your diagnosis on an analysis of the factors likely to have contributed to the problem: people, systems, structure and circumstances.

People

1. Have mistakes been made? If so, why? Is it because staff are inadequate in themselves or is it because they have been badly managed or trained?
2. If management is at fault, was the problem one of system, structure or the managers themselves?
3. If the people doing the job are inadequate why were they selected in the first place?

Systems

4. To what extent are poor systems or procedures to blame for the problem?
5. Is the fault in the systems themselves? Are they badly designed or inappropriate?
6. Or is it the fault of the people who operate or manage the systems?

Structure

7. How far has the organization or management structure contributed to the problem?
8. Do people know what is expected of them?
9. Are activities grouped together logically, so that adequate control can be exercised over them?
10. Are managers and supervisors clear about their responsibilities for maintaining control and do they exercise these responsibilities effectively?

Circumstances

11. To what extent, if any, is the problem a result of circumstances beyond the control of those concerned? For example, have external economic pressures or changing government policies had a detrimental effect?
12. If there have been external pressures, has there been a failure to anticipate or to react quickly enough to them?
13. Have adequate resources (people, money and materials) been made available, and if not, why not?

Cure

The diagnosis should point the way to the cure. But this may still mean that you have to evaluate different ways of dealing with the problem. There is seldom 'one best way', only a choice between alternatives. You have to narrow them down until you reach the one which, *on balance*, is better than the others.

Your diagnosis should have established the extent to which the problem is one of people, systems, structure or circumstances. Fallible human beings may well be at the bottom of it. If so, remember not to indulge in indiscriminate criticism. Your job is to be constructive; to build people up, not to destroy them.

Avoid being too theoretical. Take account of circumstances – including the ability of the people available now to deal with the problem, or, if you have doubts, the availability of people from elsewhere who can be deployed effectively. Your recommendation should be practical in the sense that it can be made to work with resources which are readily available and within acceptable time-scales.

You must make clear not only what needs to be done but *how* it is to be done. Assess costs as well as benefits and demonstrate that the benefits outweigh the costs. Resources have to be allocated, a time-scale set and, above all, specific responsibility given to people to get the work done. Your recommendations have to be realistic in the sense that they can be phased in without undue disruption and without spending more time and money than is justified by the results.

Take care when you apportion blame to individuals. Some may clearly be inadequate and have to be replaced. Others may be the victims of poor management, poor training or circumstances beyond their control. Their help may be essential in overcoming the trouble. It is unwise to destroy their confidence or their willingness to help.

Using management consultants

A management consultant has been described, or dismissed, as someone with a briefcase 50 miles from home. Robert Townsend (56) has suggested that consultants are people 'who borrow your watch to tell you what time it is and then walk off with it'.

Calling in consultants in desperation can indeed be an expensive and time-wasting exercise. But they have their uses. They bring experience and expertise in diagnosis. They can act as an extra pair of hands when suitable people are not available from within the organization. And, as a third party, they can sometimes see the wood through the trees and unlock ideas within the company which, sadly, are often inhibited by structural or managerial constraints.

There are, however, a number of rules which you should be aware of when contemplating bringing in consultants.

DO

Get tenders from two or three firms and compare, not only their fees, but their understanding of your problem and the practical suggestions they have on how to tackle it.

Check on the experience of the firm and, most important, of the consultant who is going to carry out the assignment.

Brief the firm very carefully on the terms of reference.

Get a clear statement of the proposed programme, total estimated costs (fees *plus* expenses) and who is actually going to carry out the assignment.

Meet and assess the consultant who is going to do the work.

Insist on regular progress meetings.

Ensure that the outcome of the assignment is a practical proposal which you can implement yourself, or with the minimum of further help.

DON'T

Be bamboozled by a smooth principal who is employed mainly as a salesperson.

Go for a big firm simply because it has a good reputation. It may not have the particular expertise you want.

Accept any old consultant who comes along. Many redundant executives have set up as consultants without having a clue about how to do it. There is a lot of skill in being an effective consultant. Check that the firm is a member of the Management Consultants Association or that the principal is a member of the Institute of Management Consultants (for UK-based firms). These provide a guarantee of professional status.

Allow the consultant to change programme without prior consultation.

Leave the consultant to his or her own devices for too long. Keep in touch. Appoint a member of your staff to liaise or even to work with the consultant.

General bibliography

1 Adair, J, *Action Centred Leadership*, McGraw-Hill, London, 1984.
2 Anderson, B, 'The visionary leader', *Management Theory and Practice*, September 1993, pp. 3–7.
3 Back, K and K, *Assertiveness at Work*, McGraw-Hill, Maidenhead, 1982.
4 Bandura, A, *Social Boundaries of Thought and Action*, Prentice-Hall, Englewood Cliffs, NJ, 1986.
5 Beckhard, R, *Organizational Development: Strategy and Models*, Addison-Wesley, Reading, MA, 1969.
6 Beer, M, 'Reward systems' in Beer, M, Spector, B, Lawrence, P, Quinn Mills, D and Walton, R (eds), *Managing Human Assets*, The Free Press, New York, 1984.
7 Beer, M, Eisenstat, R and Spector, B, 'Why change programs don't produce change', *Harvard Business Review*, November–December, 1990.
8 Bell, C, *The Conventions of Crisis*, Oxford University Press, Oxford, 1971.
9 Bennis, W and Nanus, B, *Leaders*, Harper & Row, New York, 1985.
10 Burns, J, *Leadership*, Harper & Row, New York, 1978.
11 De Bono, E, *Lateral Thinking for Managers*, McGraw-Hill, London, 1971.
12 Dignam, L, *Strategic Management: Concepts, Decisions, Cases*, Irwin, New York, 1990.
13 Dixon, N, *On the Psychology of Military Incompetence*, Futura, London, 1979.
14 Drucker, P, *The Practice of Management*, Heinemann, London, 1955.
15 Drucker, P, *The Effective Executive*. Heinemann, London, 1967.
16 Drucker, P, 'The coming of the new organization', *Harvard Business Review*, January–February, 1988.
17 Egan, G, *The Skilled Helper: A Systematic Approach to Effective Helping*, Brooks Cole, London, 1990.
18 Fiedler, F, *A Theory of Leadership Effectiveness*, McGraw-Hill, New York, 1967.
19 Follett, M P, *Creative Experience*, Longmans Green, New York, 1924.
20 Gowers, Sir Ernest, *The Complete Plain Words*, Penguin, London, 1987.

21 Hall, W, 'Survival strategies in a hostile environment', *Harvard Business Review*, March–April, 1976.

22 Handy, C, *The Age of Unreason*, Business Books, London, 1989.

23 Handy, C, *The Empty Raincoat*, Hutchinson, London, 1994.

24 Harvey-Jones, J, *Making it Happen*, Collins, Glasgow, 1988.

25 Heller, R, *The Business of Success*, Sidgwick & Jackson, London, 1982.

26 Institute of Personnel Management, *Statement on Counselling in the Workplace*, IPM, London, 1992.

27 Jay, A, *Management and Machiavelli*, Hodder & Stoughton, London, 1967.

28 Kakabadse, A, *The Politics of Management*, Gower, Aldershot, 1983.

29 Kanter, R M, *The Change Masters*, Allen & Unwin, London, 1984.

30 Kanter, R M, *When Giants Learn to Dance*, Simon & Schuster, London, 1989.

31 Katzenbach, J and Smith, D, *The Wisdom of Teams*, Harvard Business School Press, Boston, Mass, 1993.

32 Koestler, A, *The Act of Creation*, Hutchinson, London, 1984.

33 Kotter, J, 'What leaders really do', *Harvard Business Review*, May–June 1980.

34 Maslow, A, *Motivation and Personality*, Harper & Row, New York, 1954.

35 McClelland, D, *Power, The Inner Experience*, Irvington, New York, 1975.

36 McGregor, D, *The Human Side of Enterprise*, McGraw-Hill, New York, 1960.

37 Mintzberg, H, *The Nature of Managerial Work*, Harper & Row, New York, 1973.

38 Mintzberg, H, 'Organization design: fashion or fit', *Harvard Business Review*, January–February, 1981.

39 Mintzberg, H, 'Crafting strategy', *Harvard Business Review*, July–August, 1987.

40 Mumford, A, *Management Development: Strategies for Action*, Institute of Personnel Management, London, 1989.

41 Pascale, R and Athos, A, *The Art of Japanese Management*, Simon & Schuster, New York, 1981.

42 Pascale, R, *Managing on the Edge*, Viking, London, 1990.

43 Pedler, M, Burgoyne, J and Boydell, T, *A Manager's Guide to Self-Development*, McGraw-Hill, Maidenhead, 1986.

44 Peter, L, *The Peter Principle*, Allen & Unwin, London, 1972.

45 Peters, T and Waterman, R, *In Search of Excellence*, Harper & Row, New York, 1982.

46 Peters, T, *Thriving on Chaos*, Macmillan, London, 1988.

47 Pettigrew, A and Whipp, R, *Managing Change for Competitive Success*, Blackwell, Oxford, 1991.

48 Pickard, J, 'The real meaning of empowerment', *Personnel Management*, November, 1993.

49 Porter, M, *Competitive Advantage: Creating and Sustaining Superior Performance*, Free Press, New York, 1985.

50 Richardson, W, 'The visionary leader', *Administrator*, September 1993.

51 Schelling, T, *Strategy of Conflict*, Harvard University Press, 1960.
52 Schumacher, C, 'Structuring Work', *Industrial Participation*, Winter 1976/77.
53 Stebbing, S, *Thinking to Some Purpose*, Penguin Books, Harmondsworth, 1959.
54 Stewart, R, *Managers and Their Jobs*, Macmillan, London, 1967.
55 Taylor, F, *Principles of Scientific Management*, Harper & Row, New York, 1911.
56 Townsend, R, *Up the Organization*, Michael Joseph, London, 1970.
57 Walton, R, 'From control to commitment', *Harvard Business Review*, March–April, 1985.
58 Ware, J and Barnes, L, 'Managing interpersonal conflict', in J Gabarro (ed.), *Managing People and Organizations*, Harvard Business School Publications, Boston, Mass, 1991.
59 Waterman, R, *The Renewal Factor*, Bantam, New York, 1988.
60 Welch, J, quoted in J Gabarro (ed.), *Managing People and Organizations*, Harvard Business School Publications, Boston, Mass, 1991.
61 Wickens, P, *The Road to Nissan*, Macmillan, London, 1987.

Further reading from Kogan Page

Basics of a Successful Business Strategy (1994), Kerstin Friedrich and Lothar J Sweiwert

BS 5750/ISO 9000 Made Easy (1994), Kit Sadgrove

Effective Supervisory Management (series) (1994), Roger Bennett

The First-Time Manager, 2nd edition (1994), M J Morris

A Handbook of Management Techniques, 2nd edition (1994), Michael Armstrong

Implementing Strategic Change (1993), Tony Grundy

The Kogan Page Guide to Effective Management (1994), Roger Bennett

The Manager's Toolkit (series) (1994), Peter Grainger

Power (1992), Helga Drummond

A Practical Guide to Project Management (1992), Celia Burton and Norma Michael

A complete list is available from the publishers, telephone 071-278 0433.

Index